RUSSIA

BELARUS

UKRAINE

MOLDOVA

GARIA

TURKEY

Europe has a number of
climate zones, which make growing
food a different proposition in each.
For the purposes of this book, we have
broken up the land into six distinct zones
that you can use to help you reference
the recommended planting times for
each fruit and veg.

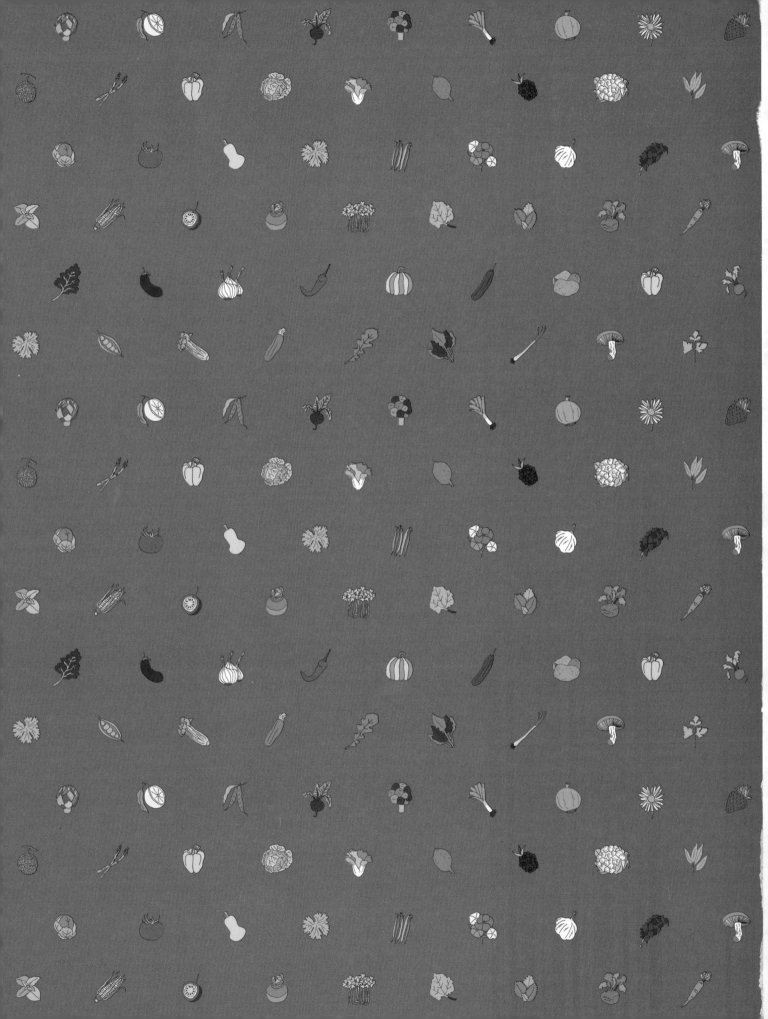

littleveggiepatchco.com.au

FOOD.
WHERE.

FOR CAROLINE,
THE APPLE OF MY EYE.

hardie grant books

GROW.
FOOD.
ANYWHERE.

At The Little Veggie Patch Co our primary interest has always been to get as many people growing food as possible, no matter their level of experience or space available. You don't have to quit your job and move to the country to enjoy a garden. Whether growing mint in a pot or farming a 3-acre block, there is a certain intangible joy in every homegrown harvest. Food simply tastes better when we grow it ourselves, and that joy is compounded if we can share it with friends and family. We want people to have success early on, so that they have the confidence to continue their own food journey.

We all grow for different reasons and no one is more or less valid than the next. For some people it is an exploration into the natural diversity of plants that are not found in a conventional supermarket. It is an opportunity to tap into varieties that are not economically viable on a large scale. We don't have to worry about transportability or regular shapes. We get to make taste and experience our sole priorities.

Others may feel that growing their own food is a middle finger to the modern system of over-fertilised, intensively farmed, mass-produced food. It's a rejection of an agricultural industry that ignores the seasons, adds travel miles by transporting over long distances (think of all that carbon!) and is more concerned with how food looks than whether it's nutritious.

Take the fruit formerly known as the tomato. Degraded through decades of intense agricultural practice, there has been no greater fall from glory. The once truly great culinary beast has become too hard, uniform and tasteless. Its evolution serves no other purpose than to transport well and look good on supermarket shelves. The saddest thing is that such paltry fruit quality has not only become acceptable, it is what we expect.

For many people, the fate of the tomato has been a tipping point that has fuelled the homegrown movement. Rather than accepting its fate, home growers are re-colouring the food spectrum, and the change is trending. More and more of the 3000 weird and wonderful varieties of tomato are finding their way to our plates – and the popularity of home growing has started to spur change in supply chains.

The purpose of this book is to help everyone make a start in growing their own food, even in the smallest of spaces. One of the biggest barriers to edible gardening is the fear of not knowing where to begin. Here we hope to dispel the mystery, because growing food is neither difficult nor time-consuming. Rather, it is something that everyone can do, no matter your location, ideology, origin or experience. It can easily become part of your daily routine.

As people who were born to immigrant families of immigrant nations, we recognise the power we have in growing food. It is how we share our culture and what bonds us so closely to our past and present. Food has a remarkable ability to break down barriers and connect seemingly different people in a shared experience. You don't even have to speak the same language to enjoy a meal with someone.

We hope to inspire growers to find the same simple practicality and enjoyment that we experience every time we are in the garden. It is an absolute luxury to be able to grow food for fun, and although your motivations can be as serious or as lighthearted as you want them to be, the food that you put on your table will make a difference to your life.

As a couple of guys who learn best from doing, we hope to show rather than tell. There are different plants and infrastructure and growing styles suited to virtually all spaces, from traditional in-ground gardens to the balconies of high-rise buildings. Whether the end goal is to grow a single radish or to feed your family for a year, we want this book to guide your exploration of modern gardening, because whatever your reason, whatever your location, whatever your ability, there has never been a better time to grow food – and it's possible to grow food anywhere.

SOIL

12

Life requires balance, and soil is no exception. Treat it like a living thing to help plants reach their maximum potential. Food can also be grown without soil, and this may just be the way of the future.

WATER

44

There is no such thing as a green or black thumb. There are only people who water and those who don't. Getting into good habits and choosing the watering style most suited to you will go a long way.

LIGHT

56

Don't throw in the towel if your space is not lit up like a Christmas tree. There are many ways to generate light, both naturally and artificially, and your space may be better than you think.

NTS NEED

GROWING STYLE
(INFRASTRUCTURE)
62

From backyards to balconies, there are more options than just pots and raised garden beds. Contemporary, efficient systems exist to suit every type of gardener and space.

PLANTING
84

Get it right – from the beginning. Covering seeds and seedlings, tubers and rhizomes, we give you everything you wanted to know but were too afraid to ask.

HARVESTING
110

All plants demand to be harvested. Knowing when and how to pick will yield more produce, making your plants happier and your belly fuller.

WHAT PLANTS NEED

Just as we all need a job, friends and strong cups of coffee in the morning, plants also need certain things to make them happy. Sunlight, soil and water are three fundamentals all plants need to thrive. Sunlight on its leaves for photosynthesis, soil from which to derive nutrition and, finally, water – the basic building blocks of all living things – which pumps life through a plant's veins. Fulfilling those requirements goes a long way towards growing happy, healthy plants.

But in the same way many people believe we need a proper job, marriage and a home to be happy, the needs of a plant are taken from a traditional reference point, too – that is, farming. Small-space gardening has evolved considerably over the past few years, but its practices are mostly inherited from large-sized farming, only scaled down. Just as farming has changed, so has the way we can grow food at home.

That's not to say that sunlight, soil and water won't keep a plant healthy, but, just like happiness, growing success can be achieved in a number of ways. So, whether you're hoping to convert a quarter-acre block into a food oasis, or simply plant a pot of herbs on your balcony, the style and means by which you grow should be determined by the amount of time, energy and resources you have available. It doesn't have to be a hard-core permaculture challenge any more than it has to be a crazy technological science experiment. The garden is whatever you make of it. Whatever you are comfortable with and whatever you want to get out of it. There is no normal – just what works for each of us.

I'D LIKE TO BE UNDER THE SEA IN AN OCTOPUS'S GARDEN IN THE SHADE

SOIL
(GROWING MEDIUM)

Many of us grow plants in good old-fashioned soil, even if that means buying it in a bag. Whether you're chipping away on a rocky outcrop or hanging a basket from your balcony railing, a little soil knowledge will go a long way when it comes to growing food. There is a whole world below the surface, but to begin, soil comes down to particle size, minerals, organic matter and pH. The perfect soil is a balance of everything, but how we get there will vary.

Plant roots need air and water, and how much they get is determined by particle size. **SAND** has large, coarse grains that allow a lot of air and water to move freely. As a result, sand drains well and is prone to rapid temperature changes. **CLAY** is at the opposite end of the spectrum. Made of extremely fine particles packed closely together, it is slow to change temperature and, once wet, holds onto moisture. Too much clay can lead to a cold, dense bog. **SILT** is a mix of the two, with more similarities to clay. The ideal garden soil is about 40% sand, 40% clay and 20% silt. This is called loam.

The reality is that most of us don't have the ideal soil mix in our yards, but if you are able to identify what kind of soil you have to start with, it will allow you to adjust your gardening practices accordingly. Many soil yards sell five-way soil blends, which consist of loam plus organic materials like compost and manure. Such blends are specifically mixed for growing vegetables and are, ultimately, what we try to create in our own gardening practices. There is the expensive fast way, or the inexpensive slow way.

Of course, many city dwellers are now growing in wicking beds or pots, and that means using potting mix. Just like a five-way soil blend, potting mix tries to create that perfect loam with organic matter. However, not all potting mixes are created equal. You generally get what you pay for. Cheap mixes use chemical fertilisers and have poor quality matter. Spending a little extra on a premium organic mix will ensure that your veggie patch has the best possible start in your first season and many more seasons to come.

MASON JAR SOIL TEST

ACTIVITY!

WHAT YOU NEED

470 ml (16 fl oz) sealable glass jar (or larger)

Water

1 teaspoon dishwashing liquid

Hand trowel or shovel

When going on a date, there are a few basic pieces of information you probably want to know before you proceed. Do they have any dietary requirements? Do they have a passport? Have they previously dated any of your friends? Although none of it is necessarily make-or-break, a little bit of information can go a long way in helping you to manage your expectations. It will also change how you approach the date. The Mason Jar Soil Test will offer similar insights for the garden. In fact, it's a bit like garden speed dating.

While not as precise as sending soil off to the lab, the Mason Jar Soil test is a quick and easy way to get a snapshot of your soil texture, which is to say, the relative proportions of sand, silt and clay. Just like potential partners, your soil will not be perfect, but understanding its flaws will guide your approach to your shared life. If the two of you are going to build an enduring relationship, then it is always going to be a work in progress.

1 Find a clean jar with a threaded lid. We like this old passata bottle. Be sure that your jar has a vertical edge, as curved jars will distort the results.

2 Dig a small hole to a depth of about 20 cm (8 in). Angle the shovel straight down to cut a thin cross section of the soil. Remember, this needs to fit in a jar, so don't get too much.

3 Remove any obvious rocks or organic debris from the sample. You want to get your soil sample as clean as possible for this test.

4 Place your soil sample into the jar, so that it is about half full and add a teaspoon of dishwashing liquid. This will work as a surfactant, which helps to separate soil particles so that you have more accurate results.

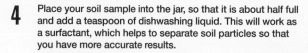

5 Fill the jar nearly to the top with water and shake well. Leave the jar overnight to allow your muddy mixture to fully settle. The heaviest/largest particles should sink to the bottom, with finer sediment at the top.

6 Note the different layers of each soil type. Sand will settle on the bottom, clay in the middle and silt on top. Knowing what kind of soil you have will make it easier to choose plants that will thrive, and to add the right amendments to help improve it.

SOIL TYPES

GET TO KNOW YOUR GROWING MEDIUM – COMMON SOILS AND PRODUCTS FOR THE HOME GARDEN

POTTING MIX

It typically comes in a bag and is our human attempt at creating the perfect soil. Usually containing a 40–40–20 mix of sand, silt and clay, it also has some added extras: coconut/pine bark fibres to make soil friable and allow for better drainage/air flow; peat moss to improve friability and moderate soil dryness/wetness; organic matter, such as compost and/or manure; and perlite for aeration and drainage. As the name suggests, it is designed to be used in pots.

LOAM

The ideal starting point for many in-ground or raised garden beds, loam consists of 40% sand, 40% silt and 20% clay. Many gardeners aspire to have a loam that is mixed with organic material, resulting in a soil that holds nutrients and water but still allows the excess to drain away. It's truly the Goldilocks of soil.

PERLITE

The popcorn of the garden world. This naturally occurring volcanic glass mineral is heat-treated and expanded into light, porous kernels (they look like tiny pieces of styrofoam). Improving aeration and drainage, it also prevents compaction. It's commonly added to potting mix to create wicking bed soil. Perlite is sterile, meaning it has been heat-treated to kill any pathogens.

VERMICULITE

This is a heat-treated and expanded mineral-like perlite. Where perlite is excellent at draining water, vermiculite is good for water retention. It will add to soil structure and help prevent soil compaction. Commonly used for germinating seeds, vermiculite is sterile.

EXPANDED CLAY

A heat-treated clay that forms lightweight aggregate balls, expanded clay is commonly used as a growing medium (instead of soil) for aquaponic and hydroponic gardening, because it is easy to use, light, porous, pH neutral, and does not compact. Expanded clay is sterile.

NUTRIENTS

Soil isn't just 'dirt'. It's a living ecosystem. Physical composters, such as worms and beetles, are readily apparent, but there is also an endless diversity of bacteria, fungi and actinomycetes (akti-gnome-e-sets) that actually changes the chemistry of soil on a molecular scale. In fact, a handful of healthy soil can contain billions of life forms, most of which are invisible to the naked eye (this is probably a good thing, because microbes tend to look like monsters or deep-sea creatures). By adding organic materials we not only add nutrients, but we also invite life into our soil, which helps to build fertility.

All of these invisible helpers work tirelessly to further break down nutrients into elements that can be utilised by plants. Just like a raw potato is almost completely useless to humans (for consumption), plants also need their food prepared in a way that they can properly 'digest'. Organic material and living creatures are the food and chefs of the veggie patch, respectively.

Once nutrition is accessible, plants are able to perform critical biological functions that allow them to grow roots, stems, leaves, flowers and fruit. In fact, many elements meet very specific plant needs and are essential for a productive veggie patch. From flower production to root growth, no elements determine a plant's health more than nitrogen, phosphorus and potassium, known in gardening circles (and your year 11 science class) as N–P–K. We can add these and other important nutrients to our soil using organic additives and the plants themselves (crop rotation).

Adding N, P and K isn't quite as simple as measuring it out and throwing it in a test tube, but we shouldn't overcomplicate it either. Focusing on these three primary elements, and some important others, will help us simplify why plants grow and why they sometimes don't grow as we desire.

TALK DIRTY TO ME

ACTIVATING YOUR POTS/GARDEN

Our ultimate goal is a well-drained, nutrient-rich, sandy loam containing an orgy of living creatures. However, purchased compost, soil blends and potting mixes are often heat-treated to kill any weeds or pathogens, making them sterile. It's like a beautiful house with no one living in it. Fortunately, all we have to do is show them the way to the front door.

Whether we are filling a new pot, wicking bed, wall garden or raised garden bed, we always add worm castings and rock minerals to help jump-start soil life. If you foster a healthy ecosystem, you will create lasting soil (even in a pot); something that remains fertile and active long into the future.

WHAT YOU NEED

Pot

Soil

Worm castings

Rock minerals

Water

1. Mat has filled a new pot today. What a boss! The soil is well drained, full of nutrients and pH neutral – almost everything that plants need to thrive. Now it's time to bring that soil to life.

2. Add worm castings and worms. Worm castings not only contain conditioned nutrients, but are full of unhatched worm eggs (the best kind). Eggs will hatch when exposed to regular moisture.

3. Invigorate the soil by adding some rock minerals. Mix it into the soil so that it doesn't blow away.

4. Water in the nutrients and maintain watering regularly. There are no bad gardeners, only bad waterers!

GUIDE TO THE ELEMENTS

PRIMARY NUTRIENTS

The big three – nitrogen (N), phosphorus (P) and potassium (K) – are essential to most of a plant's vital functions. As a general rule, you want to make sure that these nutrients are present both at the beginning and the end of the growing season. Whether this is achieved through crop rotation, mulch, soil additives or (most likely) a combination of them all, is up to you.

	HOW PLANTS USE IT	SIGNS OF DEFICIENCY	MOST READILY AVAILABLE FROM	APPLICATION
7 N Nitrogen 14.007	The key nutrient for a plant to live and photosynthesise, it is responsible for the initial growth of leaf foliage and roots, and is needed for sustained foliage growth. All plants need nitrogen, but some are much hungrier than others. All the brassica family (including kale, broccoli and cabbage) use nitrogen as their primary nutrient through their life cycle, while tomatoes and corn demand nitrogen until they need potassium for flowering and fruit production.	Symptoms include poor or stunted plant growth and leaves that turn yellow because they are unable to make sufficient chlorophyll.	Pelletised chook poo.	Plan a bi-annual application of pelletised chook poo.
15 P Phosphorus 30.9738	Critical nutrient for strong root systems. Phosphorus is known to benefit the overall vigour of a plant and help with disease resistance, and is the primary element responsible for the development of root vegetables.	The tell-tale sign in a root vegetable is lots of healthy vegetative growth but under-developed roots. Plant growth may also be visibly stunted, with plants exhibiting a bright green foliage.	Blood and bone (fast release) and rock phosphate (slow release).	Add blood and bone to the soil before planting for an immediate boost that will last a growing season or two. Rock phosphate can be applied every couple of years and will provide a slow but steady source of phosphorus.
19 K Potassium 39.098	Contributes to the reproductive plant growth, such as the development of flowers, fruit and seeds. Potassium is very important to cellular functions, specifically how well plants are able to move water, sugar and starch. As a result, it also helps plants to develop thicker skin, which improves pest/disease resistance and increases shelf life once harvested.	Mature plants, such as tomatoes, with few or no flowers visible. Other, more subtle signs include older leaves showing brown/yellow edges or veins.	Liquid or powder potash.	Mix potash into the soil at the beginning of the growing season or use the diluted liquid form before plants start to flower.

SECONDARY NUTRIENTS

Aside from the big gun N–P–K, a number of key elements need only be present in small amounts, but they play a strong supporting role and often assist with vital functions performed by N–P–K. Magnesium and calcium are the two main secondary nutrients.

	HOW PLANTS USE IT	SIGNS OF DEFICIENCY	MOST READILY AVAILABLE FROM	APPLICATION
12 Mg Magnesium 24.305	Magnesium's primary job is making the leaves green. It is necessary for chlorophyll production and without it plants are unable to capture the sun's energy to photosynthesise.	Older leaves will turn yellow-veined and lose their colour. Leaves fall off without withering.	Organic compost and Epsom salts.	Add organic compost to your veggie patch every quarter.
20 Ca Calcium 40.078	Important for cellular functions and new growth such as fruit and flower production.	Blossom end rot, dead leaf margins.	Dolomitic limestone.	Spread small amounts through the garden bed annually. Will reduce soil pH.

HOW PLANTS USE NUTRIENTS (SIMPLIFIED)

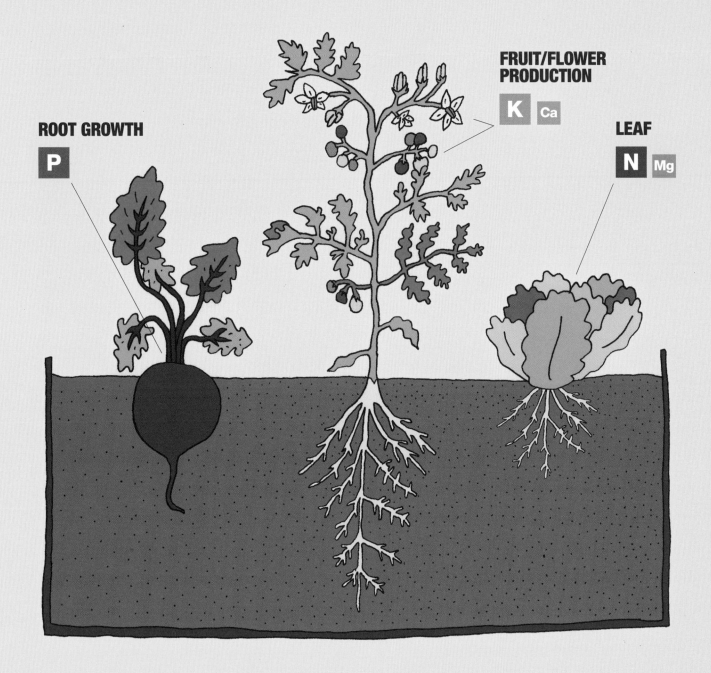

ROOT GROWTH

P

FRUIT/FLOWER PRODUCTION

K Ca

LEAF

N Mg

NUTRIENT TROUBLESHOOTING

Have you ever found yourself answering your child's provocative question with 'just because'? While some curly questions demand explanation, others should retain an air of mystery to avoid over-complication. And in the gardening world, some outcomes – such as the positive partnering of tomato and basil – also don't need a full explanation. The simple fact that they fancy each other and deserve to be together in the veggie patch is enough. And how is it possible to explain love, after all?

When it comes to what plants need, it might seem overly simplistic to concentrate on their N–P–K nutritional needs, but in doing so it does help with identifying and then troubleshooting common deficiencies. This will then make you a better grower.

NITROGEN TROUBLESHOOTING

INTRODUCING

LETTUCE

1. Lettuce is one of many leafy greens that relies on nitrogen to fulfil all of its growing dreams. When it looks stunted and begins to yellow, we know we have a deficiency.

2. Adding pelletised chook manure will provide a long-lasting, slow-burning release of nitrogen that will restore the balance.

3. While some leafy greens will dry up and become hard-stemmed, making repair difficult, subsequent plants will unleash their veggie patch glory.

PHOSPHORUS TROUBLESHOOTING

INTRODUCING

BEETROOT (BEETS)

1. Sometimes you get a lot of unnecessary attention, or in the case of beetroot, lots of leaf foliage – indicating an oversupply of nitrogen – at the expense of more desirable root growth. This indicates an undersupply of phosphorus.

2. Blood and bone provides the best, fastest-acting release of phosphorus that we have. Mix through the soil where the beetroot are growing.

3. Patience is rewarded with swelling roots.

POTASSIUM TROUBLESHOOTING

INTRODUCING

CITRUS

1. People get pretty excited when growing citrus plants, but become despondent when they produce an abundance of foliage but the plant keeps dropping its flowers. This is common when there is an oversupply of nitrogen (stop fertilising so much!). It usually means more potassium is required. This is a common problem with tomato plants too.

2. When flowers/fruit are expected but not forthcoming, add liquid potassium to the patch.

3. Potassium helps with flower production and fruit setting, so the plant's energy will shift from producing lots of leaf foliage to more desirable fruit. Now, you have something to get excited about!

SOIL AMENDMENTS

There are so many soil products on the market that it can become confusing and overwhelming. However, regularly mixing organic compost and cow manure through the garden should be enough to fulfil most of its nutritional needs and build great soil. Nevertheless, there are times when we need to target specific deficiencies. Whether trying to meet the feeding needs of certain plants or correcting an imbalance in our soil, these are some of the most common and useful soil amendments.

MANURES

Animal poo doesn't just come in different shapes and sizes. It differs in composition and the way it helps your plants grow.

PELLETISED VS RAW

By pelletising manure into small, hard granules, you have a product that provides a slow release of nutrition into the veggie patch without the fear of burning your plants. The disadvantage is that they are heat-treated to high temperatures, so any good biology in the manure is killed off.

Raw manure is packed full of microbes and is like caviar to worms. However, it needs to mellow out for a few weeks before being applied directly to plants. This can mean either allowing a pile of manure to compost off to the side, or giving the veggie patch time to rest after mixing manure through before planting.

POULTRY MANURE

The official 'super poo' of the veggie patch! Very high in nitrogen, it also contains good doses of potassium and phosphorus; the goose (or chicken) that lays the golden egg is no joke. Raw poo will burn your plants if applied directly to the patch, so don't add too much at one time. Alternatively, pelletised poo will slowly break down and should provide a steady supply of essential nutrients to your veggie patch.

Application
Mix through a handful of pelletised manure per metre of the garden bed twice a year.

Nutrients

HORSE MANURE

A powerful animal, with only a moderately powerful poo. Containing about half the amount of nitrogen of chook poo, it will burn the plants if applied directly to the patch, so will need to break down before applying. As such, composting is recommended; this will also help break down undigested weeds.

Application
Mix composted horse manure through the garden bed in spring and autumn by folding it into the top 20 cm (8 in) of soil.

Nutrients

COW MANURE

Though similar in its powers to horse manure, cow poo can be added directly to the patch in small quantities without burning the plants. However, you still need to beware of undigested weeds. On the other hand, cow poo provides a good source of bacteria and enzymes for your soil. Swings and roundabouts …

Application
Work cow manure directly into the garden bed each season by folding it into the top 20 cm (8 in) of soil.

Nutrients

WORMS

The most common types of composters are tiger worms and red worms. They are among our biggest allies in the garden and help us to physically break down organic waste to create compost. Furthermore, by digesting organic material they chemically alter nutrients, making them more accessible to our plants.

Application
Worms can be added directly to the patch or compost and will rapidly multiply with stable temperatures and organic material to eat.

Nutrients
Not applicable

WORM WEE

Not wee at all, this concentrated by-product is more accurately described as compost juice. As time, worms and microbes break down organic waste, there is a natural discharge of this dark liquid containing nutrients, enzymes and living organisms. Closed composting systems and worm farms will have a tap valve to drain off this liquid. Dilute with water, in a ratio of 1:5, in a large watering can and spread over the garden as a fertiliser.

Application
Depending on your set-up, as often as it accumulates. Once a month is about right.

Nutrients

WORM CASTINGS

Also known as worm poo or vermicast, this is the fully digested result of worm composting, which contains conditioned nutrients and unhatched worm eggs. Castings are pH neutral and loaded with nutrients that are easily accessible to plants. Castings will feel light and fluffy to the touch and will hold their shape rather than crumble when compressed in the hand. Spread over the top of the garden and water in.

Application
Once every couple of months, or as often as available. You can't overdo it.

Nutrients

OTHER AMENDMENTS

COMPOST

The single greatest thing to happen to the garden since tomatoes and basil, good-quality organic compost is pH neutral, rich in organic matter, and contains high levels of the necessary trace elements. It is just about all that any veggie patch requires.

Application
Mix compost through the garden bed at the beginning and end of each growing season.

Nutrients
N P K Ca Mg

BLOOD AND BONE MIX

One of the best organic sources of nitrogen and phosphorus, blood and bone is a slow-release fertiliser made from the waste scraps of the meat industry. A little will go a long way, so use sparingly to avoid burning plants.

Application
Dig through soil a couple of weeks prior to planting to a depth of 20–30 cm (8–12 in). One application will last about four months.

Nutrients
N P

SEAWEED SOLUTION

A concentrated liquid or powder fertiliser typically made from kelp, seaweed solution has high levels of most essential nutrients and is nitrogen-rich. Because it's plant-based, seaweed solution has natural plant hormones, which improve overall health.

Application
Apply fortnightly. For best absorption, dilute in water and use a spray bottle to mist plant foliage – or use a diluted solution in a watering can and shower the veggie garden.

Nutrients
N K Ca

FISH EMULSION

This fast-acting, concentrated liquid fertiliser is made from by-products of the fishing industry or chopped up non-native invasive species. It's an excellent source of nitrogen and helps promote good microbial growth within the soil. When diluted with water, there is little risk of burning plants, so use liberally.

Application
Dilute with water and use a watering can to apply monthly during peak growing seasons. Pour over plant foliage and the root zone.

Nutrients
N

ROCK MINERALS/ ROCK PHOSPHATE

This crushed rock is often a quarry by-product. Rock minerals (also known as rock dust) are not only rich in phosphorus, but also contain lots of other great minerals. While the entire gardening world focuses on N–P–K, the best soils don't stop there. More minerals in the ground not only means more vitamins in your vegetables, but also more diversity of life in your soil.

Application
Before planting, sprinkle liberal quantities of rock dust over the veggie patch and mix into the soil. This is very slow releasing, so don't worry about burning plants or overdoing it.

Nutrients
P K Ca Mg

EPSOM SALT (MAGNESIUM SULPHATE)

A naturally occurring mineral that prevents plant diseases such as leaf blight in tomatoes, it's good for all flowering plants. One of those 'must do' applications at the start of the warm season.

Application
Dissolve 1 tablespoon per 4 litres (135 fl oz/16 cups) of water and apply liberally every month to the root zone and plant foliage.

Nutrients
Mg

SULPHATE OF POTASH

A concentrated potassium and sulphur fertiliser that is essentially a type of salt that will dissolve when watered into the garden, sulphate of potash can be applied in a dry form (slow release) or liquid form (fast release) and should be added to the garden before plants start to flower. Be careful, as potash can increase soil pH, so don't overdo it. Many people will mix it with blood and bone to get a balanced all-purpose fertiliser that ticks all the N–P–K boxes.

Application
Apply to plant root zone prior to flowering.

Nutrients
K

GYPSUM

The naturally occurring mineral in gypsum, calcium sulphate, is used to break up heavy clays to improve soil structure. Gypsum will also help to reduce salts present in soil and should be dug into the veggie patch to a depth of 20 cm (8 in). Combine with compost for long-term benefits.

Application
A month before planting and only when dealing with especially heavy or salty soil.

Nutrients
Ca

GARDEN LIME/ DOLOMITE LIME

This naturally occurring calcium and magnesium fertiliser will raise soil pH and is often used to remediate soil acidity. It provides a shock therapy that is a last-resort attempt to increase pH when you have explored more conservative options.

Application
Dig into soil to a depth of at least 30 cm (12 in) at the end of autumn. Allow it to work through soil over winter.

Nutrients
Ca Mg

ALUMINIUM SULPHATE

This chemical compound is used as a shock method to reduce soil pH over time. When using a product like this, regular pH testing is important, and it should be used as a last resort to alter soil pH when you have exhausted more conservative options.

Application
Sprinkle over the surface and water in if plants are already established. Dig through soil to a depth of about 30 cm (12 in) in unplanted soil.

Nutrients
Not applicable

NUTRIENT WATER

A number of concentrated liquid fertilisers are used for hydroponic growing, and they come in two forms – chemical-based and plant-based. The chemical-based nutrient waters are strong in effect but about as far from organic gardening as Australia is to the North Pole. Plant- and animal-derived products are more readily available, and while still not certified organic, they are a massive improvement. Typically there are different formulas for vegetative or flower/fruit growth.

Application
Add nutrients to the reservoir and let it settle for an hour or two. Check the pH once settled to ensure water is still between 5.5 and 6.5.

Nutrients
N P K Ca Mg

MULCHES

If we could make all gardeners do one thing, it would be to water regularly. But if we could make them do two things it would be to water regularly and to mulch. Mulch suppresses weeds, insulates the soil from extreme hot and cold, regulates moisture in the soil, and slowly releases nutrients as it decomposes. While some consider it to be an extracurricular activity, the truth is if you want to be a better gardener, start mulching.

BASIC MULCHING

1   Mulching is like a blanket that stabilises the temperature underneath. When we want to insulate the soil we pull it over; similarly, when we want to allow the temperature to change, we pull it off. As all plant growth is dictated by the soil temperature, you need to use that blanket as required. During the cold months it will keep plants warm, but in the hot months it will keep plants cool and reduce evaporation. Pull much of it aside in early spring to let the sun's rays warm up the frigid soil. Conversely, pull it over once the soil is sufficiently warm and it's time to lock it in. The same process applies in autumn.

2   The type of mulch is key; we prefer something with nutritional value and that is easy to use. Pulverised pea straw, lucerne hay or sugar cane are best.

3   How deep to go? Well, if your mulch is too shallow, it's rendered ineffective and won't properly suppress weeds, retain moisture or insulate. But if you go too deep, water may struggle to penetrate, you may prohibit the growth of plants and heighten the chance of stem rot. So, this is where our 'Goldilocks principle' of ambiguous advice comes in – not too deep, not too shallow, just right! Or somewhere between your first and second knuckle – about 3–5 cm (1¼–2 in).

PULVERISED VS NON-PULVERISED VS PELLETISED

Pulverised mulch has been ground down into a finer blend and is easier to handle and apply, particularly in small spaces and around small plants. Non-pulverised (or raw) mulch, on the other hand, is bulkier and more suited to big spaces where delicate placement doesn't matter as much. And now there are also mulching pellets. These are heat-treated pellets that are dust-free, abrasive-free and pretty much hassle-free for the small-space gardener. Easy to manoeuvre around your plants, they expand into a mulch-like form once watered.

PEA STRAW

High in nitrogen and often most commonly available in large non-pulverised bales, pea straw can not only be used on the surface as an effective mulch, but is also commonly used as a layer when setting up a no-dig garden bed. As it breaks down, pea straw will restore nitrogen into the soil and will often sprout fresh pea shoots. Bonus snacks!

Application
Once per growing season, after seedlings are larger than 10 cm (4 in).

Nutrients
N

PELLETISED LUCERNE (ALFALFA) HAY

Another great basic mulch and also high in nitrogen, lucerne tends to be quite dusty, so don't wear your Christmas jumper when handling this stuff. Don't be surprised to see a few wild grasses sprouting in the lucerne, as it is grown in large pastures and grass seeds tend to come along for the journey. However, you can find pelletised lucerne these days, which is heat-treated and guaranteed to be weed-free; problem solved.

Application
Once per growing season, after seedlings are larger than 10 cm (4 in).

Nutrients
N

SUGAR CANE

A commonly available mulch that is relatively high in nitrogen, but not quite to the standard of pea or lucerne. Be sure to get the stuff that is marked as organic (commercial sugar cane production uses lots of nasty chemicals). We generally get the pulverised kind – it's easy to handle, breaks down quickly and is good for rapidly restoring nutrients to the patch. It also fits neatly into the spaces between seedlings.

Application
Once per growing season, after seedlings are larger than 8 cm (3¼ in).

Nutrients
N

BARK/WOODCHIPS

More of a landscaping mulch than an edible gardening option, bark and woodchips are very slow to break down, and are a bit of a hassle to move around every time that you replant the veggie patch. Nevertheless, if you want to mulch a garden bed and forget about it (such as an established bed filled with perennial herbs), wood chips are a viable option.

Application
Apply to perennial beds once plants are taller than 10 cm (4 in).

Nutrients
Not applicable

UNDERSTANDING pH

I've been testing pH all my life. Checking our pool's pH was my first domestic job – far more important than putting out the bins or mowing the lawns. There was always a sense of pride when my dad called upon me to determine the quality of our pool water, and to give some meaning to the yellow scum building up underwater.

Having access to pool chemicals and apparatus felt like getting the keys to my parents' car. I was sure it was powerful and in the wrong hands could cause some real damage, but with resolve and diligence I tested the water and took whatever action necessary. It later dawned on me that the scum in the pool was actually a thriving community of microorganisms that would build up as the pH approached neutrality. Playing God, I would add a bunch of chemicals to kill them and make it sterile again.

Just like that living yellow scum in the pool, edible plants need the soil to be relatively pH neutral in order to thrive. Achieving a soil that is pH neutral will allow plants to access the nutrients in your veggie patch and provide a fertile breeding ground for microorganisms, bringing your soil to life. It's the key to successful gardening in small spaces. Without a balanced soil pH, it doesn't matter what nutrients lie beneath – plants will be incapable of accessing them. It's as cruel as having a smorgasbord of delicious food in front of a hungry person who has their mouth taped shut.

Traditionally, soils tend to be acidic, while additives are alkaline. Unfortunately it's not a simple matter of mixing one acidic ingredient with an alkaline ingredient – and BINGO! – we have a pH-balanced soil. It will happen, but it takes time.

pH THERAPIES

The best way to balance your soil pH is by adding compost and organic matter. This is a softly, softly approach – sort of like talk therapy for your garden. With time and multiple visits we see real and meaningful change, and a balanced pH is just around the corner. We trade in the quick fix for lasting benefits.

Naturally, however, we all want to fix things – and the quicker the better. While we don't recommend shock therapy, we can call upon help in severe cases of pH imbalance. With very acidic soil – typical for Australian conditions – we add lime or gypsum to break it down and restore balance. For very alkaline soils – much more uncommon – there is aluminium sulphate. Be aware that if using a shock therapy to restore the balance in pH, the soil will not be agreeable to planting while that process is in action.

COMPOSTING

How good is compost? You throw a bunch of organic waste into a pile, it heats up, and these things called microbes come along to transform your rubbish into a precious garden commodity! The earth has been doing this forever, locked in an endless cycle of growth, death, decay, compost and fertilisation.

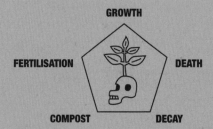

GROWTH

FERTILISATION   DEATH

COMPOST   DECAY

Nutrients are reused again and again. In this way, composting is the ultimate form of recycling, and there is no greater satisfaction than seeing those tangible results in your own garden.

GREEN WASTE + BROWN WASTE + TIME = *PLANT FOOD!*

Fully matured compost is pH neutral and can be used to propagate seeds, but when added to your patch holistically it's like a shot in the vein. It contains a broad spectrum of nutrients and all the essential trace elements, so that it not only boosts a plant's growth, but also the overall activity of life in your soil. Compost is the number one candidate for making soil into something living and correcting any imbalances. It wins Soil Additive of the Year hands down, every year.

About half of our household waste is organic – things like food scraps, coffee grounds, paper and cardboard. It all adds up. When this is mixed with waste that's not organic in a landfill, nothing decomposes properly and the end results are harmful greenhouse gases. Think of organic waste as a powerful weapon that can be used for either good or evil. The very same material can either damage the environment or improve it. Therefore, composting is just as much about avoiding the landfill as it is about creating an organic fertiliser; the time, space and appetite you have for those two outcomes will determine how you decide to compost.

TYPES OF WASTE

BROWN VS GREEN WASTE

There are two main types of organic household wastes: brown and green. The ideal ratio, 2-parts green waste to 1-part brown waste, enables composting to occur fast and efficiently. When out of balance, compost turns into a stinking den of sin (too much green) or a dusty old saloon (too much brown).

GREEN WASTE is 'wet' waste, comprised of nitrogen-rich plant material such as kitchen scraps, but also fresh garden trimmings. It's the main source of food for composting microbes.

BROWN WASTE is 'dry' waste, including carbon-rich plant material such as straw, wood chips, dry leaves, paper, cardboard and sawdust. These lightweight, dry materials help to aerate the compost bin, providing oxygen and carbon for the microbe diet.

ANIMAL WASTE (MEAT, FISH AND DAIRY)

Avoid composting animal waste. In typical urban compost bins, it tends to attract pests, such as rats. Meat also produces anaerobic bacteria, which work against oxygenated (aerobic) composting, causing odour and changing acidity. Rancid meat and dairy can also foster harmful pathogens like our old friend E. coli.

COMPOST SYSTEMS

Efficient composting systems require a minimum of 1m³ of waste to generate high internal temperatures – up to 50–60°C (122–140°F) – to then produce pure compost. Heat breaks down pathogens and also fosters an ideal environment for helpful microbes, which further aid in breaking down waste. These microbes require oxygen to work best and all parts of the pile need to be exposed to the internal high temperature, so the entire batch needs to be mixed and turned over from time to time. We call this a **BIG BATCH** system and it is textbook agricultural composting. However, it requires A LOT of waste.

As with everything in life, we have to strike a balance between best practice and what is practical in our situation. We may not be able to make perfect compost, but we can get close. Everyone has the potential to compost a little and to reduce landfill. In our households, we generate little bits of waste every day and we can dispose of it in a number of ways, which we call **SMALL BATCH** composting. It is not as hot, or as fast, and usually not as effective, but can be done on a much smaller footprint.

SMALL BATCH SYSTEMS

TRENCH COMPOSTING

Dig a deep trench in the garden bed – to 30 cm (12 in) in depth – fill with organic waste and cover with soil.

So simple and so good. Trench composting relies on worms to come and eat the waste in situ. As compost is formed, nutrients are immediately available to plants. No double-handling!

OPEN ABOVE-GROUND SYSTEM

This is a big plastic bin that sits over the ground with an open bottom and a lid on top. These systems have a great capacity – usually about 220 litres (49 gallons) – and seemingly never fill because they are in a constant state of compression and decomposition at the base. For better or worse, pests can also help to reduce the volume and have been known to tunnel great distances to get inside and feed. From a traditional composting perspective, however, it's often difficult to access mature compost at the base.

ENCLOSED TUMBLING SYSTEM

This self-contained system doesn't require any soil. The rotating function is meant to help give all the waste the chance to heat up and turn into compost, but since the units are generally so small it never quite heats up enough.

CLOSED ABOVE-GROUND SYSTEM

Like the open above-ground system, but closed on the bottom and with a low access spot to collect the compost. It also has air vents that are meant to encourage aerobic activity. In-ground compost bins provide a simple solution for avoiding all the usual compost nasties, including burrowing pests, like rats.

DIGGING YOUR COMPOST BIN INTO THE GROUND IS A LARGER-SCALE FORM OF TRENCH COMPOSTING. WHEN YOUR IN-GROUND BIN IS FULL, SIMPLY SLIDE IT OUT OF THE EARTH AND START AGAIN SOMEWHERE ELSE.

CREATING BALANCE IN THE COMPOST BIN

SKILL UP!

Most of us would like to spend more time with the people we love, pursuing activities that we are passionate about. Unfortunately, these pursuits are too often at odds with our work. Finding that perfect equilibrium is a difficult thing, thus the topic of 'work–life balance' has become such a strong theme. While we haven't yet cracked the code in our lives, balance in our compost bins is a lot easier to achieve. Sure, it's a small step, but composting may just take us all one step closer to overall contentment.

In general, we tend to have much more green waste than brown. Food scraps go into the bin every day and the result is that our compost can get a bit saucy, sloppy and stinky. When there isn't enough brown waste to balance the mix, too much moisture and nitrogen can create an anaerobic environment. Food starts to rot and ferment, rather than decompose. A good composting environment needs about two parts green waste to one part brown. Correct the balance by adding a small scoop of mulch every time food scraps are emptied into the compost bin.

1. 'Yuck, it smells like a burnt gorilla hair sandwich.' 'Eww, it's like a fish market on a hot day.' You've got too much green waste! Keep a small container of mulch next to the bin so you are reminded to use it every time you visit the compost bin.

2. Add a small scoop of mulch every time you add green waste and your compost balance will be restored.

WORM FARM

To say that worms love to eat is like saying that Elvis could dance. It is factually correct, but completely misleading in magnitude. Worms were born to eat and none of them are better consumers than tiger and red worms. These natural born composters can be bought from most nurseries and are essential allies in converting your food scraps to nourishing plant fertiliser. While the humble earthworm does an admirable job aerating your garden and processing small amounts of waste, their appetites are nowhere near the same level.

Vermicomposting/vermiculture, or worm composting, is a fast, easy and efficient way to deal with organic waste. Worms will provide unlimited free labour if you treat them well and give them a place to congregate. In fact, well-maintained worm farms can double in population every few months. Furthermore, most systems are freestanding, so it is possible to process organic waste in the absence of garden beds. The end results are nutrient-rich **WORM CASTINGS** and **WORM WEE** that are packed with good bacteria and microbial life.

Worm castings, also known as worm poo or vermicast, are the fully digested product of vermicomposting, which contains conditioned nutrients and unhatched worm eggs. Castings are light and spongy to the touch, with a subtle forest odour. Like a piece of steamed broccoli or cooked kale for humans, worm castings provide an easier way for plants to access nutrients than in their raw form. Castings are pH neutral, so can be spread in mass quantities throughout the garden bed. Worm wee is a concentrated liquid by-product of vermicompost that can be diluted with water and spread through the garden as fertiliser.

The key to maintaining a productive worm farm is providing a comfortable environment. Worms do best between 15°C and 25°C (59°F and 77°F), so it's preferable to keep your worm farm out of the sun and in an insulated container. Worms may be blind, hermaphroditic eating machines, but they still have their preferences. When it comes to feeding, we generally follow the same principles as composting, providing a mixture of green and brown waste. Nevertheless, worms have a special love for coffee grounds, tea bags, fruit and veggie scraps, paper and cardboard. They have a distaste for citrus, onion, garlic, meat and dairy.

The types of infrastructure can be loosely broken into **STACKABLE SYSTEM** and **BIG PILE**.

STACKABLE SYSTEM

Although shapes and sizes will vary, store-bought and homemade worm farms will usually consist of a number of stacking trays with a drainage tap on the bottom level. Each tray will have holes so the worms can pass between them. As the first tray fills with organic waste, worms start eating, making castings and multiplying. Once that tray is filled with scraps and primarily converted into castings, you add another tray on top and add food scraps to which they will migrate, leaving behind their castings. Eventually you should have enough worms to maintain an endless rotation of filling the trays and emptying castings/wee. As the worm population grows they will be able to consume more waste, faster. Like a swarm of bees, your population may need to be split and put in a second farm! One of the main benefits of this system is that it is freestanding and can be used indoors or outdoors.

BIG PILE

The big pile is a glorified compost mound with worms added. For anyone who already has a household compost, it is a no-brainer to add a handful of starter worms. Worms provide a little buffer from over-enthusiastic composters who add too much green waste, as they help convert scraps at a greater rate and provide aeration as they pass through the pile. As with a conventional above-ground compost, the goal here is to keep your organic waste out of the landfill, if not to have the most efficient compost possible. This method has many of the same merits and shortcomings of above-ground composting, but with the added efficiency of worms. It requires more space and soil than a stackable system, but there is very little maintenance involved.

FEEDING WORMS AND PERFECTING YOUR COMPOST

When it comes to composting and worm farming, the size of your scraps is absolutely critical to how long they take to break down. This is a matter of surface area – the finer the scraps, the more exposure they have to oxygen and, therefore, the faster their decomposition. Anyone who enjoys coffee has experienced this first hand. Whole beans keep fresh much longer than a bag of ground espresso. That's because the ground coffee has much more surface area exposed, and thus oxidises very quickly.

Many of us don't have huge back gardens to heap an enormous pile of compost, but even if we do, shouldn't we strive for the best composting practices possible? It goes without saying that worms have tiny mouths. It is indisputable. Yet, when we put organic waste into our compost bin or worm farm we often ignore this obvious characteristic. Instead, we carelessly toss whole plants, large stalks and thick rinds into the bin.

Get into the habit of chopping your organic waste before putting it into the compost bin. It will add an extra minute of kitchen time, but will save months in the compost. It's also a good activity to help develop your youngsters' erratic and inconsistent knife skills – appropriate protection worn and precaution taken, of course!

1. The usual kitchen scraps off to the farm. But remember that it's not your Yorkshire pigs you're feeding – it's your worm friends, and they're tinier than tiny.

2. Rather than throwing them to the worms as they were created, take some time to chop them well. It's great practice for aspiring chefs.

3. Let nature, and your wormies, do the work from here. They're more than capable.

COMPOST BEST PRACTICES

Good composting is all about good practices that should quickly become second nature. Many rookie errors are made by new, over-enthusiastic composters and most can be averted by adopting some of our best practices.

 Keep a sealed bin in the kitchen so that you can collect kitchen scraps indoors. Make the bin a decent size so that you accumulate a useful volume of scraps and don't be tempted to throw organic waste in the bin because it seems to be full all the time.

 The compost bin should be close enough to the house that you don't dread visiting it and not hidden among a bunch of bushes that shake their water on you after every rainfall.

 Finely chop all scraps; it's part knife skill practice, part efficient composting practice (see page 38).

 Avoid adding meat, dairy, fish and citrus. If you want to get serious about composting, by all means adopt a bokashi style of bin and ferment these wastes (see page 40).

 Add a scoop of mulch every time green waste is tossed in the bin. This can be a scoop of any brown waste such as sawdust, mulch, straw, brown leaves, etc. (see page 35).

FERMENTATION COMPOSTING 101

Fermentation is a weird and wonderful version of composting that deserves a closer look.

Commonly known as bokashi, fermentation composting is a technique with origins in east Asia and has a lot more in common with home-brewing than it does traditional compost methods. We like to call it pickled compost. Like pickling, brewing and winemaking, this method relies on a lack of oxygen and an army of anaerobic bacteria fed on yeast and sugar to break down waste. This creates an acidic environment that kills harmful pathogens and is capable of composting meat, fish and dairy.

This is often considered a 'pre-compost' method, because the end product is too acidic to spread directly onto plants. In fact, we recommend transferring your pickled compost waste into a traditional system so that it can fully mature. While it may seem like you are double-composting the waste, the fermentation process not only accelerates how long it takes for waste to break down (saving months), but it is also a safe way to treat meat and dairy scraps.

1. Use a 30-litre (6-gallon) container with an airtight lid and tap at its base. Most set-ups will include a bag of bokashi bran – a mix of dry molasses, yeast and microorganisms.

2. Add kitchen scraps to the vessel and top it off with a scoop of bran each time (two scoops if adding lots of meat). As the bin is filled, continually compress the contents to release any trapped air. Be sure to keep the lid sealed when not adding waste.

3. Once there is no more room for food, add a final scoop of bran and seal the container for 2 weeks. Do not open under any circumstances. After 2 weeks, the food scraps will be pickled. There may also be white mould growing on top, which is completely normal. Discard the batch if mould is blue or black.

4. During fermentation, a liquid by-product will develop and can be drained from the tap at the bottom. This nutrient-rich liquid can be diluted with water and spread through the garden as a fertiliser. Add the pickled food scraps to your compost bin. It will break down fast and be mature within a month.

CONVERTING A WHEELIE BIN FOR WORMS

If you have made it this far in the book, we will assume you are sold on the merits of composting. However, we recognise that not everyone has enough space for a compost bin, or even soil to rest it on. Store-bought composters also tend to be quite expensive, especially given that they are basically plastic rubbish bins with no bottom.

Nevertheless, one of the greatest assets in gardening is resourcefulness and most of us *do* have access to a large wheelie bin. These sturdy containers are designed to hold heavy household waste – making them an excellent option as a retrofitted compost bin.

WHAT YOU NEED

1 wheelie bin

1 measuring tape

1 Stanley knife (box cutter) or jigsaw if you like power tools

10 × 9 mm (½ in) stainless steel screws

1 × 50 mm (2 in) barrel bolt (simple door lock)

2 × 50 mm (2 in) stainless steel door hinges

1 electric drill/driver

1 × 25 mm (1 in) drill bit

1 × 20 mm (¾ in) threaded water tap

1 × 20 mm (¾ in) threaded back nut

10 litres (2 gallons) scoria or gravel

1 geotextile fabric (optional)

1 bag organic compost

tiger worms/red worms

1 old newspaper

food waste

1. Measure and mark a line about 20 cm (8 in) above the base of the wheelie bin. This line will be the base of your composting operation.

2. Create a compost access door using a sharp Stanley knife or jigsaw to cut out a rectangular piece just above the 20 cm (8 in) mark. The piece should be about 20 cm (8 in) x 25 cm (10 in) – at least large enough to scoop out worm castings.

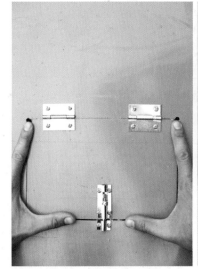

3. Use 9 mm (½ in) screws to attach barrel bolt and door hinges to the compost access door. This will keep it all secure under the weight of a loaded bin.

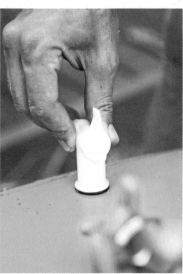

4. On the front of the bin, just near the base, drill a 25 mm (1 in) hole and fit the threaded water tap. This will be your direct source for unpasteurised, local, fair-trade, nutrient-rich worm wee. The good stuff.

5. For easier access to the tap, lift the bin onto a pedestal or elevated point. We have used a milk crate, but just about anything will suffice. The goal here is to create enough space to collect worm wee.

6. Fill the base of the worm farm with gravel/scoria up to the bottom of your compost access door. This will assist drainage, filter the worm wee, and ensure that compost is not sopping wet at the bottom. Cover the top of the scoria with a geotextile fabric to keep compost from clogging the tap.

7. Add a bag of organic compost to the bin along with your tiger/red worms (worms can be found at many nurseries and online).

8. Layer newspaper on top and wet it using a hose or watering can, so that worms have something to eat while they wait for your food scraps to start rolling in.

9. For a domestic household, you will find it takes a very long time to fill the bin, as it will continue to compress under its own weight. However, you can always use the compost access door at the base to withdraw fresh compost and worm castings, thereby freeing up some space on top.

10. Worm wee should be regularly added to your watering regime and will infuse your garden with vital nutrients.

WATER

Water is the most fundamental component of every living thing on this planet. It has a finger in every pie, from the chemical reactions in our cells, to the air we breathe, to that electrical lump we call a brain. The special someone you love is mostly water. Your favourite vegetable is mostly water. It pulls down mountains and puts out fires. Water trumps all other elements, yet why do so many people forget to add it to their gardens?

We like to say that there is no such thing as a bad gardener, only bad waterers. Plants absorb water through their roots, stems and leaves, but you still have to give them a chance to do so. Like us, plants need water for all biological functions. They need it for photosynthesis and they 'sweat' it to cool themselves (evapotranspiration). Unlike us, however, plants don't have skeletons, so they need internal water pressure (turgor) to keep their limbs and leaves firm. This is why unwatered or overheated plants droop – they don't have enough water pressure to maintain strong and sturdy limbs.

When we water can make all the difference, because plants need to have access to water when they really need it the most – during the day. Photosynthesis is how plants make their food, and it requires sunlight plus water. This means that plants can only 'eat' during the daytime. Therefore, the best practice is to water all your plants first thing in the morning.

How much we water is also an important consideration. In comparison to many decorative plants, our favourite edible crops require a lot of water. In the case of well-drained soil and potting mix, we can safely water our veggies once a day without the risk of becoming waterlogged. Denser soils with less passage for air can become anoxic and rot the roots (this is why hydroponics/aquaponics systems have aerators).

Knowing your soil and plants is the key to understanding water quantities. If your soil remains saturated days after watering (lots of clay), simply reduce watering frequency and plant varieties that enjoy extra moisture, like leafy greens. On the other hand, free-draining sandy soils will require extra soaking. In either case, regularly add compost to your soil to help improve both retention of water and drainage. Weird, right?

SURFACE WATERING

The direct application of water to the garden's surface ensures that water percolates from the top down. It's like trickle-down economics, but it actually works.

MANUAL WATERING

When most of us think of watering the garden, it is manual surface watering that comes to mind. There you are in all your glory, sun filtering through the trees, legs wide and chest out, proud grin and ready to converse with any passer-by. You spray a broad fan of water across the garden, watching fleeting rainbows form in the mist. Yes, this is the life and you are garden royalty!

The benefit of manual watering is that it provides an excellent opportunity to inspect the veggie patch. It is a moment to track progress and address any issues. Furthermore, gardening isn't all about growing things; it is equally as important to step outside and take a moment to engage with something other than a screen. Manual watering is that moment. That perfect garden bliss.

For those who choose to water manually, the best advice we can give is to water in the morning and water the base of the plants. Many pests tend to operate under the cover of nightfall and are attracted to moist plants and soil like sharks to chum. Watering in the evening is an open invitation for a feeding frenzy. Furthermore, plants will require water throughout the day, so by giving them a good drink first thing, they will be able to draw upon it as required. Think of this as giving your garden its daily cup of coffee. In fact, you can do it while drinking your coffee. Best friends forever.

Many of us, in our excitement, tend to spray water everywhere but the base of our plants. Although water does look great on the leaf foliage, it is most helpful near the roots. Directing your flow to the base of the plant will get water to the roots faster and also reduce unnecessary evaporation. Leaving your foliage wet on a hot, sunny day does add extra risk of leaf burn. So, when every drop counts, it's always better to water near the root system.

HYDROPHOBIC SOIL

The greatest challenge of small-space gardening is hydration. The smaller your pot, the more susceptible it is to drying out. Compounding that challenge is our lifestyle, which is often poorly suited to any task requiring a routine. Getting your watering wrong at the wrong time of year not only spells trouble for that generation of plants, but for the future of the soil.

Without moisture the soil can bake dry under the harsh sun, making it impervious to water. At this point it becomes hydrophobic. Try as you might, any amount of water thrown on the veggie patch is not absorbed in the soil, but rather finds the path of least resistance and drains straight through.

Once soil is hydrophobic it's a long road back. So long, in fact, that despite being able to slowly restore it using wetting agents and hydration liquids, we usually recommend starting afresh. Few people have the attention span to last an entire presidential debate, let alone wait weeks, even months, for potted soil to be useful again. At the very least, replace the top few inches of the most badly affected soil.

To insure against future hydrophobic soil, you have a few options. The first is a simple irrigation system that relies on a timer rather than yourself, the second is mulching, and the third relates to the style of growing. Wicking, hydroponic and aquaponic gardening are all self-watering systems. While they seem more complicated at first, they take care of the most critical element of vegetable gardening and the place where most people fall over – water.

1. It starts well. You buy the best quality potting mix, the perfect sized pot and plant in peak season. You water daily, and your plants are doing great.

2. A small stumble; work gets busy. But then so does the rest of your life. Your watering routine is now erratic at best and the plants soon begin to suffer.

3. The season has passed and a new one is about to break. You replace your failed twigs with fresh seedlings. Nothing but greatness ahead!

4. Despite daily watering, the plant seems to be stunted.

5. Months of neglect have rendered your soil hydrophobic and it can no longer absorb water.

AUTOMATED WATERING

Automated irrigation takes a lot of human error out of watering. It allows you to deliver a set quantity of water directly to the base of your plants at a prescribed time (quantity and timing are two of the biggest problems in the veggie patch). It also means that you don't have to ask your neighbour to water your garden while you're out of town. You can travel with the confidence that, as you sip your negroni in Tuscany, your Tuscan kale is also getting its fill back home.

While an automated system does require some investment and set-up, irrigation supplies can be readily purchased from most hardware stores and installation can be done with a few simple tools. Like all investments, it is the long-term benefit that we are after. The small cost of getting your veggie patch automated will be doubly repaid in the years of garden glory that lay ahead.

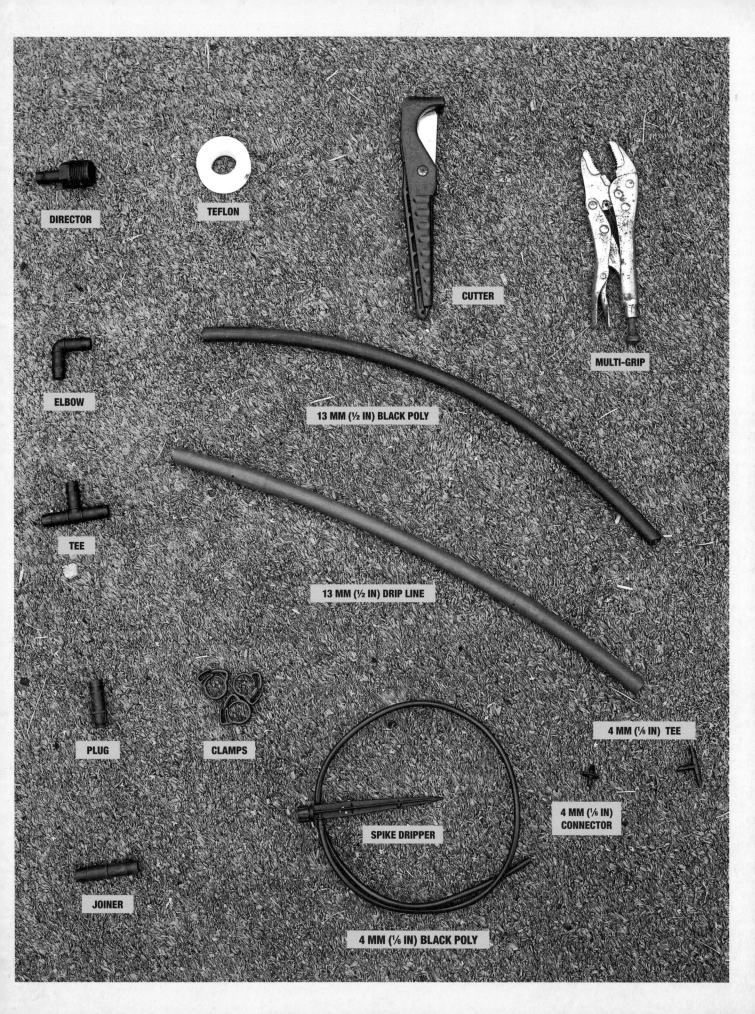

DIRECTOR

TEFLON

CUTTER

MULTI-GRIP

ELBOW

13 MM (½ IN) BLACK POLY

TEE

13 MM (½ IN) DRIP LINE

PLUG

CLAMPS

4 MM (⅙ IN) TEE

SPIKE DRIPPER

4 MM (⅙ IN) CONNECTOR

JOINER

4 MM (⅙ IN) BLACK POLY

IRRIGATION 101

 1 ## SETTING UP AN IRRIGATION TIMER + FEED LINE

You can pay a professional or be a boss and automate your dripper system to the mains water supply, or you can choose a simpler, more economical way. There are many basic timers to choose from, and installation is a cinch.

1. Make sure that you split your tap into two: one is for your timer and the second is so you can still hose down the kids when they're misbehaving.

2. All timers are pretty simple to install and have a number of setting options for multiple waterings/timings per day.

3. Use 13 mm (½ in) black poly to feed water to your veggie patch, or larger 18 mm (¾ in) tubing if your patch is some distance away (this increases the flow of water pressure). Warning: pressure may need to be regulated for small systems with few drip points.

CONNECTING THE PIECES (NO HARDER THAN LEGO)

Thankfully I'm a relatively new father whose kids have taken to Lego, but before those days I got my fix connecting up irrigation pieces (sad, isn't it?).

1. Just like Lego, all the pieces make sense and putting them together is totally intuitive.

2. Push the hose onto either end of the pieces. This is easier to do when warm and the line is soft. Remember not to cut the hose too close to a valve, as there won't be enough hose to connect your piece.

3. Because water pressure has a habit of popping off the pieces, secure each join with a clamp.

 ## SETTING UP A GRID

Even, consistent watering of the patch is the ultimate goal. So when setting up your grid system you need to ensure the drip valves are evenly spaced over the soil.

1. Drip valves are spaced out every 30 cm (12 in) on the hose length.

2. Make evenly spaced rows, 30 cm (12 in) wide, to ensure even distribution of water through the soil.

3. This means that young seedlings will need surface watering initially.

✦ POT IRRIGATION

Most pots will be too small for grids of the poly tubing, so a spike dripper will be the best way to irrigate these. It's still very much child's play, though not as satisfying as Lego.

1. A spike dripper is an adjustable fan spray that is best used to irrigate pots.

2. They can be added directly into the poly tubing by making an incision using a small punch tool or delicate work with a small knife. Insert a 4 mm (⅛ in) connector into the cut hose.

3. Then use 4 mm (⅛ in) plastic tubing to feed the water to your pot, to which the spike dripper is attached.

4. The size of the plant/tree will determine how many spike drippers to use and the flow rates, but be aware that while the brown drip holes release 2–3 litres (½–¾ gallon) of water every hour, a fully opened spike dripper releases 50 times that amount!

5 WALL GARDEN IRRIGATION

Gravity can often lead to our downfall – like when jumping out of a plane without a parachute, standing on your head for too long, or even trying to get out of bed in the morning – but when it comes to irrigating wall gardens, it works in our favour. The key is to provide a water source at the top and let simple physics do the rest.

1. Using your skills acquired so far, irrigate the top boxes using our adjustable spike drippers.

2. As each box becomes saturated, water drains onto the next below, until all have been watered. Set the watering duration to the time it takes for the bottom box to become saturated (or even a few moments earlier), as any excess will be a waste of this precious resource.

WICKING RESERVOIR

Wicking beds, or self-watering gardens, have gained a lot of popularity and for good reason – they are essentially a garden built on top of a self-administering water reservoir (more on pages 72–75). Soil 'wicks' extend into the water below and draw water upwards through the physical process of capillary action (also called wicking). Just as a lantern's wick draws oil, soil draws water up into the plant's root zone.

Wicking is an extremely efficient watering system because water is available for mature plants whenever they need it and, unlike surface watering, minimal water is lost to evaporation, particularly when mulch is applied. As a result, little to no moisture is present near the surface. This not only benefits the plants that are growing, but inhibits the presence of weeds and pests. Furthermore, less maintenance is required and gardeners will only need to fill the reservoir a couple of times per month.

Wicking beds are not a silver bullet, however, as seeds and seedlings will still need to be surface watered until they become established. Once plants mature enough to have larger root systems, they can be weaned from surface watering and will be able to draw from the water reservoir below. These are great for thirsty summer plants like tomato, eggplant (aubergine), pumpkin (winter squash) and zucchini (courgette).

FLOW SYSTEM
(AQUAPONICS/HYDROPONICS)

Flow watering systems are completely unlike any other watering practice in that there is no soil present. The water itself carries all of the nutrients to plants and is enhanced with synthetic and/or organic fertilisers. In this way, our water acts both as hydration and growing medium. Nevertheless, some of our basic watering principles still apply – namely, that roots require oxygen. In these systems water is oxygenated with air pumps – like in an aquarium – or by the flow of water itself, and many systems will also operate on timers so that water levels periodically drop enough to aerate plants' roots.

Because water circulates through mostly closed pipes/trays, flow systems have virtually no evaporation and are extremely water efficient. Watering is entirely automated and systems will only require minimal top ups, about once per month. However, set-ups can be quite costly and complicated. And the need to continually run pumps is not only energy-intensive, but also limits the places where systems can operate.

LIGHT

MacGyver is legendary for his ability to combine a bunch of everyday items to make something useful. Like when he used a sleeping bag, tank of oxygen and vodka to blow himself out of a snow cave. Or when he used a candelabra, microphone cord and a rubber mat to make a defibrillator. Well, when it comes to the use of light, plants make MacGyver look like Huckleberry Finn.

Plants use photosynthesis to convert light energy into chemical energy. A simplified explanation is that when light hits a plant's leaves, CO_2 from the air reacts with water in the plant to create sugars (plant food) and oxygen. Oxygen is the by-product, which is why we talk about places like the Amazon rainforest as the 'lung' of the earth. A lot of photosynthesis happening at one time can produce a lot of oxygen. The sugars then spur the growth of the plant.

Just like we need essential vitamin D to be healthy, photosynthesis is essential for the successful growing of edible plants. But there's a belief among some would-be growers that only direct sunlight can achieve these outcomes. Thinking they don't possess the environment in which to grow food, they resort to soulless indoor plants, even terrariums, to get their growing fix. It's a crying shame.

As our cities continue to build up and our living spaces dwindle, direct sunlight is becoming more of a scarce commodity. Thankfully, that doesn't mean you can't grow food.

> PAINTING A DULL WALL WHITE WILL CREATE MORE REFLECTIVE LIGHT TO BOUNCE OFF AND ONTO YOUR PLANTS. IT CAN MAKE ALL THE DIFFERENCE!

FULL SUN VS PARTIAL SUN/ SHADE

Our fruits, veggies and herbs all have their own respective light requirements, but in general, more light is always better. Even if a plant's tag states its requirements as partial shade, let it be known that full sun is always preferable. Yes, it just may demand some elevated maintenance, more water for example, but more rays almost always translates to better growth.

So, when a plant's tag indicates it wants partial shade, what it's really saying is that it may become stressed by hot afternoon sunlight. For these varieties, try to find them a space that collects the gentler morning sun.

DIRECT LIGHT VS INDIRECT LIGHT

If there isn't a direct beam hitting a space, it doesn't mean that it is dim. Different colours and materials will reflect light in varying brightnesses. If your wall is bright white and smooth, it will bounce light much better than one that is dark and irregular. While both may not have direct sunlight, one will be brightly lit and suitable for growing food.

For that reason you shouldn't become preoccupied with only direct sunlight in the patch. Although much gardening literature will attest to needing 4–6 hours of direct sunlight to grow tomatoes, for example, you really don't need to grab a stopwatch and measure the rays hitting the patch.

Just like MacGyver can find his way out of a snow cave, light has a habit of finding its way to your veggie patch, and reflective light can play a big part in bolstering stocks. So, while we can all make the educated guess that a tomato will not grow in complete darkness, you are never going to know what will grow in your space without trying.

Our advice is to start with plants that are known to be less needy, and then when you succeed, graduate. We've seen bananas and avocados grow in the temperate south of Australia, so why can't a tomato grow between two buildings?

If you happen to be left with a dud of a growing space, with little direct or indirect light, there are still options available. A bright wall will bounce so much more light than a dark one – creating a new spectrum of growing opportunities – and in the event that fails, technology and a host of artificial lights are there to give us a helping hand.

ARTIFICIAL LIGHT

Our expanding cities mean that natural sunlight, whether direct or indirect, is becoming a scarce commodity. However, artificial lighting is one way to meet the increasing demand for locally and organically grown food without the energy, expense and loss of freshness associated with long-distance transport. Most importantly, it is a way for people to grow food year-round in places where it was previously impossible.

We've been generating artificial light for centuries, and flicking a switch to create light is as natural as pulling a carrot from the veggie patch. Well, probably more natural to most. So then, why does the idea of artificial light for growing food seem so unnatural, or at the very least only reserved for those *secretly* growing plants in their homes?

We tend to be sceptical about new technology, but eventually most people come around. Unlike the clunky, hot and expensive-to-operate technologies of old, LED and fluorescent bulbs have made artificial lighting more accessible than ever before. It doesn't have to be a complete replacement for old growing techniques, but it is yet another tool. When considering lighting, it is important to think about how natural, visible light affects plants. There are three main attributes:

INTENSITY
Can be thought of as the power of a light source. Anyone who burns easily has a good understanding of the difference between morning full-sun and midday full-sun. It's still bright, but there is a difference in intensity. Grow lights also offer a range of intensities.

DURATION
Length of time that the sun is out. Plants only photosynthesise in the presence of light, so duration becomes very important. Our summer plants are tuned to long days, while winter crops thrive on short days. Grow lights can customise day length to best suit crops, no matter the season.

COLOUR OF LIGHT
As rainbows and prisms often remind us, visible light is actually composed of different coloured wavelengths – red, orange, green, blue, indigo, violet. Blue wavelengths are important for vegetative growth, while red wavelengths promote fruit and flower development. Grow lights can enrich specific light colours to maximise productivity.

FLUORESCENT

By far the most economical to buy, but can be inefficient to run. Generic bulbs provide more of the blue spectrum, but you can get 'full spectrum' lights or those that specialise in blue and red. The lights stay cool, allowing you to position them close to the plant where they maximise their growing effect on your plants.

LED

More expensive to buy, but more efficient to run. Customised LED lights provide all the wavelengths that plants need and are low heat, meaning you can place them close to your plants. The effectiveness of LED light stays stronger over a greater distance from the plant than their fluorescent counterparts. The most promising technology yet and widely used in commercial operations.

WHILE VIRTUALLY ALL EDIBLE PLANTS ARE SUN WORSHIPPERS AND WILL THRIVE IN BRIGHT CONDITIONS, SOME CAN GET BY ON LESS DIRECT LIGHT THAN OTHERS.

A DIM CORNER	UNITED KINGDOM LIGHT CONDITIONS. WHAT IS SUNSHINE?	BRIGHT SPACE, BUT LIMITED DIRECT LIGHT	A COUPLE OF HOURS DIRECT LIGHT EACH DAY	LOTS OF LIGHT MAKES US THRIVE! OFTEN GROWN IN THE SHADE OF TALL SUMMER CROPS	LOTS OF LIGHT! BRING ON THE SUN AND HEAT! ALL SUN. ALL DAY. EVERYDAY. WE ARE TANOREXIC
Mint	Potato	Leafy vegetables	Broad beans	Zucchini (courgette)	Chilli
Lemon/lime balm	Horseradish	Alliums	Beans	Cucumber	Capsicum (bell pepper)
	Ginger	Root vegetables	Peas	Squash	Eggplant (aubergine)
	Jerusalem artichoke	Cauliflower	Deciduous fruit trees	Melon	Citrus
	Turmeric	Broccoli	Coriander (cilantro)	Strawberry	Tomato
		Cabbage		Perennial herbs and vegetables	Basil
		Kale			Corn
		Brussels sprouts			

BASIC INDOOR GROWING

SKILL UP!

Sometimes I think about all of the perfect waves that go unsurfed at night. It is usually around sunset when conditions are amazing and you wish that you could stay out for a few more hours. The best conditions in the world are often missed because of one major barrier: light. Sure, I understand that there is a certain romance to limitations, but sometimes I just want to surf! The same is true with growing plants indoors. We live in an insulated, almost pest-free environment, yet without the right light conditions it is very difficult to grow edible plants indoors.

One of the main things that we tell our clients is to grow food as close to the kitchen as possible – that way it is easier to access. Using artificial lights, we can actually grow food in the kitchen. We don't need synthetic fertilisers, chemicals or frankenscience seeds. It's just normal plants, on a windowsill, with a little bit of extra light. Don't be afraid.

1. Most flat dwellers only have the kitchen space to grow food.

2. We use a self-watering pot with potting mix, perlite (for aeration) and some vermiculite (for water retention).

3. We've bought a simple LED panel from a local hydroponics store. It has a bit of a college dorm room vibe, but it's also charming in a futuristic growing kind of way. LED grow-light heaven. We run the lights on a timer for 6 hours per day.

4. Try to keep the lights about 25 cm (10 in) from foliage, though distance isn't nearly as important with LEDs as fluorescents. Herbs anyone?

GROWING STYLE (INFRASTRUCTURE)

We are judged by many things in life. The type of car we drive is one of them. Our choice of political party is another. But just because I'm a Volvo-driving Greens voter doesn't mean I'm a hippie who has trouble navigating my vehicle at pace.

The type of growing infrastructure you choose has typically defined you as a food gardener, too. People who grow in pots are seen as hoarders; people who plant in the ground are considered resourceful; and people who grow indoors using hydroponic systems … well, we don't have to say.

However, the dynamic of food growing is changing and the type of system you choose isn't necessarily a representation of who you are. Rather, it's a solution to your food-growing proposition and the aspirations that you harbour.

So, while homeowners living on the idyllic quarter-acre block would tend to grow in-ground or in raised beds, renters with only a balcony space and limited budget would mostly use pots. And then there are the apartment dwellers, with no more than a kitchen benchtop as their real estate. Traditionally, the idea of growing edible plants indoors sat in the 'too hard' basket but, as more and more people flock to cities and downsize their dwellings, indoor growing will soon be the only option available to most. It can be done.

Just like the Volvo – what a car! – growing food has reinvented itself over the last couple of decades, and you may be surprised that regardless of the space at our disposal or the skill set that you possess, growing food is something that we are all capable of doing.

RATINGS EXPLAINED

ᗦ COST: Initial outlay to build/obtain infrastructure

◎ COMPLEXITY: Intricacy of the set-up

◊ WATER USAGE: Amount of regular watering required

$ MAINTENANCE: Ongoing work to keep crops growing

IN-GROUND

COST $

COMPLEXITY   ◉

WATER USAGE   ◊ ◊

MAINTENANCE   ⌂ ⌂ ⌂

👍 Advantages

- The most cost-effective way to get started, because you don't have to go out and buy soil ... it's already there!
- Soil temperature is more insulated, creating a more stable, user-friendly environment for the plants.
- More room to move – for you, your plant friends, and their roots.
- Greater water retention than potting mixes (unless it's very sandy).
- In most cases, there will be good-natured microorganisms housed in the soil, living their lives and making it more hospitable for plants.

👎 Disadvantages

- Difficult to tend, particularly for those with back issues, which is pretty much everyone.
- Compaction as a result of constant foot traffic.
- Most soils tend to be acidic and in need of a lot of work.
- Potential contamination due to unknown history of soil.
- Generally not as presentable and less well defined.

An idea of permaculture is to start with what you have, and then improve it – which implies you have something to work on in the first place, such as a patch of earth. It's a slow burn, but a very satisfying progression – from naked and probably infertile land, to a patch fully clothed and absolutely teeming with life. Soil that has been worked on and grown in for years is blue chip. Even the saddest-looking plants or most challenging varieties will grow well in this magical stuff.

However, growing in-ground in urban areas isn't without its difficulties and inherent risks. Many soils – particularly those that haven't contained plant life for some time – tend to be baked hard and acidic. This makes the food-growing proposition a difficult one. And then there's the potential for contaminants, which will compromise the safety of the food you intend to eat. Cities have a long and mixed history of residential/industrial occupants, and urban soil can contain anything from asbestos and lead, to arsenic. These are not things we want in our food systems, and there are plenty of ways to test and then mitigate risk.

So, if you're lucky enough to walk the bare earth at the place you live, or in the place you are considering to grow food, in-ground vegetable gardening tends to be the most economical and most rewarding. Just make sure you do your due diligence before jumping in.

RAISED GARDEN BED

COST $ $ $
COMPLEXITY   ◎ ◎
WATER USAGE   ○ ○ ○
MAINTENANCE   ♥ ♥ ♥

👍 Advantages

- Allows for the importation of new growing medium.
- Ergonomic.
- By elevating the growing height, there is greater access to sunlight.
- Excellent drainage.
- Less competition from ground-level trees and shrubs.
- Building an enclosed space for growing food builds ownership/accountability, which we find improves the likelihood of success.

👎 Disadvantages

- Can be costly and/or time consuming to build.
- Having the base open to the soil still exposes you to the risk of contaminants and creeping tree roots.
- Space is required to accommodate one.
- Bulk soil can have fluctuating pH levels.

Where would our business be without the humble raised garden bed? The answer: with more back problems and less satisfied customers. The raised garden bed was what our business was built on and in the early years we couldn't escape the smell of cypress pine or red gum timber. It was our bread and butter, and always served with cups of tea and biscuits.

We remember those early years fondly; an uncomplicated life of power tools, timber and bolts. You'd leave early in the morning hungry for the feel of a circular saw, then return home with a nose full of sawdust. Despite the occasional flesh-seeking splinter missile, there were few hiccups along the way.

In terms of lifestyle changes and starting to grow your own food, the humble raised garden bed is often the protagonist for change. And while our raised bed has almost become an extinct beast at the Little Veggie Patch Co, if you have the space and a hunger for the taste of sawdust, this one is for you.

WHAT IT IS: It's any constructed or salvaged structure that elevates the growing height of the garden, allows for the importation of new soil medium and is open to the ground. The last part of that definition is the key difference between a raised garden bed and a pot. When we talk about raised garden beds we're usually referring to sizeable growing infrastructure.

MATERIALS: Materials need to be cost-effective and functional, so 99% of the time it will be timber – but you can also use rock, metal or plastic. One of our best, and worst, raised garden bed experiences involved bluestone blocks, in which we underquoted, underestimated the difficulty of building, and undid and then redid the grout to finally get the colour right. We ultimately left this job so satisfied, knowing that we'd probably never do another or come back, because we'd left them with a bed that would last for generations to come.

SIZE: Your bed can be as long as your space can accommodate or your garden bed ego demands. Width is different. Ideally you don't want to have to walk in the growing space, nor do you want to struggle to tend your crops, so without Inspector Go-go-gadget arms, the maximum width is 1.5 metres (approximately 5 ft). Height should be dictated by budget and usability. Optimum tending height is around 60 cm (2 ft), but be conscious that the higher you go the more costly it becomes.

POT

COST $

COMPLEXITY   ⊚

WATER USAGE   ◊ ◊ ◊ ◊ ◊

MAINTENANCE   ♧ ♧ ♧ ♧ ♧

👍 Advantages

- Most cost-effective starting point.
- Most space-efficient option.
- Allows for importation of good quality growing medium – that is, potting mix.
- Many types of pot with many different aesthetics, so not limited by choice.
- Excellent drainage.

👎 Disadvantages

- Plants are more likely to become root-bound.
- Soil dries out quickly.
- Difficult to irrigate.
- Dangerous in the hands of hoarders.

🪣 Know your pot

Terracotta
Made from moulded, baked clay. Terracotta is porous and prone to drying out. Glazed pots are watertight, but will cost more.

Timber
Timber boxes make beautiful planters, but be sure they are not made from treated wood that could contaminate your food. To avoid this, consider nesting a plastic or polystyrene box within to carry water and soil.

Plastic
Cheapest to buy, but costly to the environment. Be sure that pots are UV stabilised and made from recyclable PE plastic.

Recycled polystyrene
So ugly, but so good for growing plants. Well-insulated and durable, you'll get about 10,000 years out of one of these. Nest inside a timber box for a combination of function and fashion.

When I think of a potted garden I can't shake the memory of one hoarder's playground. I was transfixed and unable to concentrate. Everywhere I stepped I stumbled – on either a small pot or a box (terracotta, glazed, plastic, styrofoam or timber). So many things, everywhere … it shook me right up.

The arrangement of pots was completely wrong and it troubled me. It was a large space filled with a lot of small pots, and in them a lot of small, dehydrated, stunted plants. It seemed more a testing of the gardener's ability to hoard than a food-growing exercise. Nothing about that garden was user-friendly, and the evidence was there, in the form of sick and abused plants.

A good use of pots, however, is a very adaptable and effective way to garden. We have grown everything from mint to fruit trees in pots, which can vary in size from the classic terracotta vessel to a wine barrel to a 50-gallon drum. For many city gardeners and renters, this may be the most obvious growing method, if not the only starting point. Pots can complement a larger garden or be the main feature; it just depends on the space.

Like many things, however, growing in pots comes with its own set of complications and responsibilities. Pots have relatively small volume and excellent drainage, which means that they are prone to drying out, making it very important to water them each morning. Different materials only exacerbate this propensity. As a result, pots generally require the most care and attention of all the growing infrastructures – a level of care that is inversely correlated to the size of the pot. That means, the smaller the pot, the more care that is required.

We don't like to grow in anything smaller than 30 cm (12 in) in diameter. After all, a small pot is like the relationship that is destined to fail. It seems like a great match, but there is ultimately no room for growth and it turns out to be a lot of hard work with very little reward. A large pot, on the other hand, is a keeper. Sure, it's an investment and you will need to make changes in your life to accommodate it, but this is something that will help you grow things that last.

WALL GARDEN

COST $ $ $
COMPLEXITY   ◎◎◎
WATER USAGE   ◌◌◌◌◌
MAINTENANCE   ⸙⸙⸙⸙

👍 Advantages

- Maximises ground-level real estate.
- Saves space.
- Chases the sunlight.
- More out of reach from certain pests.
- Simple modular systems available.

👎 Disadvantages

- Engineering challenges (particularly for people who struggle with handiness).
- Can be costly to set up.
- Dries out very quickly so needs lots of water.
- Plants become root-bound quickly.

Sometimes when space is lacking, your only option is to go up. George A Fuller – the inventor of the modern-day skyscraper – was well aware of this. He showed that you're not limited by ground-level real estate; rather, you're limited only by imagination, engineering and cost. The same applies when creating a wall garden.

All challenges create invention, and the modern-day challenge of growing food in our cities has seen much creation in the area of wall gardening – and gardening in general. Any wall that basks in the glory of sunshine is a wall waiting to have things grown on it. It goes without saying that a green wall is a far better alternative to an empty one, giving you meaningful growing real estate in the most unlikely of places. What's more, if you live in an urban environment, this may be one of a few available options.

Wall garden systems are constantly improving, both from a growing and aesthetic point of view. Nevertheless, to minimise loading they are often constructed from low-volume, shallow containers, and are thus afflicted with many of the issues that challenge pots.

Things to consider

CHOOSING A WALL

Choose a wall that receives sufficient light and is preferably north-facing so it gathers the lower winter sun. If you have many sunlit walls, choose one that takes in the gentler morning light rather than an afternoon heat trap.

ACCESSIBILITY

Let the height of your wall be determined by what is manageable to harvest. While the idea of a ladder to gather food seems plausible when your enthusiasm is at its peak, harvesting quickly becomes a chore.

WATERING

Wall garden units tend to have shallow soil depths that dry out quickly. Irrigation is highly recommended – almost essential. Watering twice daily is par for the course.

TYPES OF PLANTS

Shallow soil depth limits the types of plants that you can successfully grow. Lettuces and other leafy greens are perfectly suited, while herbs will do well for some time until they become root-bound. Smaller root vegetables – radish, baby carrots – are fine, and then it's a gamble for most others.

HOW IT WORKS

LID
To prevent mosquitoes laying their larvae on the surface of the water.

PLANTS
Your bounty of choice!

FILL POINT
Used to fill up the reservoir from an external water source, such as a hose; you could also connect up your stormwater to this point.

GROWING MEDIUM
The soil in which you grow your plants; we favour an organic potting mix (10 parts) broken up with perlite (1 part), which provides aeration and reduces compaction of soil over time.

GEOTEXTILE
A felt-like fabric that prevents soil from spilling into the reservoir but also allows water to pass up through it; it acts like a wick.

DOWNPIPE
Leads down to the reservoir of water.

WICKS
Materials that extend between the growing medium and the reservoir will enhance the wicking effect. Can range from densely packed plugs of soil to folded geotextile.

COARSE AGGREGATE OR SAND
Fill material in the reservoir, which allows the water to breathe and to provide a sturdy platform on to which the growing medium will sit.

DRAINAGE HOLES
In down pipe – allows even distribution of the water through the reservoir.

CONTAINER
Made from a watertight material or lined with an impermeable layer (such as pond liner).

OVERFLOW VALVE
Indicates when the reservoir is full as it begins to overflow.

WICKING BED

COST $ $ $ $
COMPLEXITY   ☺ ☺ ☺
WATER USAGE   ⬯
MAINTENANCE   ⚘ ⚘

👍 Advantages

- Plants always have access to water.
- Low-maintenance.
- High-yield.
- Water-efficient.
- A self-contained system means that invasive tree roots and grasses are not a threat.
- It's suited to balconies because of no messy drainage.

👎 Disadvantages

- More expensive and labour-intensive to build than a conventional raised garden bed.
- Not ideal for vegetables that prefer dry conditions.
- Not suitable for deeper-rooted plants.
- Soil tends to compact if not prepared properly.

The wicking bed, or self-watering garden, is not that mirage of water in the desert. Rather, it is one of the most user-friendly growing infrastructures for all the lifestyle, time-poor, lazy gardeners out there. Using the age-old idea of capillary action, water in a reservoir below is drawn up and into the soil, to be used by the plants as required. Ever dipped a tissue in a glass of water and watched the moisture climb up the fibres, defying gravity? A wicking bed works in the same way.

Water and soil are typically separated by a permeable membrane – such as geotextile fabric – that allows easier passage of moisture up from the reservoir and prevents spillage of soil down below. The wicking process will be aided by having more 'wicks', like that of a candle, that grab water from lower levels of the reservoir and distribute it to different points within the growing medium.

The self-watering function, however, is not instantaneous. It's a slow journey of moisture from the bottom of the soil right up to the top, so initial surface watering for new seeds and seedlings is required. Once plants are established, the wick will be in effect and ready to switch over to autopilot. In summer, when we revel in an abundance of warm-season crops AND a week or two of holidaying, the wicking bed really earns its keep. As long as your reservoir is topped up and the surface has been well mulched, your plants will welcome your return with garnishes for your homecoming cocktails.

While size, materials and construction vary, the underlying principle is that plants' roots can draw water whenever they need it. As long as there is water in the base, plants will essentially water themselves. As water – or the lack of it – always seems to be at the crux of unsuccessful food gardening, the wicking bed may well be the answer to one of our greatest gardening problems.

MAKING A WICKING BED GROWING MEDIUM

WHAT YOU NEED

1 × 5 litre (1 gallon) bag perlite

2 × 30 litre (8 gallon) bags
organic potting mix

1 × 100 g (3½ oz) sachet rock minerals

2 handfuls worm castings

When growing in the city, we often find ourselves managing environments that aren't particularly conducive to gardening, such as a balcony or concrete patio. Fortunately, there are many good systems that we can now use to grow food above ground. Wicking beds are one of our favourites and are readily adaptable to suit most spaces. Although there are a multitude of different system shapes, sizes and designs, getting the right kind of soil, or growing medium, is a matter of knowing the right recipe.

Our wicking bed growing medium recipe makes enough for a 70 litre (15 gallon) container.

1 Combine 1-part perlite and 10-parts potting mix into the growing container. Perlite's size and structure will improve soil aeration and drainage, while also helping to reduce soil compaction.

2 Spread a sachet of rock minerals over the top. This will add nutrients and vital rock minerals to the perlite/potting mix, taking it one step closer to real soil.

HOT TIP

How far can my water wick?

Water can only wick so far, and there is a point where no matter how fine or irresistible the particles that it is climbing, or depth and pull of the wicks, the moisture will be unable to travel any further. The optimal depth for the bed is about 20–25 cm (8–10 in). Water is able to wick up and it's deep enough to accommodate larger rooted vegetables and herbs.

3 Mix through a couple of handfuls of worm castings. In addition to being a soil conditioner, worm castings contain worm eggs. With time and water, the worm eggs will hatch and begin to transform the sterile potting mix into a living ecosystem.

4 Remember, wicking beds will only work when plants have mature root systems that extend deep into the bed. Until then, be sure to water seeds and seedlings by hand.

HOW IT WORKS

GROW TRAY

Holds your growing medium and flushes of water; can be purpose built or more DIY.

GROWING MEDIUM

'Soil' substitute in which the plants grow – can be a combination of expanded clay, perlite, vermiculite and/or coconut coir.

WATER INLET

For inflow of water from the the water tank. Water is aerated as it falls into the growing bed.

NUTRIENT WATER

(FRUIT/FLOWER GROWTH)

Fuel for fruit/flower growth of the plant, typically a chemical, but can also be found in a plant-based derivative.

(VEGETATIVE GROWTH)

Fuel for vegetative growth of the plant, typically a chemical, but can also be found in a plant-based derivative.

DRAINAGE POINT

For the outflow of water back to the reservoir.

WATER TANK

Reservoir where water and nutrients are added.

AIR PUMP

Provides additional oxygen to water (and plants). Especially important when operating a growing tray that is continually flooded.

AERATOR/ AIR STONE

Diffuses air into the water tank.

SIMPLE WATER PUMP

Cycles water from the tank to growing tray. Many growers will set it on a timer so that roots aren't continually flooded.

HYDROPONICS

COST $ $ $ $
COMPLEXITY ◎◎◎◎
WATER USAGE ◊
MAINTENANCE ♐♐

👍 Advantages

- Space-saving systems – plants can be grown in very shallow vessels.
- PRODUCTIVE!
- Very water efficient.
- Very limited weeding (boom!).
- Less pests and diseases because it's soil-free growing.
- Fast growing.
- Self-contained system.

👎 Disadvantages

- Difficult set-up.
- Nutrient liquids are inorganic, often pharmaceutical chemicals.
- Hard-to-get materials.
- Can look a bit 'scientific' or 'experimental'.
- Most systems require a power source.

Tip

No matter how plants are grown, it is important that their roots are oxygenated. When using hydroponics/acquaponics systems, it is important to either a) have cycles of flooding and draining in the grow tray, whereby roots are exposed to fresh air; or b) oxygenate the water with an airstone.

The pastime of growing vegetables at home generally follows the basic farming techniques related to water, soil and sun. Most home gardeners will use all those elements – in either their pot, raised garden bed or wicking bed – to grow food and then eat it. Hydroponic growing – which, let's be honest, is most often associated with growing dope plants – relies on different elements, such as nutrient water, vermiculite and artificial lights, mostly for reasons of stealth. One growing method seems legitimate and the other completely illegitimate.

However, regardless of the stigma, hydroponics is still worthy of your attention. In fact, hydroponic systems are some of the most progressive and resource-efficient systems to be found, and can grow food using up to 90% less water in less than half the time of conventional systems. They require no arable land and can produce abundant food in minimal space. Furthermore, hydroponics doesn't necessitate the use of artificial lights – you can grow hydroponically under natural light if you possess it.

Farming practices have changed a lot in the past few decades and today some of the most innovative farms are those using hydroponic systems to grow the produce that we eat. This is quickly filtering into home growing, with hydroponic growers harvesting much more than just pot. While some work is still needed to substitute the inorganic nutrient waters that fuel the plants' growth, we're certain it will get there.

TOP 5 PLANTS FOR HYDROPONICS

LETTUCE

STRAWBERRIES

TOMATOES

PEAS

CORIANDER (CILANTRO)

SIMPLE HYDROPONICS

During the hot months, the water wars will be well underway. Plants will need water at least every morning, especially those in pots and wall gardens, which dry out very quickly and are vulnerable to changing temperatures. Small containers are particularly susceptible to hydrophobia, whereby soil becomes so irredeemably baked due to prolonged heat and neglect that it can no longer absorb any water (see page 47). At this point, all you can do is throw away the soil and start again. Don't let it get this far. Just mulch and water.

The ultimate answer to hot weather growing may well be hydroponics – that is, growing plants without soil. While the abundance of synthetic fertilisers is off-putting, the tremendous water efficiency and high yields make this system extremely tempting. Those looking to dabble in the dark arts, but not wanting to make their garden look like a science experiment, should try a simple hydroponics set-up anywhere that the mercury rises.

WHAT YOU NEED

1 × 4 litre (135 fl oz/16 cup) bag of perlite

20 litres (4 gallons) coconut coir or palm peat

1 × 30 litre (6 gallon) felt planter bag

1 × 1 litre (34 fl oz/4 cups) of concentrated supplemental calcium (liquid or powder)

1 × 1 litre (34 fl oz/4 cups) bottle of foliage/ blossom nutrient water – plant/animal derived products are best (available online and at hydroponics shops)

1. Wet briquettes of coconut coir in a bucket. Quantities will vary depending on the size of the briquette, but you should get 50 litres (11 gallons) of coconut coir from two briquettes.

2. Mix a growing medium using 70% coconut coir and 30% perlite. Perlite will help to aerate and add structure so that roots can breathe and the growing medium doesn't compress over time.

3. We've transported the medium to a felt planter and planted our prized herbs. Felt is a terrific hydroponic growing container, as it has the benefit of being both inexpensive and highly breathable. Oxygen flows through the container, dramatically decreasing chances of root and stem rot.

4. Water with a supplemental calcium mixture once a month, then alternate between nutrient water and regular watering every three days.

5. Expect robust productivity and much less heat stress. Expect compliments on your beautiful garden and produce.

AQUAPONICS

COST $ $ $ $ $

COMPLEXITY   ☺ ☺ ☺ ☺

WATER USAGE   ◌

MAINTENANCE   ♀ ♀

👍 Advantages

◆ Highly water-efficient.

◆ No chemical inputs.

◆ Food grows very fast.

◆ Raise hard-working pets that you can eat.

◆ Self-contained system.

👎 Disadvantages

◆ Complicated to set up.

◆ Expensive.

◆ Have to keep plants AND fish alive.

◆ Needs to be connected to a power source (heater + aerator + pump).

Tip

Fill the reservoir with rainwater rather than tap water, which will have high levels of chlorine in it that isn't compatible with your fish friends.

Aquaponics derives its name from aquaculture (farming fish) and hydroponics (growing plants without soil). Together they fulfil two great passions in life: growing food and catching fish. It's like shooting fish in a barrel. The great news is that growing food is made easier too.

Although the infrastructure itself can seem a bit cumbersome, the principles are very simple. Fish eat food and generate poo (ammonia). Waste water is circulated up to the growing tray where it is broken down by bacteria and converted into nitrates and nitrites. The plants then use these as nutrition. As plants use the nutrition, they filter the water, which is recirculated down to the fish pond below. Everyone wins.

The efficiency of a well-oiled aquaponics set-up is simply mind-boggling, as a perfectly run system is closed loop (you do have to feed the fish). This means that there is no water wastage and all the nutrients are provided by the aquatic life that you farm. At their peak, food will grow two to three times faster, as plants thrive on the nutrient-rich water, giving gardeners with short attention spans the instant growing gratification they crave. But there are challenges getting the balance right between fish and food because, like in any relationship, too much of one thing can be detrimental to the other.

When starting out, plants' young roots will have a limited ability to process and filter fish waste solids, so overfeeding will create toxic water for the fish. At the beginning, don't feed your fish every day (most aquaculture species can go a week without food). Once plants start to grow, you can ramp up to a daily or twice daily feeding regime and even increase your fish stocks. If plants start to turn yellow, it's a sign they are not getting enough nutrients and fish should be fed more.

Sure, there are some complexities in keeping any pet healthy and happy, let alone sensitive creatures like fish. Indeed, it is quite disheartening to find your fish friends floating on the surface or, perhaps worse, stuck in the pump. However, we believe that such a basic, commonsense idea will one day completely change the way we grow food.

HOW IT WORKS

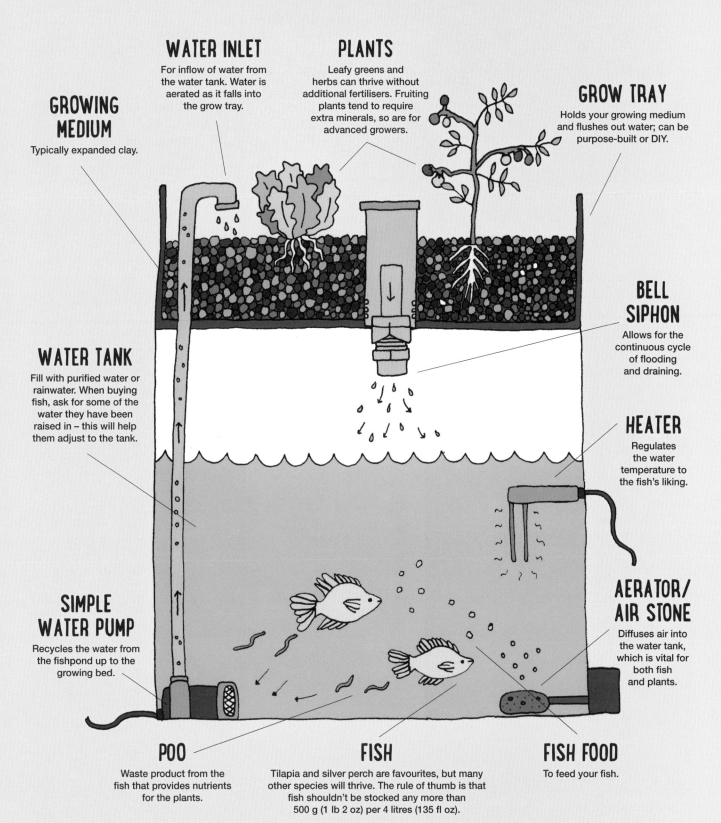

WATER INLET
For inflow of water from the water tank. Water is aerated as it falls into the grow tray.

PLANTS
Leafy greens and herbs can thrive without additional fertilisers. Fruiting plants tend to require extra minerals, so are for advanced growers.

GROW TRAY
Holds your growing medium and flushes out water; can be purpose-built or DIY.

GROWING MEDIUM
Typically expanded clay.

BELL SIPHON
Allows for the continuous cycle of flooding and draining.

WATER TANK
Fill with purified water or rainwater. When buying fish, ask for some of the water they have been raised in – this will help them adjust to the tank.

HEATER
Regulates the water temperature to the fish's liking.

SIMPLE WATER PUMP
Recycles the water from the fishpond up to the growing bed.

AERATOR/ AIR STONE
Diffuses air into the water tank, which is vital for both fish and plants.

POO
Waste product from the fish that provides nutrients for the plants.

FISH
Tilapia and silver perch are favourites, but many other species will thrive. The rule of thumb is that fish shouldn't be stocked any more than 500 g (1 lb 2 oz) per 4 litres (135 fl oz).

FISH FOOD
To feed your fish.

COURTYARD MAKEOVER

Unlock the potential of your low-maintenance courtyard into a low-maintence kitchen garden. More than just a space to sit and ponder life, it can easily become productive with a few simple additions.

1 Another day in paradise. Otherwise known as a low-maintenance rental property.

2 The two most important things to consider are space (which is why we're going to espalier the apple) and not scarring those precious pavers.

4 Empty space + plants = friends. Let the good times grow.

3 Raised beds built off the ground will capture more sunlight and create decent growing real estate.

BALCONY MAKEOVER

ACTIVITY!

The balcony is often considered a 'too hard' space. However, by choosing infrastructure that works in small spaces and adopting a simple routine, even the smallest of balconies can become an edible oasis.

1 A small balcony with an amenity eyesore but lots of north-facing potential. None of it is being realised in those undersized pots!

2 First thing's first. Cover up the air con unit, making it a bench space or the perfect place to position a pot.

3 Working in confined spaces means choosing smart systems to ensure growing success. This hanging wicking system looks after the watering for you.

4 The key is not to over-clutter. It's your space and you take priority. Make sure there is still room to put your feet up and enjoy a glass of pinot.

I WANT TO LOVE YOU
(P-Y-T)
PRETTY YOUNG THING
YOU NEED SOME LOVIN'
(T-L-C)
TENDER LOVIN' CARE

PLANTING

This is the glory we all come for – the plant out. As a business we often take people right up to this edge. We set up their infrastructure until it's purring like a well-oiled machine, only to have this moment taken from us. But with good reason, because if we're going to do everything for you, we may as well be a paid gardening service rather than a helping hand. Planting builds ownership, and learning about the diverse range of plant species and the different ways you can plant them builds confidence.

Whether you plant seeds or seedlings hinges on a couple of things – the time and effort at your disposal, and the varieties you're choosing to explore. Seedlings are by far the easiest to start with – bypassing the sometimes tedious and demanding infancy stage, and jumping straight to a level of maturity that is more tolerant. As a parent it's like skipping the first year of nappies and milk, and being given a toddler who can walk and sit still while watching a game of premier league football with you.

However, planting from seed gives you a wider choice, as there's a complete gene pool you can access via seed that won't be found in seedling form. If we're going to loop back into the parent analogy, it's like choosing your child and the qualities you had always hoped for. Now, we don't doubt that you love your children the way they are, but wouldn't that be incredible?

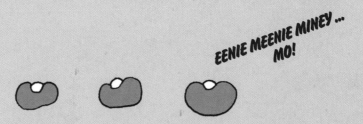

SEEDS

This is where it all begins, in a seed. Or did it begin in a plant? Whether chicken or egg, plant or seed, what is important to realise is that if you want to experience the huge spectrum of food that can easily be grown at home, you need to learn how to grow it from seed. Then you need to learn how to save them for the following year, to grow even better food.

I'm sure most of you are aware of large seed companies and their purportedly 'bad' practices with genetically modified (GM) seeds, or the unsustainable practices of commercial farming. And most of you will likely have heard of heirloom seeds, and the fact that we should all be growing them. But why are heirloom seeds so much better?

Heirloom seeds represent the huge diversity of food that exists and make up literally thousands of varieties that have both subtle and pronounced differences to each other. Let's take the tomato as an example. While there may be only a few dozen varieties (at best) that we're accustomed to, there are actually more than 3000 varieties that exist. Some are yellow and pear-shaped, others black and ribbed. Some are no bigger than your smallest fingernail, while you can find others that would weigh more than a baby's head. Without home growers saving heirloom seeds, not only is our gene pool diminished, but meal time becomes far less interesting.

The effects of consuming GM foods are still unproven but if current practices continue, the only tomato we'll have to choose at the supermarket will be the hard, tasteless red thing that transports well. The seeds that survive will be the ones demanded by the big businesses that sell them, not the ones that are demanded by the home grower: the ones that excite us because of a unique taste or aesthetic, the ones that have a certain *je ne sais quoi*.

But we can all do something to restore the balance. Growing heirloom seeds in the home garden makes you part of the movement towards unique, tastier and more exciting food. An increased awareness and expectation of better quality food puts pressure on mainstream food producers and suppliers to meet the growing demand. By growing from seed, you are doing more than just growing great food.

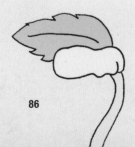

WHAT IS AN HEIRLOOM SEED?

Much like an heirloom possession – something of value that has been passed down from generation to generation – heirloom seeds represent our heritage of diverse plants, whether in relation to their yield, flavour, resistance to disease or something else entirely. They have been saved year by year, generation by generation for a reason.

An heirloom seed is an old variety (by definition pre-dating the 1960s) that is open-pollinated – by wind, insect or animal (including our good selves) – meaning that it produces a true copy of itself. Seeds collected will then produce an exact copy of their parent plant. So, by saving seeds from last season's best tomato plant, we can enjoy a whole garden of them this year. In this way, we can slowly select for qualities that we like and evolve our gardens over time.

In order to keep the varieties pure, they must not be grown too closely to plants of the same species, with which they can cross-pollinate.

Cross-pollination is how hybrids originate. Now, let us be clear – hybrids are not bad things. This is how all heirlooms originally came about, by cross-pollination in nature or by human. Once that new variety of seed is saved for several generations, without further cross-pollination, it may then be classified an heirloom.

Genetically modified organisms (GMOs) are different again – these are organisms (or foods) that have had alterations made to their DNA using genetic engineering techniques. Desirable qualities are taken from other species to modify the plant. Like taking a gene from salmon to make your tomatoes redder. It's very frankenscience, and just a little too freaky.

When growing from seed, make sure you select the very best heirlooms or hybrids you can find. Choose your seeds for yield, flavour and variety. Your tastebuds will thank you for it.

SEED SAVING

Seed saving is a basic gardening skill that is deeply programmed into all of us, albeit tucked away in the attic of our heritage. Seeds are very important. So important, in fact, that when people emigrate from their homelands, they often carry seeds with them. Seeds represent security, continuity and hope. They represent a long-standing agreement between humans and plants to contribute to one another's mutual prosperity. Which begs the question, did we domesticate plants or did they domesticate us? Woah, man, what's in these cookies?

By collecting and saving seeds from the best-performing plants in your garden, you will slowly evolve varieties that are better adapted to the local environment. This practice will not only allow you to grow better food, but also save money in the process. It's not hard to do and ultimately comes down to a few simple principles and practices.

Most plants seed through fruit or flower. Though there are some exceptions – see Tubers (page 105) and Rhizomes (page 104) – many of us are probably familiar with fruit seeds, such as tomato, eggplant (aubergine), squash, chilli, etc. Plants like lettuces, herbs, garlic and onion are a little less obvious, because they often only produce seeds at the end of their life. Collection varies slightly between the two.

1. Fruit seeds are continuously produced and can be scooped out of the flesh with a spoon, knife or finger.

2. Separate fruit seeds from other pieces of tissue by placing them in a sieve and running water over the top.

3. Seeds can be quickly dried on a plate when placed in a sunny position.

4. Non-fruiting plants, such as leafy greens, coriander (cilantro), broccoli and radish, will produce flower heads at the end of their lifetime. In this case, we are harvesting the seed head of a leek. Flowers will vary with each plant. Coriander and broccoli produce beautiful edible flowers, while others, such as cos (romaine) lettuce, will produce a thick tower. However, no matter how the flowering looks or tastes, the process is always the same – leave your best plant in the garden until the flowers/pods start to dry and brown off.

5. Hang the flower in a cool dry place. We use the same technique for pods such as peas and beans. It can take a month for plants to become brittle enough to release their seeds, so be patient.

6. Fruit seeds, on the other hand, will dry within an afternoon and can be transported straight into a sealed container (more on this to come).

7. Once flowers or pods are dry and crunchy, you can break them apart with your hands or mash them into a sieve. This is called threshing and is an age-old method used to separate seeds from brittle plant material.

8. Seed collection is mostly just an exercise in labelling. It's hard to tell the difference between a capsicum (bell pepper) seed and a ghost chilli seed a few months down the road, so always write down the variety.

9. Store seeds in a cool dry place. Humidity and warmth shorten a seed's life. Many people store seeds in a refrigerator, but anywhere cool and dry will be stellar. The garage, pantry or a closet are all great.

SEED BASICS

SOAKING

Just like us, all seeds are different. Some are small and circular while others are long and flakey. Some are also significantly larger than the standard, and typically these seeds will benefit from an overnight soaking in water prior to planting.

Soaking helps to break down the seed's exterior coating, promoting faster and more successful germination. It also means that the seed is able to absorb and store a reserve of water itself, aiding the seed through what is a delicate and often thirsty process.

Seeds we'd recommend for soaking include beans, peas, beetroot (beets) and corn.

DEPTH

Some seeds need light in order to germinate, while others rely on darkness. Some will like to set up larger root structures before announcing themselves to the world, while others are happy to pop up and get on with it almost immediately. Rather than delving into the planting psyche of each seed, some people smarter than us came up with a simple rule.

The rule of thumb is to plant twice the depth as the diameter of the seed. This means that a pea seed with a 7 mm (¼ in) diameter should be planted 14 mm (½ in) deep, or a broad bean that is 2 cm (¾ in) across goes down 4 cm (1½ in). Now you're probably thinking, how do I measure a hole that is exactly 14 mm (½ in) or 4 cm (1½ in) deep? And perhaps more concerningly, how do I dig a hole for a seed that is no bigger than a bee's penis?

So, now we introduce the second rule of thumb: the minimum depth for sowing all seed is anywhere between 5 mm (¼ in) and 1 cm (½ in); enough to prevent them being blown away by the wind or picked out by birds.

SPACING

Is less ever more? In the case of growing vegetables, it certainly is. Overcrowding plants, which limits air flow and creates competition between plants for moisture and nutrition, means more seeds and seedlings often result in less produce. Therefore, spacing is paramount to maximising the yields of your precious seeds.

But you also need to be conscious that not all seeds will germinate, and so we sometimes need to plant more as a backup. Our common practice is to plant twice as many seeds as necessary, whether that means planting two in a hole (and then culling one if both germinate) or spacing them half as far apart as recommended.

The type of plant dictates which method we use. If growing plants that ultimately produce a fruit and no other part can be eaten – for example, tomatoes, chillies, eggplant (aubergine) and capsicums (bell peppers) – we plant two in the same hole and cull the weaker if they both germinate. Otherwise, if growing plants that produce foliage or parts that can be eaten when juvenile, we plant them half as far apart and cull the middle plants as meaningful produce when they begin to compete.

When it comes to sowing root vegetables, our methods have changed. Rather than scatter along a trench line and then cull to the required spacing, we've accepted that most people are too busy or too sentimental to act at a later date. So, we carefully space out to the advised distance. This may seem like a tedious process when you're there with a handful of tiny carrot seeds, but it will ultimately save you effort and time (that you don't often have) and may be the difference between a straight root and a bent, gnarled and twisted one.

WATERING

Water is the most critical element when growing from seeds. The idea of watering is to keep the soil moist rather than soak it, and to do it sensibly using a fan water spray that won't dislodge the seeds or blow the soil apart.

Watering a seed is much like feeding a newborn. A lot of short feeds several times a day is necessary. If you've ever heard the spine-tingling shrill of a hungry newborn baby, you will know the distress of a tiny, germinated seed if the soil mix dries out. If young parents could put their newborns in a greenhouse to ensure each feed stays with them longer, believe me, they would.

TEMPERATURE

Soil temperature dictates the growth of each plant, and is the reason why some varieties grow in the warm season and others in the cool. This idea indicates that keeping a consistent and relevant temperature will aid the seed you are trying to germinate. Another idea worth considering is that the smaller the body of soil, the more exposed it is to fluctuations in the air temperature (and the quicker it dries out).

For all these reasons, germinating seeds in a greenhouse environment will infinitely assist the process, and your greenhouse doesn't have to be any bigger than the seed tray you're propagating in. If growing in a small unit, portability is a great aid in helping it escape the hot sun in autumn (when you're getting a head start on cool-season varieties) and the cold nights in spring (when we're eagerly looking forward to the warm season).

CULLING

When challenged by the cull of your healthy, strong, beautiful tomato seedling, it's hard not to get sentimental. But in the same way culling four million kangaroos each year preserves the land and ensures the survival of those that remain, culling seedlings is essential for the greater good. By spacing the seedlings to their required distance, it ensures that those remaining produce to their potential.

To cull a young seedling you need to be quick and get the timing right. If you try culling too young, you risk dislodging nearby plants. Leave it too late and roots become intertwined; as you remove the weaker seedlings, damage to the remaining is inevitable.

Here we like to use a quite arbitrary rule of fat thumb, and that is cull when a seedling is large enough to handle with fat fingers. Bracing the strongest seedling with one hand, pull out the competing plants, leaving the chosen one to realise its potential.

SOWING METHODS

Some plants are hardy enough to sow directly into the patch (in situ) when the time is right, while others need some individual care before a move in the veggie patch. The plants you choose to grow will dictate whether they begin their life in a seed tray or whether you immediately set them free in the garden.

IN SITU

In situ growing means that the seeds begin their lives in the garden. This can be done with varieties such as leafy greens, root vegetables and gourds, which generally have little trouble germinating and are tough enough to set up camp from a young age. Of course, the type of seed will determine how you introduce them into the patch.

BROADCAST

Broadcasting is the most free-loving way of spreading your seed, and is a technique used when seed is plentiful and hardy. Simply scatter them over the patch of earth in which you intend to grow them, rake them through and water in. There's no real plan here, but with a lot of seed spread through the soil the odds of a successful outcome are stacked in your favour. Only problem is that there will be so many seed babies popping up all over the place, you'll have the heartbreaking practice of culling for the greater good.

This is really the lazy person's method for sowing seed, but with both seed stock and real estate becoming more precious commodities, this is not something we like to practise in the garden itself.

DRILLING

This method is more us – ordered and regimented. 'Drilling' seed in organised rows and columns is the best way to maximise the seed you have. It also lessens the amount of required culling once they have germinated.

You can drill seeds in either shallow trench lines made from the point of your finger, or in spaced-out individual holes. The method you use will be determined by the variety you are planting. Smaller produce such as root vegetables and leafy greens are best suited to trench line planting, while larger varieties with larger seeds – beans, corn, gourds – are better to plant in individual holes. When using this method, ensure you place two seeds in each hole in the event that one does not germinate.

SEED TRAYS

When seeds, and the forthcoming seedlings, need a little special care before introduction into the patch, propagating in seed trays is recommended. This is a common method to get plants started before the last frost and for more temperamental plants – those that appreciate a head start on their growth before ultimate plant-out or those that need some hardening off. Hardening off simply refers to the maturing of the plant so they are tougher and more able to cope with transplant.

We propagate all the brassicas and nightshades in seed trays for this reason, but seed tray propagation may simply be a way to get a head start on growing seed in a controlled environment – such as a greenhouse, big or small – when the patch conditions are not conducive to their introduction.

Growing in seed trays demands a nutritious, friable, free-draining and pH-neutral soil mix. This can be achieved using easily purchased 'seed raising mixes' from a nursery or in compost and worm castings. Worm castings (see page 25), in particular, are a fantastic propagation medium, not only for their fertility attributes, but their ability to retain moisture for the germinating seeds.

OPEN TRAY

Any seedling tray can be easily converted into a propagation device. Measuring approximately 30 cm x 30 cm or a square foot, with adequate drainage below, it is the cheapest and more readily available form of seed tray. Filling up the tray with a soil medium provides a blank canvas of growing opportunities in which you can broadcast or drill your seeds, depending on the variety and your mood. Using an open tray also allows the plant to become more established before transplanting into the garden and will reduce transplant shock. Most nurseries will happily pass on a seed tray or two if you politely ask.

CELL TRAY

To step it up to the next level you can use a purpose-built seed tray with inbuilt seed cells. Separating the cells means that root growth will be kept separate, translating to a less stressful transplant when the time comes. These are more suited to the larger, more delicate varieties, such as the brassicas and nightshades.

SOWING IN JIFFY POTS

For the ultimate care for germinating seeds, use decomposable cells/pots. This allows the plant to become more established before transplanting into the garden and drastically reduces any transplant shock. Simply bury the pot in the patch and the roots will pass through into the soil as it breaks down. There's no need to pull them free and compromise the roots.

Most gardening shops will sell small 'jiffy pots' that are tailor-made for this job, but common household rubbish can also be recycled. Egg cartons, and the individual cells that the eggs sit in, are almost custom-made seed cells. So, when seed propagation comes calling, don't let this item go to waste.

SEEDLINGS

Seedlings are young plants raised from seed and can typically be bought in small, light plastic containers called punnets. On a per plant basis, they definitely cost a lot more than propagating plants from seed. However, for most of us, gardening isn't a purely economic proposition and a lot of other factors have equal importance, namely convenience and practicality.

To put it simply, some plants are difficult to grow from seed. Growing from seed can involve a lot of preparation and foresight. Sometimes it is just too late in the season to start from seed, but you still want to grow tomatoes. Am I right or am I right? Whatever your reason, growing from seedlings is just another part of gardening with its own set of skills to master.

HOT TIP

Spreading a layer of potting mix over the top of a new garden bed will allow seedlings to establish themselves in a balanced soil. By the time their roots extend into the rich organic layer below, the mix will have already mellowed and abundant nutrients will be accessible. Just remember that you get what you pay for, so be sure to get the best quality organic potting mix available.

CHOOSING THE RIGHT SEEDLING

Transplanting can be hard enough on seedlings, so give them and yourself the best chance at success by starting with healthy plants. These are some of our trade secrets for getting top quality plants.

1. VISIT A NURSERY MIDWEEK It's a fine line between being an informed gardener and being the creep that fondles every single plant. Since opening our nursery, we have met our fair share of both and the best insider's advice that we can offer is to visit a nursery mid-week. It's not as busy on weekdays, so staff will be more helpful. Furthermore, many nurseries will have stock delivered before the weekend, so if you go on a Thursday or Friday you will have first pick of the freshest stock.

WE ARE THE CHAMPIONS

2. AVOID TALL, SPINDLY PLANTS Although it is tempting, don't choose the biggest, tallest seedlings. Tall, spindly growth is a tell-tale indicator that plants have been competing for light, especially if they are pale green. Such plants will be weaker and won't transplant as well.

3. AVOID SEEDLINGS ALREADY BEARING FRUIT OR FLOWERS A plant will valiantly try to produce a few seeds before it dies, so that its short life won't have been for nothing. Next time you see a fat chilli hanging from a tiny seedling or florets on some young broccoli, alarm bells should sound.

4. CHECK UNDER THE LEAVES FOR ANY HITCHHIKERS There is no need to bring any extra pests back to your home.

5. CAREFULLY INSPECT THE ROOTS To inspect the roots in a non-invasive way, simply have a look at the punnet's drainage holes. If brown roots (white are OK) are protruding from the bottom, then the seedling has probably been in its container too long and is likely to be root-bound (also called pot-bound). It's not a death sentence for the plant, but it is yet another valuable indicator of how the seedlings have been raised.

TRANSPLANTING SEEDLINGS

Transplanting can be difficult, whether you are a human or plant, and the older you get the more taxing it can be. I learn this every time my mother visits from New Mexico. The 21 hours of travel and absence from her comfortable home routine sends her into a loopiness that ensues for days. Not even the strongest Melbourne coffee can save her. But put my younger sister through the same cycle, and there's a notable decline in loopiness. A day later she's back to normal. Meanwhile, mom is still trying to find answers in a cup of coffee.

The same is true in the plant world. Mature plants always suffer from collateral damage during a transplant and require much more nursing to bring them back to health. Meanwhile, young seedlings are strong and resilient so you shouldn't be afraid of hurting them!

Many seedlings are packed into a single punnet and ideally they should be separated into individual plants, which will require some manhandling. However, just as there'd be a difference if I booked mom in first class, there are some best practices to follow to ensure that you have the highest possible rate of success.

1. Seedlings can come in any number of shapes and sizes. Some will have lots of plants, tightly packed, while others will have a few distinct plants neatly divided.

2. The trick to planting seedlings is to keep them hydrated. Try not to plant in the heat of the day and always water seedlings before separating.

3. Break off excess roots and soil at the bottom of the punnet.

4. Separate seedlings carefully by gently grabbing near their base and slowly wiggling the roots apart. This is a lot like disentangling the cord to a pair of earphones in your pocket. Roots and earphones alike will release with gentle jiggling, rather than abrupt pulling.

5. Space according to planting instructions and, with any luck, those seedlings will mature into full-sized plants that don't compete for sun or water. However, we often plant closer together, in case some of our seedlings die. Once plants have proven themselves we pull out a few to create ideal spacing.

6. Water after planting. The seedlings have just had the equivalent of 21 hours of international travel and they deserve a drink.

GROWING PLANTS FROM CUTTINGS

Growing from cuttings is a special class of propagation that allows you to cultivate a new plant by using a trimming from an existing plant – essentially creating a clone. This method is most commonly used for flowering, aromatic culinary plants such as mint, marjoram, sage, rosemary, thyme, hyssop and lavender. These plants have naturally occurring growth hormones that allow them to create roots from broken stems. It's like a lizard regrowing its tail – only in this case, it is like another lizard growing from a discarded tail. Cuttings are robust and much faster than growing from seed. This process allows you to quickly multiply your plants without costly trips to the nursery.

Many herbs are dormant over winter and do all of their growing from spring to autumn. Therefore, when we propagate cuttings it is good to start before mid-summer so that they can soak up as much light and warmth as possible.

THE BEST THINGS IN LIFE ARE FREE

1. Choose healthy, mature plants from which to collect your cuttings. We've had our best success with new growth, so look for young, green stems at the tip of each plant.

2. To test whether the stems will be effective, a 'bend test' suffices. Simply bend the stem back on itself – anything that breaks before turning 90 degrees is too woody. Anything that can turn 180 degrees back on itself without breaking is too young. You are ideally looking for snappage to occur somewhere in between.

3. Collect a number of cuttings approximately 20 cm (8 in) in length.

4. Once you have enough cuttings collected, strip the bottom few leaves from each one. Removing the leaves exposes nodes along the stem, from which new roots will grow.

5. These plants all have naturally occurring growth hormones that help cuttings to regenerate. However, some gardeners will use synthetic hormones to help stimulate the process. Gel and powder rooting hormones are available at most hardware stores and nurseries. Another option is to dip the plant stem into honey or cinnamon, both of which are known to work as natural root stimulants and are easily found in the pantry.

6. Any free-draining container filled with organic potting mix or seed raising mix can be used for sticking – the technical term for planting a cutting. Be sure that the depth of the container is more than 10 cm (4 in) and drains freely. Compostable jiffy pots work great because they can be planted directly into the veggie patch once the cutting matures. A mini-greenhouse can help to maintain warmth and moisture. Water the soil thoroughly after sticking your new plant.

7. Place cuttings on a warm windowsill or in a mini-greenhouse and water daily. If stems begin to form flowers or leaves die off, don't get concerned – these forms of plant stress are ways the plants cope with the transplant. Just remove the flowers or dead leaves to help it refocus on the root growth.

8. It will take anywhere from a few weeks to more than a couple of months to develop meaningful roots. When cuttings begin to form new leaves, or visually chase the sun, the plant is nearing readiness. Once roots begin to hold soil – if you pull at the stem and the soil bulges with it – the plant is ready for transplant.

RHIZOMES

COMMON RHIZOMES Asparagus | Ginger | Turmeric | Galangal | Horseradish | Rhubarb | Hops | Mint

Plants like ginger, asparagus and rhubarb are grown from rhizomes. Although they are easily confused with roots, rhizomes are actually underground stem systems. They invade areas around the parent plant, extending horizontally and producing above-ground shoots. In this way, new 'clone' plants are created. In the case of ginger and turmeric, we eat the underground rhizome itself, whereas the above-ground shoots are what interest us when it comes to asparagus and rhubarb. When it comes to hops, another famous rhizome, its flower cone is the object of our desire.

Rhizomes are often called 'creeping rootstalks' and by dividing them it is possible to grow new plants from each piece. In nature, rhizomes are known to survive fire and drought, laying dormant underground until good growing conditions are available. As a result, they are very hearty and can be transported easily without water or soil. Many people order seed rhizomes online or buy them from a local nursery to ensure that they don't contain any disease/pesticides/herbicides. However, it is also possible to plant a piece of (organic) ginger from the grocery store – though success will vary.

HOW TO PLANT

1   Soak the rhizome for a few hours in water or compost tea.
2   In well-drained soil, dig a shallow hole or trench and plant the rhizome horizontally with any shoots pointing upward.
3   Cover the rhizome with about 3 cm (1¼ in) of soil.
4   Water in thoroughly. Continue to water every second or third day, as overwatering can cause rot.
5   Edible rhizomes are slow growing, so don't expect any visible growth for a couple of weeks.

TUBERS

COMMON TUBERS Potato | Sweet potato | Yam | Cassava | Jerusalem artichoke

'It's not a tuber!' shouted Arnold Schwarzenegger in the perennial classic *Kindergarten Cop*. At least that's what we heard. Potatoes, on the other hand, are tubers. As are yams and the poorly named Jerusalem artichoke.

Tubers are neither roots nor rhizomes, but are often found in their company and are, in fact, a growth of reserve nutrients. Like an underground doomsday bunker, tubers store plant energy for an uncertain future. They are rich in simple carbohydrates (starches) and sugars, which is what makes them so delicious. It is this stored energy that gives them the potential to grow a new plant at a moment's notice or lay dormant until conditions improve.

Anyone who has left a potato long enough has seen it start to produce sprouts. Seed tubers from a nursery are often well sprouted and guaranteed not to contain any soil-borne disease, which is not the case for market-bought varieties. For those with small spaces, we recommend planting tubers in a felt pot or other container so that growth cannot invade the rest of your garden. Keeping tubers in a separate container also guarantees that you won't miss any produce when it comes to harvest time.

HOW TO PLANT

1 Select a collection of your favourite seed tubers.
2 Larger pieces can be cut in half, but make sure that there are a few sprouting eyelets on each piece.
3 Dig a 15 cm (6 in) trench in nutrient-rich and well-drained soil, and space seeds about 25 cm (10 in) apart.
4 Cover over with soil and water.

RUNNERS

Strawberries get right to business by producing no-nonsense, ready-to-plant seed-lings on the vine and ready for our use – thus saving us from the tedious process of collecting, drying and labelling seeds. There are not many varieties that are in the habit of throwing up bonus planting opportunities, but the strawberry is one such variety.

As your strawberry plant grows, it will begin to send out wiry 'runners' or 'daughters' – that is, long stems with small clumps of foliage. These will sprawl outwards from an established plant, eventually settling on the ground to colonise new territory. If you feel like you've had a guardian patch angel planting more strawberries in your garden, sorry to kill the idea but it's just the runners getting on with their regular course of business.

While the best use for these runners is to grow more strawberries, simply cutting them from the existing plants frees up energy to focus on less foliage growth and more fruit – which seems to be an outcome that is in everyone's best interest.

BABY I WAS BORN TO RUUUUUUUN!

TRANSPLANTING STRAWBERRY RUNNERS

Rather than just growing outwards from its centre, mature strawberry plants also grow long, thin stems with a sort of pioneer seedling at the end. When allowed to go wild, the runners will implant into the ground and grow new roots, like a little strawberry colony. However, they can also be cut from the parent plant and used as fresh seedlings.

1. Identify runners.

2. One simple propagation technique is to place a small pot filled with organic potting mix underneath a runner. The seedling will form roots and can then be cut free in a couple of months when it's able to stand on its own two feet. However, this means taking vital growth energy from the parent plant that could be dedicated to delicious fruit.

3. We prefer to cut the runner early so that the parent can direct all possible energy into fruit production. To do this, we cut the stem a few centimetres either side of the bonus seedling.

4. Although cut runners will implant directly into soil with the right care, we find it best to sprout fresh roots in a glass of water before transplanting into soil. New roots should grow almost immediately, but it's best to wait a few weeks until they're strong enough to transplant.

5. Once strong roots have formed, transplant into the garden and water frequently. Because the runner already has developed roots, it should establish quickly and maybe even start throwing off runners of its own!

CLOVES

Garlic and shallots can be grown from cloves. This will likely come as no surprise to people who have left garlic in the pantry for a long time, only to see it sprout a bright green shoot. Even without any assistance, plants always seem to find a way. The most important thing to remember is that each individual clove will grow an entire bulb.

HOW TO PLANT

1 Plant cloves with the pointy end facing up and flat end down.
2 Push cloves a few centimetres into fertile, well-drained soil, spacing them about 15 cm (6 in) apart.
3 Water in.

HARVESTING

Make no mistake about it, our plants are domesticated. Just like a golden retriever, edible plants want to please. Remember that plants in the patch want to be eaten. In fact, they NEED to be eaten to remain productive.

Saying that, it is surprising how many gardens go unharvested. Whether it is people revelling in patch pride or simply getting too sentimental to cut off pieces for consumption, one of the most common mistakes in the veggie patch is not harvesting regularly enough. Harvest with frequency and sensitivity and you will discover that plants respond by producing even more prolifically. A plant that is not harvested will not only feel unwanted, it will believe that the season is over and go to seed. It's in everyone's best interests to harvest your food.

To paraphrase JFK, 'Ask not what your garden can do for you, but what you can do for your garden'.

HOT TIP

A plant can only hold so much fruit, just like we can only lift so much weight at the gym. Once a plant reaches its limit of 'muscle' for producing fruit, it must free up energy. Picking developing fruit or pinching growth tips redirects energy towards further fruit production. If a plant is left to grow to its limit unpicked, it becomes stressed and the yield, stagnates. This is why harvesting truly is in everyone's best interests.

TECHNIQUES + TIMING + COLLECTION

GOURDS

Zucchini (courgette) | Squash
Pumpkin (winter squash)

TECHNIQUE
Gourds are all connected by thick and fibrous stems, particularly the more developed fruit, so secateurs are not just advisable, they're essential. Bear in mind that the leaves and stems have spikes, so some form of hand protection will also be necessary.

TIMING
There is a sliding scale of harvest timing that applies to these three. Pumpkin sits at the end, and should be harvested as close to mature size and colour as possible, whereas zucchini can be picked anytime – and, in fact, zucchini flowers and small fruit are among the most desirable. Squash sits somewhere in between and will depend on variety and definition of squash (as most of our pumpkins are considered squash in the northern hemisphere).

COLLECTING
The fruit on the plant keeps well, but so does the picked fruit. Store in a fruit bowl, keeping an eye on fruit that sits there for too long. Mouldy fruit will attract unwanted indoor visitors, such as composting and/or fruit flies.

MELONS

Rockmelon (netted melon or canteloupe)
Honeydew | Watermelon | Cucumber

TECHNIQUE
The vine that connects the fruit to the plant is often thick and fibrous, which means it can be difficult to pull off. You have a far better chance of pulling out the entire vine than a single fruit, so save everyone the anticipation of what you're going to prise free and use secateurs.

TIMING
Readiness is usually defined by size but often colour, too. A smell test is also advisable, but a lot of the ripening happens off the vine, so it's not paramount. The ultimate indication of readiness for melons (excluding cucumbers) is when the fruit literally falls off the vine, however it is important to free up energy to help subsequent fruit grow, so picking earlier is advisable.

COLLECTING
Fruits will ripen off the vine, so can be harvested in advance of consumption. The exception is cucumber, which should be picked when ready and will overcook (blister or discolour) when left for too long.

HONEYDEW YOU LOVE ME?

CANTALOUPE TONIGHT?

NIGHTSHADES

Tomato | Capsicum (bell pepper)
Eggplant (aubergine) | Not potato

TECHNIQUE
Other than the cherry tomato, which will come easily off the vine, all other nightshades should be harvested using scissors or secateurs. When picking eggplants, be aware that they have surprisingly nasty spikes – not as bad as a flathead fish, but quite close.

TIMING
Harvest once the fruit is at a mature size and colour – the best indicators of readiness. With tomatoes you will need to let them develop to their mature size before contemplating a harvest. However, with capsicum, chilli and eggplant, an early harvest at small size is completely valid. A plant can only hold so much fruit, and picking will free up energy to keep producing, so it may be best to pick some fruit unripened if there is a lot on the plant.

COLLECTING
Choosing to let them vine-ripen will be a gamble that may require trial and error. It seems that every pest, including your next-door neighbour, has a heightened awareness of vine-ripened tomatoes (particularly early in the season). If you notice ripening fruit becoming victims to attack, pick early and let them ripen next to your fruit bowl of bananas.

PODS

Peas | Beans

TECHNIQUE
Break free with sharp fingernails, bracing the plant with the non-picking hand. There is always a risk of pulling an entire tendril off a plant, so if you harbour a more conservative style of thinking, use scissors.

TIMING
This is dependent on the variety and whether you are after the entire pod or the seeds within. For snow peas (mange tout) and string beans, which are picked for their pods, it's a fine balance between size and flavour. Younger pods are sweeter, but if you're hungry, you may need to let them mature more. Seeded varieties, such as snap peas or kidney beans, need time to develop the large edible seeds within. Once again there is a balance between size and flavour. Quite often a simple feel test through the pod will help reveal the size of the seeds.

COLLECTING
Nothing beats fresh pods, so pick these as required. If storing, use a snap-lock bag and keep them refrigerated. Seeding varieties will store better and most beans will require a drying process, so pick once ready for that process.

LEAFY GREENS

Lettuce | Rocket (arugula) | Spinach |
Silverbeet (Swiss chard)

TECHNIQUE
Leaf by leaf, perpetual harvesting is possible for all leafy greens, regardless of whether they're classified as hearting (iceberg) or non-hearting (rocket) varieties. Take the outer, more mature leaves first, freeing up energy for the next generation of leaf foliage to come through. Leafy greens are mostly shallow-rooted so it's always advised to brace the plant with one hand while picking or cutting with the other. Make sure you leave enough foliage on the plant, allowing it to photosynthesise and reproduce efficiently.

TIMING
Depending on the season, leafy greens can be harvested in this fashion as early as 2 weeks after transplant from seedlings and a month after sowing. Leaving a plant holding its bounty of foliage for too long can cause stress, sending it off to seed and turning the taste bitter. It's therefore in everyone's best interest to harvest with regularity.

COLLECTING
These are best picked fresh as required, but if needing to store, keep sealed in a snap-lock bag in a refrigerator. Leaves quickly dry out and turn limp if left out for more than a couple of hours.

HOW TO HARVEST LEAFY GREENS TO GET A PERPETUAL HARVEST

The joy of growing things at home is that we have a steady supply of fresh, seasonal produce to call upon at any moment. This is, perhaps, most true of leafy greens – lettuce, spinach, kale, rocket (arugula), silverbeet (Swiss chard), beetroot (beet) greens, etc. When harvested properly, just a few plants can yield consistent foliage over an entire season. The trick is to pick leaf-by-leaf, rather than exhuming the whole plant. In fact, we find plants that have regular harvesting of leaves will produce more, which in turn should encourage you to pick more. Win–Win.

1. Harvest older, larger leaves from the outside of the plant, leaving plenty of foliage to continue growth. Brace the plant with one hand while you pick with the other. After all, a clean break is a good break, or at least that is what ex-girlfriends always tell me …

2. Harvest from a variety of plants for a range of different textures, colours and flavours. This will also prevent you from taking too much from any one plant.

3. Plants, stimulated by frequent picking, will regrow quickly. Try rotating through a few plants each week so that each one has time to regenerate.

ROOTS

Beetroot (beets) | Carrot | Swede (rutabaga) | Kohlrabi | Turnip | Parsnip

TECHNIQUE

Many root vegetables present a double harvesting opportunity, both roots and foliage being perfectly edible. Harvesting a root bulb is like pulling a giant weed. Simply grab the base of the foliage nearest to the root bulb and gently pull up. Wipe away any excess soil from the bulb. If you are shocked to find a wimpy root in your hand, you probably should have done a scratch and inspect first.

Although they are often discarded, most leaves are delicious and packed with nutrition. Turnip greens, for example, are a highly regarded superfood akin to kale. Accordingly, leaves can be harvested in just the same way as lettuce and other greens. However, be sure to always leave some behind so that the roots continue to grow. Leaves will offer a perpetual harvest until the buried treasure is ready to be exhumed.

TIMING

An important thing to know is that there is no direct relation between the amount of foliage and root size, as each growth is governed by different, albeit connected, processes. Therefore, roots can present an interesting challenge, given that what you want to harvest is hidden beneath the soil. To reveal the bulb, simply scratch away soil at the base of the foliage to get a rough approximation of size. Roots are edible at any time and sweetest when they are small, gradually becoming more 'woody' as they get larger. This is the classic garden trade-off between taste and quantity. Experiment with your own palate to determine what you like best.

COLLECTING

Roots keep best in-ground, as does their foliage, so if they are not in jeopardy of becoming too big, you can consider the veggie patch to be your root refrigerator. However, once harvested you can store the whole plant in a cool, dark place, such as a crisper drawer. Leaves will wilt after about a day and root bulbs will soften after about 4 days.

TUBERS

Potato | Sweet potato | Yam | Cassava | Jerusalem artichoke

TECHNIQUE

Tubers grown in the garden bed are best harvested with a garden fork, which lifts away much of the plant while allowing excess soil to fall through its tines. When harvesting, sink the fork into the ground – giving a fairly wide berth from where you expect the first tuber (you don't want to spear it!) – to lift the earth and reveal the tubers growing beneath.

Many city gardeners will plant potatoes in a felt pot or other containers, which can simply be dumped upside down to reveal all of the contents inside. This allows growers to quickly sift through the soil with their hands and ensures that no tubers will be missed.

TIMING

Depending on the variety, tubers will have reached the end of their life cycle after 70–120 days, and foliage will start to yellow and die back.

COLLECTING

Tubers are typically collected all at once. Leave dirt on them and store in a cool, dark place. Decent ventilation is important because tubers will continue to breathe and repair bruises/blemishes for a couple of months after harvesting. Keep away from sunlight.

BRASSICAS

**Broccoli | Cauliflower | Kale
Brussels sprouts**

TECHNIQUE
Nearly all brassicas will prefer to be set free using a sharp harvesting blade than to be snapped and/or twisted off the plant. A clean cut will lessen plant stress, which is important for broccoli, kale and brussels sprouts, which have a continuous state of harvest.

TIMING
As the risk of seed heading and pest infection is high, we take a more conservative approach to harvesting and pick when young. Colour has little influence over ripeness in the world of brassicas; it's all about size. Younger produce has a much smaller chance of carrying caterpillars, which have a tendency of occupying the centres of the heads. Like in common real estate, possession is nine-tenths of the law.

COLLECTING
Homegrown, organic brassicas will quickly wilt and become rubbery once picked so ensure you pick just prior to use. If you are rescuing young produce from an encroaching pest attack and have no immediate use for it, store in a snap-lock bag in a refrigerator.

FLOWERS

TECHNIQUE
Another job for sharp fingernails and a bracing hand. Alternatively, without the appropriate manicure, use scissors or secateurs. Some flowers, such as borage, can be pinched free from an otherwise tough and unpalatable stem/casing.

TIMING
A flower will open up and bloom when it is ready. This is the primary indicator of readiness and the best time to harvest. You can also pick flower pre-bloom, as they will continue to open once freed from the plant. Once the flower has bloomed it will stay open a day or two and then quickly decline. Shrivelled flower heads on the plant take up energy that prevents it from reproducing, so breaking off those heads should go hand in hand with your harvesting routine.

COLLECTING
It's always best to collect as you need, but if your plants are producing an abundance of flower heads that are doing nothing other than shrivelling and then dying, pick for preservation. Fresh flowers will keep best in a snap-lock bag in the refrigerator for 3–4 days.

GROW. ADMIRE. EAT.

PRESERVING FLOWERS

Many of the best gifts are simple things that you would never get for yourself. I have a friend who always brings flowers when she comes over for dinner. Not a drink. Not dessert. Just some freshly cut flowers. I love it and can't help but smile.

Growing flowers can give you that feeling every day. Not only have they become an essential part of the edible gardening scene to attract pollinators, but many chefs have long embraced them as a way to add colour, flavour and texture to our foodscape. There are a lot of different ways to use flowers but, no matter their use, it is important to know how to preserve them.

1. Flowers are best preserved on the plant. The best thing about growing our own is that we can harvest as needed, rather than stocking up all at one time.

2. If we do need to stock up, the simplest method is to store cut blossoms in a plastic container. Place a damp cloth in the bottom and pile flowers on top. This will prevent wilting and compression. Store the container in a refrigerator and flowers should remain fresh for about a week.

3. For cocktails, we like to freeze whole blossoms or just a few petals in ice cubes. Borage, for example, is highly regarded for its subtle, cucumber-like taste. Gin and tonic, anyone?

4. For long-term storage, many chefs will preserve flowers by simply washing each flower with egg whites and coating in caster (superfine) sugar. After 48 hours, the sugar will draw out the moisture and, once dried, most sugar crystals can be brushed away. Voila!

5. Candied flowers not only look great. They taste delicious, too.

CITRUS

Orange | Lemon | Lime | Mandarin | Cumquat

TECHNIQUE
Most of us will harvest citrus on a whim and come armed with nothing more than bare hands and some enthusiasm. If you find yourself in this situation, twist the fruit until it breaks free from the plant, as a rough pull will usually take a limb along for the ride. If you have more time to prepare, use secateurs or scissors.

TIMING
All citrus fruit keeps well on the plant, so pick when ready for use. If you've left the plant loaded with mature fruit for a number of months, a clean sweep of the citrus will be necessary to allow the plant to develop next season's flowers and subsequent fruit.

COLLECTING
The fruit on the plant keeps well, but so does the picked fruit. Store in a fruit bowl, keeping an eye on fruit that sits there for too long and becomes mouldy. Mouldy fruit will attract unwanted indoor visitors, such as composting and/or fruit flies.

ALLIUMS

Onion | Garlic | Leek

TECHNIQUE
SHOOTS The pull or cut down are the two harvesting methods. The pull signals the end of the plant's life, but it takes the entire body, including the highly prized stem and roots. The cut down gives the plant the chance to re-sprout and give further flushes of produce.

BULB Loosen the soil around the bulb, as it has been growing a long time and soil tends to become compacted. Then, gently pull on the foliage, prising it free.

TIMING
SHOOTS From 6 weeks, you can harvest any time you're hungry.

BULB When the leaf foliage begins to die, the bulb is approaching readiness. Scratch down with your finger to inspect the size before harvesting.

COLLECTING
SHOOTS Once cut off the plant, the produce will be at its peak for 2 days. Keep in a snap-lock bag in the fridge.

BULB Bulbs need to be hung out to dry – not as bad as it sounds – in order to be kept over long periods of time. Hang in a cool, dry place for up to a month. They will then be good for six more.

HERBS

Parsley | Basil | Coriander (cilantro)
Thyme | Rosemary

TECHNIQUE
Use the same equipment that is used for a haircut (i.e. scissors) or extremely sharp fingernails. Given that harvesting your herbs might be necessary a few times a day, sharp scissors and some care will be required.

TIMING
Much like a haircut, we sometimes groom lightly to stimulate new growth, or get inspired by the need for complete change and cut it all off. Light stimulation is the best method for perpetual harvesting throughout the warmer times of the year, but as herbs become woody and go dormant in winter, a severe cutback is required to bring on fresh growth once the good times return. A new you – and a new herb plant.

COLLECTING
Take as required. Herbs keep well on the plant and quickly decline once taken from the plant, so small, dish-sized harvests are advised. The only time we tend to take large quantities is when the plant is loaded and we want to dry herbs.

PICKING HERBS TO MAXIMISE THEIR VALUE

The beauty of growing your food is that it's always in your best interest to eat it. Harvesting regularly encourages more growth by freeing up the plant's energy for more production, so leaving food on the plant and admiring it well past its best is not a habit we recommend. Pick often and you eat often.

This also applies to our herbs, but we often see erratic harvesting practices that set back their progress. Over-enthusiastic haircuts and premature harvests leave them in a bigger state of shock than the time you had that horrific haircut when you started high school – a disaster! While a rebound is inevitable, the worse the haircut the longer it takes everyone to get over the physical and psychological shock.

It's worth noting that not all herbs are made the same and each has its own particular style of harvest. For herbs to love you back they need to be treated like the individual plants they are. Rather than taking to them with your finger and thumb, bring in a pair of surgical scissors for maximum precision.

ROSEMARY, THYME & OREGANO
A little trim to stimulate new growth, or a harder cutback before spring hits.

PARSLEY & CORIANDER (CILANTRO)
The outer, more mature leaves, harvesting leaf by leaf working in.

BASIL, SAGE & MINT
Cut down to the next junction of leaves. Sage and perennial basil will need a big cutback once they go dormant, just before spring hits.

MICRO GREENS

TECHNIQUE
Use nimble, flat scissors (not bulky secateurs) to cut at ground level. Micro greens are just as easy to pull free from the soil, but do bring a lot of soil matter with them (fine if the taste of grit is in high demand).

TIMING
All plants develop a first set of immature leaves that will subsequently drop off as growth continues, but it's when the first true leaves begin to develop that signals the time to begin harvesting the micro greens. These leaves will look distinctly different to the immature first leaves, so they are easy enough to identify.

COLLECTING
Being so small and delicate, you ideally want to harvest micro greens and then literally throw them on top of your dish. If preparing for a long day of highbrow culinary dishes, keep them in a snap-lock container within a damp tea towel (dish towel). We've seen chefs do this, so it must be a good idea. Actually, we've also seen chefs commit vegetable genocide, so thankfully we researched it ourselves.

STONE FRUIT

TECHNIQUE
Call us conservative, but when it comes to fruit picking we're big fans of sensible harvesting that mitigates the potential for spoilt fruit. Stone fruit bruises so easily that it requires some care during picking. Use scissors rather than a 'pull' method that will tend to dislodge other ripe fruit from the tree. This will send them hurling towards the ground and into your next batch of jam, rather than pride of place in the fruit bowl. Of course, if it's jam you're making and you're inherently lazy, by all means do what you have to. We'll look away as you set up a tarp and shake down the tree in question.

TIMING
Stone fruit is best enjoyed once ripened on the tree. Skin colour, smell and a gentle squeeze of the fruit will give you all the information needed to make the assessment.

COLLECTING
Depending on the grade of ripeness, the fruit should keep OK in the fruit bowl or in the fridge if well developed. Routinely turn the fruit as the undersides tend to ripen more quickly and will rot if not aired sufficiently.

OLIVES

TECHNIQUE
As most fruit is picked unripened and won't bruise too easily, we favour the Mr Bump technique of harvesting, which is to bump into, shake or hit the tree. Rather than scavenging for fallen fruit within the grass and/or dirt, remember to lay a catching sheet. If harvesting ripened fruit, use a ladder and pull the olives free by hand.

TIMING
Once the olives are fully formed in size, they are ready for harvesting. Olive size will vary depending on varieties, so check up on what you are growing and what is expected. These unripe olives will suit both curing in a brine and olive oil production. Ripe olives tend to become mushy when brined and are lacking in oil content.

COLLECTING
Unripe olives will keep for a number of days, or up to a fortnight in a cool, dry place, without spoiling. They can therefore be picked in advance of curing and/or olive oil production. And, to be honest, bumping into trees will take a lot out of you so a small recuperation may be necessary.

FRUIT & VE

Artichoke

128

Asparagus

130

Basil

132

Beans

134

Beetroot
(Beet)
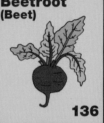
136

Berries

138

Capsicum
(Bell pepper)

148

Carrot

149

Cauliflower

150

Celeriac

152

Celery
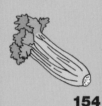
154

Chilli
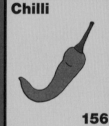
156

Fennel

168

Flowers

170

Fruit trees

176

Garlic

182

Herbs

184

Kale
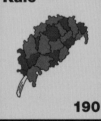
190

Micro greens

200

Mint

202

Mushroom

204

Nasturtium

208

Onion

210

Parsnip

211

Rhubarb

222

Rocket
(Arugula)

224

Silverbeet

226

Spinach

228

Spring onion
(Scallion)

229

Squash
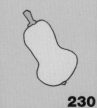
230

G TO GROW

Broad beans
140

Broccoli
142

Brussels sprouts
144

Cabbage
146

Citrus
158

Coriander (Cilantro)
162

Cucumber
166

Eggplant (Aubergine)
167

Kohlrabi
192

Leek
194

Lettuce
196

Melons
198

Parsley
212

Passionfruit
214

Peas
216

Potato
218

Pumpkin (Winter squash)
219

Radish
220

Strawberry
232

Swede
234

Sweet corn
235

Tomato
236

Tubers
240

Zucchini (Courgette)
242

GROW, GROW, GROW YOUR BOAT

FRUIT & VEG TO GROW

At our nursery in Melbourne we come into contact with all types of growers, from grizzled garden gurus that visit for a chat, to shy novices looking to grow their first radish. However, of all the people we have met, one interaction will always remain in our minds. We were helping a customer to choose seeds for their garden and suggested that they grow kale. To this they responded, 'Oh no, too hip'. Pardon? Not 'no thanks, it tastes like green leather'. Not 'nah, that stuff gets stuck in my teeth and I only realise it's there four hours later'. Their statement implied a common insecurity: the fear of other people's judgement. It is something that we all feel, especially when we try something new. In the case of kale, it was the feeling that a vegetable was too popular to enjoy. So, let's set the record straight – people have grown kale since before it was fashionable. The same goes for gardening. Don't let someone tell you that it is trendy, or just for hippies or old Italian grandmothers. Growing food is for all people.

Nevertheless, it is fair to have our preferences and understand our limitations. It's important to recognise early on that there will be plenty of gardening failures, but that the judgement we fear is probably coming from within. Getting things wrong is always a step in the right direction. Some plants are more demanding than others. Some plants are suited to specific conditions. Some plants taste like old work boots. We can't know until we try.

Think of this section as a recipe book that can be referenced for inspiration and guidance. It is an all-you-can-eat buffet of possibility. Accordingly, we encourage improvisation to your own experience and taste. There is no sure way to grow food, but there are some basic principles to follow that will make it easier, which in turn will make gardening more successful and a lot more fun.

YOUR PLANTS' SURVIVAL GUIDE

GROW WHAT YOU LIKE TO EAT

If you are excited about the food that you grow, then you will take better care of it. There is no point having that prize-winning cabbage just to feed the caterpillars (although that would be very considerate). More kimchi, please.

PROVIDE NUTRIENT-RICH, WELL-DRAINED SOIL

Some plants are certainly more tolerant than others, but getting your soil right goes a long way when it comes to edible plants. Add organic compost and various manures at least once a year and you shouldn't need any additional additives. You can improve the soil that you have or import something new. See Soil (Growing medium), page 12.

CONSIDER QUALITY

The quality of ingredients always makes a difference to the final product and we strongly encourage using non-chemical growing methods. After all, what you put in the garden will ultimately be put in your mouth (see pages 24–27 for information on organic fertilisers).

DONT LET SEEDS AND SEEDLINGS DRY OUT

Many seeds need to remain damp until germination and then will require daily water as seedlings. Once plants become established they will be fine on water every couple of days.

WATER REGULARLY

We say it all the time – there are no bad gardeners, only bad waterers. Most established plants will need water every couple of days and every day in hot weather. No excuses. Make it part of the routine (see Watering, page 44).

CHALLENGE YOURSELF

Grow what you like to eat, but try things you don't like as well – you might be surprised how good something tastes when you grow it yourself. How many of us grew up eating vegetables boiled to mush? I didn't realise I loved eggplant until someone other than my mom prepared it. Don't let a couple of bad experiences rule your palate or your garden.

RATINGS EXPLAINED

SCALED 1-5 *(WHERE 5 IS THE BEST)*

EASY TO GROW
Amount of effort or skill required to grow:

1   5

Making a soufflé   Frying an egg

SMALL SPACE SUITABILITY
Minimum spatial footprint requirements for a healthy plant:

1   5

Requires about 1 m   Can be packed into close quarters
(3 ft 3 in) of space   and/or shallow soil depth

YIELD VALUE
Relationship between effort required and final product value:

1   5

The artichoke is   Fresh herbs cost a lot to buy but
high-maintenance and a long are very easy to grow and can
wait for a single flower that be continuously harvested
doesn't have much flesh

JE NE SAIS QUOI/PLEASURE
An undefinable quality that often has more to do with
emotions and feelings than any real gardening attribute:

1   5

An awkward first kiss   Falling in love

THE LITTLE VEGGIE PATCH CO RATING
We've combined all the above to come up with an
all-encompassing veggie patch rating.

NONNO'S TIP
Practical, everyday gardening wisdom passed down
from Mat's no-nonsense Italian grandfather.

KITCHEN TIP
Our favourite ways to prepare and eat produce
from the garden.

☮ WHEN TO PLANT
Best time of the year or season to plant for your zone.
Reference the map on the inside front cover to identify
the correct climate zone in your country.

⚘ BEST GROWN FROM
Ideal starting point for growing. While most plants
can be started from seed, many plants are easier and
more productive to start from a different growth stage.
Growing rosemary from seed, for example, is tedious
and can take a long time to germinate, but it is easily
grown from a cutting.

↓ DEPTH
Optimal seed planting depth: seeds should be planted
to twice the depth of their diameter.

⌇ SPACING
Optimal spacing for mature plants and seedlings.
We often sow seeds much closer together and then
thin out the successful seedlings once they become
established.

♂ TIME TO 1ST HARVEST
Length of time from planting to first harvest.

△ IDEAL pH LEVEL
Best pH conditions for plant health and productivity.

♡ FAVOURITE SMALL-SPACE VARIETY
Plants that are well suited to keeping close quarters
with other crops and/or do well in shallow soil.

⊔ BEST SUITED TO
Three main types of infrastructure from largest
to smallest – in-ground, pot and wall garden.

☼ COMMON PROBLEMS
Pests, diseases and conditions that will most likely
challenge your plant.

TIMELINE
Timelines show the different stages of propagation, soil
preparation, planting, growing and time of first harvest
for each fruit and veg.

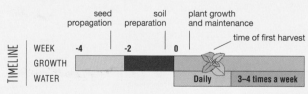

ARTICHOKE

	1	2	3	4	5
EASY TO GROW					
SMALL SPACE SUITABILITY					
YIELD VALUE					
JE NE SAIS QUOI/PLEASURE					

When to plant
ZONE 1 Sep–Nov   ZONE 3 Aug–Oct
ZONE 2 Sep–Nov   ZONE 4 Not suitable

Best grown from
Seedling

Depth
1.5 cm (½ in)

Spacing
1 m (3 ft 3 in)

Time to 1st harvest
18–30 weeks

Ideal pH level
6.0–6.8

Favourite small-space variety
None – they're all so bloody huge

Best suited to
In-ground

Common problems
Aphids, ants

There are some plants that just don't belong in the small-space garden, and unfortunately dear friend, you (artichoke) are one of them. But that's not to say that they don't belong in the garden, because an artichoke is a majestic plant and a fierce culinary weapon – not to mention a purple flower that will make you swoon.

Growing artichokes requires patience and planning. It's generally not the type of plant you purchase on a whim, but it would be the first variety we put on the drawing board when designing our future market garden for our future dream Tasmanian property. You can build the rest of the vegetable growing team around it.

To accommodate this monster plant you need a succession plan. Some plants can grow in and around it early, but as it gets established it appreciates nothing more than its own space. The artichoke will also need a 12-month concession for its lack of productivity, as few hearts develop until the second year. However, for the next 5 years it'll repay the faith with an increasing output of hearts, and if left to flower it will attract bees and predatory insects like the complete stud it is. American artist Georgia O'Keeffe never got to paint *this* flower, but there is no doubt that she would have given it two thumbs up.

NONNO'S
TIP   They can grow quite lanky if not kept in check, so prune them like a fruit tree to keep a strong shape.

KITCHEN
TIP   Stuff them, literally.

TIMELINE

WEEK	-2	0	4	8	12	20	32	52

Prepare soil with compost and organic slow-release fertiliser. (−2)

Plant as a seedling. (0)

Mulch to a depth of 3–5 cm (1¼–2 in) using pea straw, lucerne hay or sugar cane mulch. (4)

Feed with slow-release organic fertiliser. (12)

Begin harvesting flower buds (hearts), cutting them off about 5 cm (2 in) down the stem. Feed them fortnightly with liquid potash while they are flowering. (20)

Moderately prune back the plant to maintain a healthy shape and stake if necessary. Any extra plants that shoot from the root zone can be carefully taken from the plant and grown elsewhere in the garden. (32)

Feed with slow-release organic fertiliser and re-mulch the plants. (52)

GROWTH

WATER: **Daily** | **3–4 times a week**

ASPARAGUS

	1	2	3	4	5
EASY TO GROW					
SMALL SPACE SUITABILITY					
YIELD VALUE					
JE NE SAIS QUOI/PLEASURE					

When to plant
ZONE 1 Oct–Dec   ZONE 3 Aug–Oct
ZONE 2 Sep–Nov   ZONE 4 Not suitable

Best grown from
Crown (rhizome stock)

Depth
Dig crown in so that the top-most points can be
covered with a few centimetres of soil.

Spacing
50 cm–1 m (1 ft 7 in–3 ft 3 in)

Time to 1st harvest
If grown from crown, 1 year. If seed/seedling,
2 years. Productive for 20 years!

Ideal pH level
6.0–7.0

Favourite small-space variety
Purple

Best suited to
In-ground, larger pots

Common problems
Relatively exempt to pests, but overwatering or wet
boggy soils make them susceptible to crown rot.

Committing to this vegetable means you are effectively putting yourself in a long-term relationship. Tomatoes, pumpkins (squash) and cucumbers are just simple warm-season flings – the types of vegetables you would meet in a bar and spend a summer with. You won't encounter asparagus on the bar scene. This is a plant of real substance.

Though asparagus is a long-term investment, particularly in a small-space garden, that doesn't necessarily mean it isn't worth your effort and a piece of your precious real estate. It's best to plant from established root balls, or crowns, which will give you a headstart on expected yields. However, it can be grown successfully from seedling and seed.

You can choose female varieties that are slenderer and more beautiful looking, or the stumpier, stockier male version. We have a fondness for both, because variety (in asparagus) is our spice in life.

All asparagus are white unless exposed to sunlight. So, for those who prefer the more delicate and tender flavour of white asparagus, mound up mulch around the shoots as they emerge from the ground. This is a process called blanching and we often use it for onions and leeks as well.

NONNO'S TIP
Asparagus used to grow wild all over the old country. Those were the days ... It was cut young and regularly and it tasted like sunshine.

KITCHEN TIP
Freshly picked spears sautéed in olive oil and garlic with a squeeze of lemon to finish.

TIMELINE									
		Prepare soil with compost and organic slow-release fertiliser.	Plant as a crown.	Slender asparagus begin to shoot. Do not harvest as we want to concentrate purely on foliage growth for the first 12 months.	Mulch to a depth of 3–5 cm (1¼–2 in) using pea straw, lucerne hay or sugar cane mulch.	Feed with organic slow-release fertiliser.	As the soil cools the plant begins to die back. At this stage, cut it back to ground level and cover with mulch.	Feed with compost and organic slow-release fertiliser.	Harvest slender first-year shoots at ground level. Cover the cut over with soil to help repair the rhizome. Repeat each year for 15+ years of productivity.
WEEK		-2	0	4	8	16	28	48	52+
GROWTH									
WATER				3–4 times a week		2–3 times a week			

BASIL

	1	2	3	4	5
EASY TO GROW					
SMALL SPACE SUITABILITY					
YIELD VALUE					
JE NE SAIS QUOI/PLEASURE					

When to plant
ZONE 1 Nov–Jan   ZONE 3 Aug–Feb
ZONE 2 Oct–Feb   ZONE 4 Anytime

Best grown from
Seed – propagate in trays and transplant into the patch.

Depth
1 cm (½ in)

Spacing
20 cm (8 in)

Time to 1st harvest
30–45 days

Ideal pH level
6.5–7.5

Favourite small-space variety
Mini Greek

Best suited to
Pots, wall, in-ground

Common problems
Caterpillars

Life is often defined and then separated by moments, both good and bad. There are pivotal 'sliding door' occasions that will change life forever, so there exists the time before and the time after. Anyone with kids could quite easily split their life into pre-kid and post-kid existence. Similarly, jobs, ex-partners or even flashy new cars can define people and their lives. But when it comes to the garden, there is a seasonal sliding door that always throws me into turmoil – the time when there is basil and the time when there is none.

Over the years I've learnt to broaden my horizons, so I'm not just the tomato and basil man I used to be. However, these varieties continue to have a profound impact on my gardening psyche and that of life in general. When these plants are around, things just seem a little brighter. Sure, it could be that it happens to coincide with late spring, summer and holidays, but our culture – that of an Italian and an Italian/Australian – is so affected by both, it feels like there's more to it.

Basil simply changes a garden for the better. Each year in February or March, my bond with sweet basil peaks as we push oversized, bittersweet leaves into the VB bottles we've so diligently prepared for the pasta sauce. But it's not just sweet basil. Others have found a place in my garden, varieties that I've come to know and love, such as the red-leafed Sapphire or small-leafed (almost bonsai-style) Greek, even the anise-flavoured Thai variety. This is not a monogamous relationship.

NONNO'S
TIP
Plant in and around the canopy of your tomato plants. It's a companionship made in heaven.

KITCHEN
TIP
Pick only as required, as leaves will quickly wilt.

TIMELINE									
		Propagate in a seed tray.	Prepare soil with compost and organic slow-release fertiliser.	Transplant the seedlings into the patch well after the last frost and position around the base of your tomato plants.	Mulch to 3–5 cm (1¼–2 in) with lucerne hay, sugar cane mulch or pea straw.	Begin to harvest moderately. The best way is to pick down the stem to the next junction of leaves, helping it regenerate most efficiently.	Apply liquid seaweed fertiliser.	If seed heads begin to form, pinch them back to redirect energy towards foliage production.	Make pesto.
WEEK	-4		-2	0	4	6	8	12	16
GROWTH									
WATER				Daily		3–4 times a week			

BEANS

	1	2	3	4	5
EASY TO GROW					
SMALL SPACE SUITABILITY					
YIELD VALUE					
JE NE SAIS QUOI/PLEASURE					

When to plant
ZONE 1 Oct–Jan
ZONE 2 Sep–Jan
ZONE 3 Aug–Feb
ZONE 4 Apr–Jul

Best grown from
Seed

Depth
2–3 cm (¾–1¼ in)

Spacing
30 cm (12 in)

Time to 1st harvest
75 days

Ideal pH level
6.5–7.0

Favourite small-space variety
Bonaparte

Best suited to
Pots, in-ground

Common problems
Rats

In the world of growing vegetables there are two types of people: bean people and tomato people. Between them is a giant divide. Each year, as spring approaches, we again need to decide what side of the fence we sit on.

However, this is one occasion when fence-sitting is acceptable and actually encouraged. While there's no hiding from the fact that we are fanatical tomato lovers, this doesn't mean we turn our back on the bean. With even more heirloom varieties to choose from, why miss out on one of the veggie patch's greatest treasures?

While most beans are runner varieties that will climb high on a trellis, there are still a number of more compact bush style varieties that produce well in a small-space garden, and are perfectly suited to pots. This makes maintenance a more manageable proposition.

Where we truly get rewarded for our fence-sitting is in the nitrogen-fixing quality of the bean, which leaves the patch primed for the cool-season brassicas to follow.

NONNO'S TIP Once the plant is on the cusp of production, with flowers forming, pinch off growth tips to redirect energy to pod production.

KITCHEN TIP Remember to leave a little crunch for the dinner table. Have a bowl of icy water ready for plunging after boiling/steaming.

TIMELINE

WEEK	0	4	8	10	12	20
GROWTH	Add compost and some blood and bone. Sow seeds directly to the patch where you have previously grown brassicas, such as broccoli, cabbage and cauliflower.	Thin out seedlings to a spacing of 30 cm (12 in) and mulch using sugar cane mulch to a depth of 3–5 cm (1¼–2 in).	Climbing varieties will need trellising. Even some bush varieties can do with some staking. This is also a good time to apply epsom salts to help with magnesium.	To encourage flower and then pod development, apply a dosage of liquid potassium.	Pick pods when at a desirable size, being careful to brace the plant while doing so. Harvesting frees up energy on the plant to produce more fruit.	If planting in-ground, chop up the plants and dig them through the patch. This will help fix the soil with nitrogen for the subsequent crops.
WATER	3–4 times a week					

BEETROOT (BEET)

	1	2	3	4	5
EASY TO GROW					
SMALL SPACE SUITABILITY					
YIELD VALUE					
JE NE SAIS QUOI/PLEASURE					

When to plant
ZONE 1 Sep–May   ZONE 3 Anytime
ZONE 2 Sep–Jun   ZONE 4 Mar–Sep

Best grown from
Seed

Depth
1 cm (½ in)

Spacing
10 cm (4 in)

Time to 1st harvest
45+ days for leaves, 75+ days for roots

Ideal pH level
6.5–7.0

Favourite small-space variety
Detroit dark red

Best suited to
Pots, wall, in-ground

Common problems
Rats

Vegetables that carry the gourmet tag tend to be either difficult to grow or seasonal – and usually both. However, beetroot is one exception. Rather, it throws up a premium culinary experience with only basic growing requirements and can be grown at most times of the year.

Google 'interesting beetroot facts' and you will find that beetroot may improve your libido, cure hangovers and regulate garlic breath. We generally eat it after a boozy, French degustation when we're not in the mood.

Because it is suitable to grow in most climates at most times of the year, beetroot is always ready to fill a void in your veggie patch and will do so with little fuss. While we often prize beetroot for its dense, richly coloured root bulb, it has a versatile offering. Freshly germinated seeds can be harvested as micro greens and the foliage of mature plants are a food source in their own right.

This is one vegetable that should certainly be in your gardening bag of tricks.

NONNO'S TIP Grow closely together and harvest every second one early for small beets and foliage to let the remaining plants mature to full size.

KITCHEN TIP Great seed for micro greens. One of the best veggies to pickle.

TIMELINE

WEEK	0		4		8		12
GROWTH							
WATER	Daily				3–4 times per week		

Add compost and blood and bone for phosphorus and sow seeds directly to the patch.

Thin out seedlings to a spacing of 10–15 cm (4–6 in) and mulch using pea straw, lucerne hay or sugar cane a depth of 3–5 cm (1¼–2 in).

Begin harvesting leaves as salad greens. However, do so in moderation so you don't disturb the overall growth of the root.

Harvest roots, bracing plants nearby that will remain in the ground for further growth. Roots keep well in-ground, particularly when the soil temperature is cool, so only harvest as required.

BERRIES

BLUEBERRY

BLACKBERRY

	1	2	3	4	5
EASY TO GROW					
SMALL SPACE SUITABILITY					
YIELD VALUE					
JE NE SAIS QUOI/PLEASURE					

When it comes to berries, perspective is everything. For those who grew up on farms, berries would sprawl across the land and grow feral. They'd eat up anything that entered – kites, footballs, the pet dog – but in return they would throw up a feast that was unparalleled.

For city folk, on the other hand, berries are a rare treat. They're (expensive) lollies dressed up as fruit, and any offering to a child is immediately accepted. As a kid it felt illicit to be eating berries – mostly because they were usually taken from my uncle's patch. It didn't make sense that something so good was actually a 'piece of fruit'.

Growing them in a small space is a challenge, albeit not an insurmountable one. Though a berry bush will flourish when space allows it to sprawl, all berries can be grown in pots and provide enough treats to earn their place.

THE LITTLE VEGGIE PATCH CO RATING
3.5

BLUEBERRY

When to plant
ZONE 1 Apr–Aug ZONE 3 Not suitable
ZONE 2 Jun–Sep ZONE 4 Not suitable

Best grown from
Mature plant (from nursery)

Depth
Dig hole slightly deeper than the root ball, place in the hole and cover back over until ground level is restored. Make sure that the stem is vertical.

Spacing
40 cm–2 m (1 ft 3 in–6 ft 6 in)

Time to 1st harvest
350+ days

Ideal pH level
4.0–5.5

Favourite small-space variety
Sunshine blue dwarf

Best suited to
In-ground, large pots

Common problems
Children, birds

NONNO'S TIP
Need to be planted in groups to remain fertile. Grow at least three plants together to ensure viability. Blueberries need a highly acidic soil, so try digging in some pine needles prior to planting, which will pull down your pH.

KITCHEN TIP
To preserve, spread blueberries across a baking tray and freeze. Frozen berries can then be transferred to a bag or tub, without any risk of sticking together.

BLACKBERRY

When to plant
ZONE 1 Apr–Oct ZONE 3 Jun–Aug
ZONE 2 May–Sep ZONE 4 Jun–Aug

Best grown from
Bare-rooted cane

Depth
Dig hole slightly deeper than the root ball, place in the hole and cover back over until ground level is restored.

Spacing
1–2 m (3 ft 3 in–6 ft 6 in)

Time to 1st harvest
350+ days

Ideal pH level
5.5–7.0

Favourite small-space variety
Black satin

Best suited to
In-ground, large pots

Common problems
Grey mould, viruses from wild blackberries

NONNO'S TIP
Ask your local nursery for erect cultivars. These varieties are much easier to manage, as they can be cut back right to the ground each year. Thornless varieties should also be available.

KITCHEN TIP
Cheat's blackberry syrup: mix 4 cups of blackberries and 1 cup of sugar in a saucepan. Simmer, stirring continuously, until sugar is dissolved. Add to pancakes and waffles or eat by the spoonful.

CRANBERRY

🌱 **When to plant**
ZONE 1 Apr–Sep   ZONE 3 Not suitable
ZONE 2 Jun–Aug   ZONE 4 Not suitable

🌾 **Best grown from**
Rooted cutting

↓ **Depth**
Dig hole slightly deeper than the root ball, place in the hole and cover back over until ground level is restored.

〜 **Spacing**
60 cm–1 m (2 ft–3 ft 3 in)

♂ **Time to 1st harvest**
350+ days

△ **Ideal pH level**
6.2–6.8

♡ **Favourite small-space variety**
Howes

🪴 **Best suited to**
In-ground, large pots

☼ **Common problems**
Birds

NONNO'S TIP
Requires a winter freeze to produce fruit.

KITCHEN TIP
They're great served warm on top of vanilla ice cream.

LOGANBERRY

🌱 **When to plant**
ZONE 1 Apr–Oct   ZONE 3 Jun–Aug
ZONE 2 May–Sep   ZONE 4 Jun–Aug

🌾 **Best grown from**
Bare-rooted cane

↓ **Depth**
Dig hole slightly deeper than the root ball, place in the hole and cover back over until ground level is restored.

〜 **Spacing**
1–2 m (3 ft 3 in–6 ft 6 in)

♂ **Time to 1st harvest**
350+ days

△ **Ideal pH level**
5.5–7.0

♡ **Favourite small-space variety**
American thornless

🪴 **Best suited to**
In-ground, large pots

☼ **Common problems**
Birds – otherwise, quite disease- and pest-resistant

NONNO'S TIP
Fruit production occurs on second year growth, so it is most efficient to divide the plant into two sections. After one section fruits, cut it right back. Harvest fruit from the other section the following year and then cut that one back. Go about alternating the harvest and cutting every year to get a steady harvest.

KITCHEN TIP
Loganberries are great for making a drinking vinegar.

RASPBERRY

🌱 **When to plant**
ZONE 1 Apr–Oct   ZONE 3 Jun–Aug
ZONE 2 May–Sep   ZONE 4 Jun–Aug

🌾 **Best grown from**
Bare-rooted cane

↓ **Depth**
Dig hole slightly deeper than the root ball, place in the hole and cover back over until ground level is restored.

〜 **Spacing**
1–2 m (3 ft 3 in–6 ft 6 in)

♂ **Time to 1st harvest**
350+ days

△ **Ideal pH level**
6.2–6.8

♡ **Favourite small-space variety**
August red

🪴 **Best suited to**
In-ground, large pots

☼ **Common problems**
Birds

NONNO'S TIP
Soak raspberry roots for a couple of hours before planting to decrease transplant shock.

KITCHEN TIP
Raspberry pavlova, of course!

STRAWBERRY SEE PAGE 232

BROAD BEANS

	1	2	3	4	5
EASY TO GROW					
SMALL SPACE SUITABILITY					
YIELD VALUE					
JE NE SAIS QUOI/PLEASURE					

When to plant
ZONE 1 Mar–May
         Oct–Nov
ZONE 2 Mar–Jun
ZONE 3 Apr–Jul
ZONE 4 Not suitable

Best grown from
Seed

Depth
3–4 cm (1¼–1½ in)

Spacing
20–30 cm (8–11 in)

Time to 1st harvest
90+ days

Ideal pH level
6.5–7.5

Favourite small-space variety
Crimson red for its edible flowers

Best suited to
Pots, in-ground

Common problems
Rats like the seeds and young seedlings

The broad bean is to autumn what the tomato is to spring. It's the veggie we get unusually excited about when the leaves start to fall. As a youngster I remember the clumsy swagger of the broad bean plant alongside my itchy knitted threads. In winter I'd wander through my nonna's garden and a forest of 'bob' – as she would call it – and the battle would be on to protect her greatest autumn asset. She would have to use all her powers of distraction, persuasion and the wooden spoon to keep my mittens off her 'bob'.

Thankfully, we now have raised garden beds to make it an unfair fight with the next generation and my broad beans are more than safe. While my nonna only used the beans in the pod (double shelled, of course), whether it's impatience or our quest for more value from the plant, we are equally committed to the beans, pod, foliage and flowers. The broad beans throw up a multitude of feasting opportunities, none of which should be ignored.

Given that my nonna was obsessed with broad beans and tomatoes, it made the rotation between seasons the smoothest of transitions. The broad bean – a nitrogen fixer – should always be planted in the soil where the tomatoes once lay. In the small-space garden, where we seldom promote permaculture practices, this is a rule we always follow.

NONNO'S TIP The number one crop to precede and follow tomato for its nitrogen-fixing quality.

KITCHEN TIP Eat the whole plant. Young pods are great either fresh or cooked. Foliage has an earthy pea flavour and can be eaten raw or lightly sautéed. Flowers are delicate and should never be heated, but they offer a subtle sweetness to any fresh dish.

Add compost and some blood and bone. Sow seeds directly to the patch where you have previously grown nitrogen-hungry tomatoes.

Thin out seedlings to a spacing of 20–30 cm (8–11 in) and mulch using sugar cane to a depth of 3–5 cm (1¼–2 in).

Plants are tall and a bit clumsy, so will need trellising. This is also a good time to apply a dose of liquid potassium to help with flowers setting and turning into pods.

Pick pods when at a desirable size, being careful not to dislodge developing flowers. Harvesting frees up energy on the plant to produce more fruit. Another way to encourage better pod growth is to cut the tops of the plant to help redirect energy. These shoots are edible.

If planting in-ground, chop up the plants and dig them through the patch. This will help fix the soil with nitrogen for the subsequent crops.

TIMELINE	WEEK	0	4	8	12	20
	GROWTH					
	WATER			3–4 times a week		

BROCCOLI

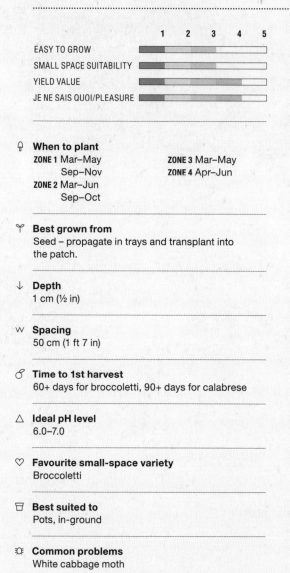

	1	2	3	4	5
EASY TO GROW					
SMALL SPACE SUITABILITY					
YIELD VALUE					
JE NE SAIS QUOI/PLEASURE					

When to plant
ZONE 1 Mar–May
     Sep–Nov
ZONE 2 Mar–Jun
     Sep–Oct

ZONE 3 Mar–May
ZONE 4 Apr–Jun

Best grown from
Seed – propagate in trays and transplant into the patch.

Depth
1 cm (½ in)

Spacing
50 cm (1 ft 7 in)

Time to 1st harvest
60+ days for broccoletti, 90+ days for calabrese

Ideal pH level
6.0–7.0

Favourite small-space variety
Broccoletti

Best suited to
Pots, in-ground

Common problems
White cabbage moth

Of the brassicas – which include nutrient-dense, cold-tolerant vegetables with an appetite for nitrogen, such as cauliflower, cabbage and brussels sprouts – broccoli is the most accessible to grow. On top of that, it is the only one that regenerates a number of times, allowing a prolonged harvesting period. You shouldn't need any more reason to give it a shot.

But don't fall into a false sense of security. Despite the advantages broccoli has over its brassica counterparts, it is still a favoured target of the white cabbage moth – and this is a battle all broccoli growers inevitably will have to face.

The level of warfare with the white cabbage moth is generally determined by what variety of broccoli you choose to grow. Larger heading varieties, known as calabrese broccoli, require longer growing and maintenance periods than sprouting varieties, or broccoletti. This gives the caterpillar a larger window of opportunity to strike – and more cover to hide – so bear that in mind when selecting your variety.

Broccoletti looks like the beautiful love child of broccoli and asparagus. Not only is it a vegetable, but it is also a sacred gardening mantra that should be spoken three times aloud. Broccoletti, broccoletti, broccoletti. Try it. At the very least it should produce a smile, and in some rare cases it is known to summon a miniature Italian man to dance across your tongue. Whatever the effect, the plant's magic should not be denied.

NONNO'S TIP Net the plants so that the moths cannot lay their larvae on them, and so the caterpillars cannot strike. It's amazingly effective.

KITCHEN TIP Broccoli will provide subsequent florets after the primary harvest and, if anything, these are sweeter and tastier. The flowering florets, sautéed in chilli olive oil with fresh garlic shoots, are next level.

TIMELINE							
	Propagate seeds in a seed tray and prepare the patch with plenty of compost and high-nitrogen manures.	Plant the seedlings into the patch. Use netting to deter white cabbage moth. Mulch to 3–5 cm (1¼–2 in) with pea straw or lucerne hay.	As hungry feeders, the broccoli plants will appreciate monthly feeds with liquid fish emulsion.	Thin out the seedlings to the required spacing.	As the heads begin to form, apply compost to ensure they get required nutrients during this critical phase.	Harvest the heads by cutting them at the base of the stem. Leave the plants in-ground as they will generate subsequent smaller florets until they turn to flower.	
WEEK	-4	0	4	8	12	16	24
GROWTH							
WATER		Daily		3–4 times a week			

BRUSSELS SPROUTS

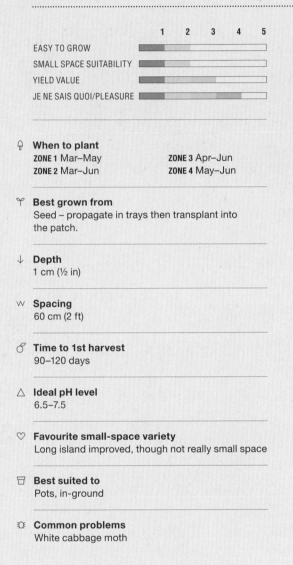

	1	2	3	4	5
EASY TO GROW					
SMALL SPACE SUITABILITY					
YIELD VALUE					
JE NE SAIS QUOI/PLEASURE					

When to plant
ZONE 1 Mar–May   ZONE 3 Apr–Jun
ZONE 2 Mar–Jun   ZONE 4 May–Jun

Best grown from
Seed – propagate in trays then transplant into the patch.

Depth
1 cm (½ in)

Spacing
60 cm (2 ft)

Time to 1st harvest
90–120 days

Ideal pH level
6.5–7.5

Favourite small-space variety
Long island improved, though not really small space

Best suited to
Pots, in-ground

Common problems
White cabbage moth

Someone, somewhere once gave bad advice on cooking brussels sprouts and it stuck. People everywhere began overcooking the sprouts, turning them into a sulphur-emitting mush. This made them smell no better than an overcooked sports kit that had been enclosed in an airtight bag. With few people having the appetite for soggy wet socks, this bad rap still lingers today.

If you still have the smell of a dirty sports bag imprinted on the back of your nasal palate, it's time to cleanse it and begin to realise the true beauty of a brussels sprout. For us it's one of the perfect vegetables, the very best of the brassica family in a textured, bite-sized parcel. It's like small mini hearts of cabbage, but without the fodder of leaves everywhere. It gets right to business and is perhaps the perfect accompaniment to butter and garlic.

Growing brussels sprouts at home is a test of your gardening aptitude, but success comes with reward. Seeing the sprouts spiral around the stem of the plant is real viewing pleasure – one of the garden's best – and then there's the anticipation of the butter and garlic.

NONNO'S TIP
Net to prevent white cabbage moth from laying its larvae. Don't over-fertilise once the sprouts begin to form as this turns them loose and puffy.

KITCHEN TIP
Develop an intimate relationship with butter and garlic and don't overcook them!

Propagate seeds in a seed tray and prepare the patch with plenty of compost and high-nitrogen manures.

Transplant the seedlings into the patch. Use netting to deter white cabbage moth. Mulch to a depth of 3–5 cm (1¼–2 in) with pea straw or lucerne hay.

As hungry feeders, the sprouts will appreciate monthly feeds with liquid fish emulsion.

Thin out the seedlings to the required spacing.

Apply compost to the patch, but don't over-fertilise with nitrogen, as this will cause the sprouts to become loose and puffy.

Harvest by cutting the sprouts loose, starting at the base, which is where the more mature ones will be. As the plant produces, pick off any yellowing leaves.

TIMELINE	WEEK	-4	0	4	8	12	16	24
	GROWTH							
	WATER		Daily		3–4 times a week			

CABBAGE

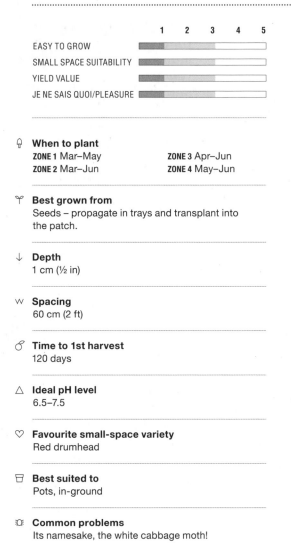

	1	2	3	4	5
EASY TO GROW					
SMALL SPACE SUITABILITY					
YIELD VALUE					
JE NE SAIS QUOI/PLEASURE					

When to plant
ZONE 1 Mar–May   ZONE 3 Apr–Jun
ZONE 2 Mar–Jun   ZONE 4 May–Jun

Best grown from
Seeds – propagate in trays and transplant into
the patch.

Depth
1 cm (½ in)

Spacing
60 cm (2 ft)

Time to 1st harvest
120 days

Ideal pH level
6.5–7.5

Favourite small-space variety
Red drumhead

Best suited to
Pots, in-ground

Common problems
Its namesake, the white cabbage moth!

Cabbage is a versatile vegetable that can be eaten steamed, raw, fermented, pickled and barbecued. It is also an honest vegetable that is high in vitamin C and is said to be able to help heal ulcers and prevent cancer. Something cabbage will also help you with is flatulence, as it has been tagged 'the windy vegetable'. This quality is largely abated with fermentation.

We have always been in love with cabbage – for all its qualities – but particularly the way it can turn a meal almost meaty. Few people know that the great Australian dim sim is almost entirely filled with cabbage. Like all brassicas, in the veggie patch it's a constant battle keeping up nutrition for this hungry feeder, while at the same time swatting away hordes of attracted white cabbage moths.

In Italian the word for cabbage, cavolo, can be used as a mild swear word, once again demonstrating its versatility.

NONNO'S
TIP
Net to prevent the moth from laying its larvae –
that's half the battle won.

KITCHEN
TIP
So versatile, from coleslaw to cabbage rolls,
kimchi to dim sim, explore all that it has to offer.

TIMELINE

	Propagate seeds in a seed tray and prepare the patch with plenty of compost and high-nitrogen manures.	Transplant the seedlings into the patch. Use netting to deter white cabbage moth. Mulch to a depth of 3–5 cm (1¼–2 in) with pea straw or lucerne hay.	As hungry feeders, the cabbage will appreciate monthly feeds with liquid fish emulsion.	Thin out the seedlings to the required spacing.	Apply compost to the patch, but don't over-fertilise with nitrogen, as this will cause the heads to grow loose, rather than compact.	Harvest by removing the entire plant from the patch. It will not regenerate well, so it's best to take out roots and all and start replenishing the soil for the next crop. When eating, beware of caterpillars or slugs that may be hiding within the head.
WEEK	-4	0	4	8	12	18	24
GROWTH							
WATER		Daily		3–4 times a week			

CAPSICUM (BELL PEPPER)

	1	2	3	4	5
EASY TO GROW					
SMALL SPACE SUITABILITY					
YIELD VALUE					
JE NE SAIS QUOI/PLEASURE					

When to plant
ZONE 1 Nov–Jan   ZONE 3 Sep–Feb
ZONE 2 Oct–Feb   ZONE 4 Apr–Jul

Best grown from
Seed – propagate in trays then transplant into patch once conditions are warm.

Depth
1 cm (½ in)

Spacing
50 cm (1 ft 7 in)

Time to 1st harvest
75–120 days

Ideal pH level
5.5–6.5

Favourite small-space variety
Sweet banana

Best suited to
Pots, in-ground

Common problems
Blossom end rot, root-knot nematodes

A member from the *solanaceae* family that includes chilli, eggplant (aubergine) and tomato, capsicum is a crop that is best planted once the soil temperature has balanced out at a balmy 20°C (68°F) and above. Much like its cousins, it is a heat-loving variety that will prefer a sunny place in the patch with a little airflow to help avoid any fungal disease. However, that does not mean it enjoys baking out in the hot sun without refreshments.

As you may have seen at the markets, capsicums come in a small rainbow of colours. However, all start out green. As a slow ripener it can be a frustrating wait, but at least it helps you understand the price difference between a red and green capsicum. Plants will produce for an extended period of time – sometimes well into winter depending on where you live – but the rate of production and rate of ripening will slow down even further as the weather cools down.

Rather than rip out the plant and sow again the next season, high-performing plants can be cut back to a bare skeleton and left dormant in-ground through winter (a bit like a polar bear). Next season the plant will reshoot and be a little stronger and a little hardier (much like a polar bear) – and a little better at producing. Unfortunately, the wait for vine-ripened capsicums will be just as tedious.

NONNO'S TIP Unless you like the idea of a plant imitating a polar bear, just save the seeds from your best-performing fruit. Even though your dormant capsicum plants don't use up any veggie patch fuel, they do hoard space that could be better utilised.

KITCHEN TIP Roasted vine-ripened red capsicums are a delight.

TIMELINE								
WEEK	-4	0	4	8	12	16		24
GROWTH								
WATER			Daily			3–4 times a week		

Propagate seeds in a seed tray and prepare the patch with compost and slow-release organic fertiliser. Apply rock minerals to supply trace elements, helping prevent blossom end rot.

Transplant the seedlings into the patch long after the last frosts, at half the spacing of mature plants. Then mulch to a depth of 3–5 cm (1¼–2 in) with pea straw or lucerne hay.

As hungry feeders, the capsicums will appreciate monthly feeds with liquid seaweed fertiliser.

If all plants take, thin out the seedlings to the required spacing.

Apply liquid potassium to the patch to encourage flower growth and fruit development.

All capsicums start off green and then mature to their ripe colour. The ripening process is long – harvest some green while allowing others to mature. Picking encourages further growth.

If the space is not required, cut back the plant to a bare skeleton and leave it dormant in-ground. This only works in more temperate areas, so in colder climates, incubation will be necessary.

CARROT

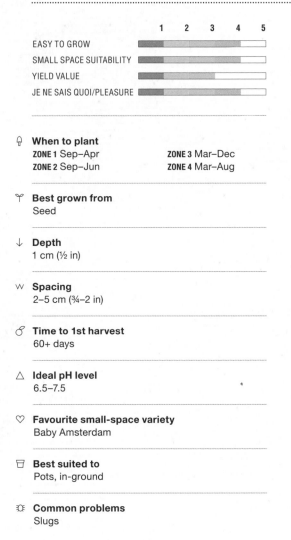

	1	2	3	4	5
EASY TO GROW					
SMALL SPACE SUITABILITY					
YIELD VALUE					
JE NE SAIS QUOI/PLEASURE					

When to plant
ZONE 1 Sep–Apr   ZONE 3 Mar–Dec
ZONE 2 Sep–Jun   ZONE 4 Mar–Aug

Best grown from
Seed

Depth
1 cm (½ in)

Spacing
2–5 cm (¾–2 in)

Time to 1st harvest
60+ days

Ideal pH level
6.5–7.5

Favourite small-space variety
Baby Amsterdam

Best suited to
Pots, in-ground

Common problems
Slugs

Each carrot is a lottery. The ones you pull from your patch will look nothing like the long, waxed things you buy from the supermarket. They will be bent and twisted and hooked – contorting themselves in an effort to find moisture and nutrition, something we all bitterly keep away from our plants from time to time. You never really know what shape will come out. The only guarantee is that they're rarely straight.

Growing carrots successfully, and straight if you wish, hinges on soil preparation and watering. You're after a soil that is not too friable, making it too easy for the carrot to chase pockets of nutrition and moisture as it begins to fork or curl. But at the same time you don't want it to be too compacted. This is another time when we use the 'Goldilocks principle' for giving ambiguous advice. Yes, we want a soil that is just right.

Despite typically being slender and orange, a carrot can be short, stumpy, round and long, as well as yellow, purple, pink, black, white and, yes, orange. Unfortunately, unless you're eating a carrot while undergoing laser eye surgery, they will not improve your vision.

NONNO'S TIP
Sow from seed, but rather than the freehand scatter method, take the time to space seeds properly. It seems like extra work but it means thinning (a job most people don't do) is not necessary and tips the chances of growing straight carrots in your favour.

KITCHEN TIP
Pick as you need them, as fresh garden carrots quickly turn limp.

Thin out seedlings to a spacing of 3–5 cm (1¼–2 in) and mulch using pea straw, lucerne hay or sugar cane to a depth of 3–5 cm (1¼–2 in). As carrots are an all-year-round vegetable in most climates, begin your next planting of seeds if space is available. This way you can get a staggered, regular harvest.

Begin the carrot lottery by harvesting roots that feel the most developed. A simple inspection at the base of the foliage will give you girth, which is a good indication of length (or so they say).

When harvesting, brace nearby carrots to prevent them from becoming dislodged. Roots keep well in-ground, particularly when the soil temperature is cool, so only harvest as required.

Add compost and blood and bone for phosphorus.

Sow seeds directly to the patch.

TIMELINE	WEEK	-2	0	6	12	16
	GROWTH					
	WATER		Daily	3–4 times a week		

CAULIFLOWER

	1	2	3	4	5
EASY TO GROW					
SMALL SPACE SUITABILITY					
YIELD VALUE					
JE NE SAIS QUOI/PLEASURE					

When to plant
ZONE 1 Sep–Nov
Mar–May
ZONE 2 Mar–Jun
ZONE 3 Apr–Jul
ZONE 4 Jun–Aug

Best grown from
Seeds – propagate in trays and transplant into the patch.

Depth
1 cm (½ in)

Spacing
60 cm (2 ft)

Time to 1st harvest
90–120 days

Ideal pH level
6.5–7.5

Favourite small-space variety
Purple graffiti

Best suited to
Pots, in-ground

Common problems
White cabbage moth, aphids

Who would've thought 10 years ago that the humble cauliflower would be the vegetable on everyone's invite list? It is a culinary and cultural chameleon, reinventing itself and deftly adapting to any situation with grace and ease. Thankfully, it has not let fame get to its head and our beloved cauliflower continues to provide great culinary value, no matter how it's dressed.

In fact, as a wine lover (and drinker), I have welcomed the renaissance and found my own connection. Did you know that the cauliflower – aside from its ability to be turned into rice – can also detoxify your liver? Yep, that's right. If you're like me and enjoy the occasional extra glass of wine with your meal, there is now a way to mitigate the damage.

Like its brassica counterparts, cauliflower presents all the usual spectrum of growing advantages and challenges. It is cold tolerant and nutrient rich, but is also very hungry for nitrogen and the whipping boy for the menacing white cabbage moth.

NONNO'S TIP Once the head begins to develop, fold up the leaves into a bunch over it (pin it with a long toothpick or stick), which will protect it from frost and pest damage.

KITCHEN TIP Charring it on a barbecue sweetens it up and draws out another flavour dimension.

TIMELINE

Propagate seeds in a seed tray and prepare the patch with plenty of compost and high-nitrogen manures.

Transplant the seedlings into the patch. Use netting to deter white cabbage moth. Mulch to a depth of 3–5 cm (1¼–2 in) with pea straw or lucerne hay.

As hungry feeders, the cauliflower will appreciate monthly feeds with liquid fish emulsion.

Thin out the seedlings to the required spacing.

Apply compost to the patch. Pull up the outer leaves around the developing head to protect it from pests and severe frost. Use a toothpick or clothes peg to hold them in place.

Harvest by removing the entire plant. Take out roots and all and start replenishing the soil for the next crop. Wash well before eating – beware of caterpillars or slugs that may be hiding within the head.

WEEK	-4	0	4	8	16	20	24
GROWTH							
WATER		Daily		3–4 times a week			

CELERIAC

	1	2	3	4	5
EASY TO GROW					
SMALL SPACE SUITABILITY					
YIELD VALUE					
JE NE SAIS QUOI/PLEASURE					

When to plant

ZONE 1 Mar–Apr
        Oct–Dec
ZONE 2 Mar–May
        Sep–Nov
ZONE 3 Mar–Aug
ZONE 4 Jun–Jul

Best grown from
Seed – propagate in trays and transplant into the patch.

Depth
1 cm (½ in)

Spacing
30–40 cm (1 ft–1 ft 4 in)

Time to 1st harvest
90–120 days

Ideal pH level
6.0–7.0

Favourite small-space variety
White alabaster

Best suited to
Pots, in-ground

Common problems
Slugs, celery leaf spot

In the veggie garden we generally go by the rule that the uglier the produce, the more alluring it is. This always rings true among tomatoes, with the ribbed and knotted brain-like tangle of beefsteak varieties by far the tastiest (but with a face only a mother could love). The same rings true with celeriac, a close relative of the more commonly grown, and conventionally attractive, celery.

The moment you pull celeriac from the ground there is the universal assumption among fair people that it must taste good. The tangle and knot of roots is so damn ugly that it'd be cruel if it only tasted mediocre. Fortunately, things work out for this vegetable, and the smooth interior of the root is like a fresh salad of apples, walnuts and, of course, celery. Whole celeriac makes for a simple, earthy treat when roasted under low heat.

Despite its foliage, celeriac should be thought of as a root vegetable from a gardening perspective. It is particularly hungry and thirsty, so be generous with compost and manure in preparing your soil. This will not only provide the extra nutrients, but will also improve water retention and soil structure in the patch. Celeriac can be kept in ground well into winter because cold weather will help the flesh to sweeten (as natural starches are converted to sugar). Once harvested, it will keep for a number months in the crisper drawer of a fridge, so you can admire its unconventional beauty whenever you want.

NONNO'S TIP
It loves water, so don't deny it. The success of growing celeriac will directly correlate to your diligence as a waterer.

KITCHEN TIP
Roast in foil with olive oil, thyme and garlic, then purée to make the perfect mash.

TIMELINE

WEEK	-4	0	4	8	16	20
GROWTH						
WATER			Daily			

Propagate seeds in a seed tray and prepare the patch with blood and bone.

Integrate compost into the patch and then transplant to the required spacing.

Apply monthly applications of liquid seaweed solution.

Mulch to a depth of 3–5 cm (1¼–2 in) using pea straw, lucerne hay or sugar cane mulch.

Harvest from the size of a tennis ball to that of a large fist, using a hand fork to loosen the ground and taking care not to disturb other plants. The foliage can be used as a strongly flavoured celery.

CELERY

	1	2	3	4	5
EASY TO GROW					
SMALL SPACE SUITABILITY					
YIELD VALUE					
JE NE SAIS QUOI/PLEASURE					

When to plant
ZONE 1 Feb–May
Oct–Dec
ZONE 2 Mar–May
Sep–Nov

ZONE 3 Mar–Nov
ZONE 4 May–Jul

Best grown from
Seed

Depth
1 cm (½ in)

Spacing
40 cm (1 ft 3 in)

Time to 1st harvest
60 days

Ideal pH level
5.8–6.8

Favourite small-space variety
Amsterdam

Best suited to
Pots, in-ground

Common problems
Snails and slugs

A stick of celery is one of the ultimate vegetable snacks, so having it growing in your garden will provide it at its absolute peak. Beyond snacking, celery is a culinary heavyweight and one of the 'big three' in French cooking, along with carrot and onion. Though it has such a seemingly mild taste, it adds an intangible depth to almost every soup or casserole and even has a place in our Sunday night ragu. The theory is that celery helps draw the acidity of the tomatoes and sweeten the sauce, so you can usually find a stick or two swimming around.

Stalks are clearly the most prominent feature and can be harvested continuously by cutting outer growth as needed. However, celery leaves should be revered just as much given their abundance, rich flavour and nutritional value. When the plant goes to seed, it presents yet another opportunity. Seeds are high in calcium and thought to help with arthritis.

Celery is generally a cool-weather crop, and will tolerate boggy conditions better than most edible plants. So, reserve that low-lying part of the garden that collects the excess water run-off. Nevertheless, it also can cope well during the warm times of the year as long as it is kept hydrated. Along with water, celery will also appreciate a fortnightly dose of liquid seaweed solution.

NONNO'S TIP
It's a real water lover, so don't deny its guilty pleasure.

KITCHEN TIP
To keep the stems and heart tender, you can blanch them by building up mulch around the base of the plants. This will prevent exposure to the sun and ensure that stems retain their supple white flesh.

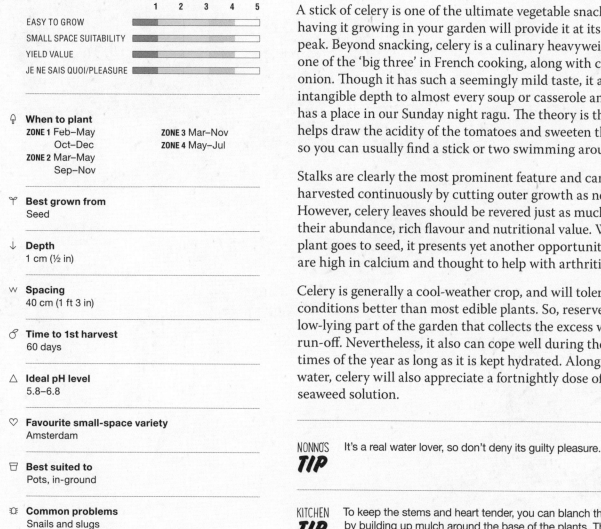

TIMELINE

	WEEK	-4	0	4	8	12	20
	GROWTH						
	WATER				Daily		

Propagate seeds in a seed tray.

Integrate compost into the patch and then transplant, making sure the conditions are neither too hot nor too cold. Space seedlings at half the distance needed for mature plants.

Apply monthly applications of liquid seaweed solution.

Mulch to a depth of 3–5 cm (1¼–2 in) using pea straw, lucerne hay or sugar cane mulch, and thin out seedlings to required spacing.

Blanch the stems of celery by building up extra mulch around the plants. You can begin harvesting, taking the more mature outer stalks first, allowing the younger inner ones to further develop.

CHILLI

	1	2	3	4	5
EASY TO GROW					
SMALL SPACE SUITABILITY					
YIELD VALUE					
JE NE SAIS QUOI/PLEASURE					

When to plant
ZONE 1 Nov–Jan   ZONE 3 Aug–Mar
ZONE 2 Nov–Feb   ZONE 4 Apr–Aug

Best grown from
Seed – propagate in trays and transplant into the patch.

Depth
1 cm (½ in)

Spacing
40 cm (1 ft 3 in)

Time to 1st harvest
90 days

Ideal pH level
6.5–7.5

Favourite small-space variety
Cayenne plus the bloody hot ones that my nonna's brother's niece smuggled back from Italy.

Best suited to
Wall, pots, in-ground

Common problems
Fruit flies in warmer parts

The chilli is *the* summer pro. It originated in the Americas and was spread across the globe by Portuguese explorer Christopher Columbus. Chilli was seen as a meaningful substitute for the pepper spice and was so valuable in the fifteenth century it had become a currency in its own right. These days it is often used as a sort of social currency, whereby friends and family try to one up each other in their chilli heat tolerance.

Chillies derive their spice from chemicals collectively known as capsaicinoids, and are measured in intensity by Scoville heat units (SHU). But in reality no one pays too much attention to the specific ratings. There are mild ones, hot ones, those that tingle the backs of your eyeballs, and the chillies that compromise your everyday survival.

Heat is key for growing chillies and they require a hot, sun-drenched space, preferably up against a heat-reflecting wall that helps to collect extra rays of warmth. Those in cooler climates often produce the best chillies in hoop houses or any other insulated environment. However, do not let its heat infatuation distract you from the basic demands of the plant. Even the toughest dudes need food and water to survive and the chilli is no exception.

NONNO'S TIP
Chilli is known to be an aphrodisiac but to arrive there you have to be persistent. For a long time you may just burn your mouth and ruin your meals, but there will be a turning point when you begin to understand how sexy a chilli can be.

KITCHEN TIP
Make chilli oil – finely chop chillies and place them into a jar with red-wine vinegar. Cure them overnight. Drain the vinegar and top the chillies with good quality olive oil. Chilli oil is delicious and highly addictive. Add to any meal, including your morning toast.

TIMELINE								
		Propagate seeds in a seed tray and prepare the patch with compost and slow-release organic fertiliser. Apply rock minerals to supply trace elements.	Transplant the seedlings into the patch long after the last frosts, at half the spacing of mature plants. Mulch to 3–5 cm (1¼–2 in) with pea straw/lucerne hay.	As hungry feeders, the chilli will appreciate monthly feeds with liquid seaweed fertiliser.	If all plants take, thin out the seedlings to the required spacing. Give away extra plants as lame 'Christmas gifts that keep on giving'.	Apply liquid potassium to encourage flower growth and development of the chillies.	Begin harvesting. The difference between a green and ripe chilli is about 6 weeks, so we suggest striking a balance.	Save the plant for next year by cutting back to a bare skeleton and leaving it dormant in-ground. This only works in more temperate areas, so in colder climates, incubation will be necessary.
WEEK	-4	0		4	8	12	16	24
GROWTH								
WATER			Daily			3–4 times a week		

CITRUS

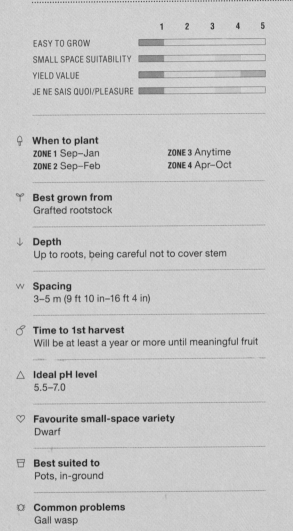

	1	2	3	4	5
EASY TO GROW					
SMALL SPACE SUITABILITY					
YIELD VALUE					
JE NE SAIS QUOI/PLEASURE					

When to plant
ZONE 1 Sep–Jan
ZONE 2 Sep–Feb
ZONE 3 Anytime
ZONE 4 Apr–Oct

Best grown from
Grafted rootstock

Depth
Up to roots, being careful not to cover stem

Spacing
3–5 m (9 ft 10 in–16 ft 4 in)

Time to 1st harvest
Will be at least a year or more until meaningful fruit

Ideal pH level
5.5–7.0

Favourite small-space variety
Dwarf

Best suited to
Pots, in-ground

Common problems
Gall wasp

Each year we indulge in a gardening phenomenon that never seems to lose its shine – citrus in winter. It's a relief to harvest when the sun, temperature and our morale are at their absolute lowest. Try not to limit citrus to the common varieties found in the markets (lemon, lime, orange, mandarin, grapefruit) or littered through the inner-city neighbourhoods by our early migrants. Citrus is a diverse family and all are perfectly suited to our climate. Finger limes, sinton and yuzu are all varieties you may not have grown, but should consider doing so.

GROWING CITRUS

HEAT

It just can't get hot enough for citrus so you should reserve the best planting position for it – somewhere that faces north west, if you have it, and preferably up against a brick wall that will collect and rebound some residual heat. All citrus have an equal liking of heat, but some varieties are more tolerant of cooler conditions. Lemons and kumquats, for example, seem to thrive in the southern parts of our country more than limes and grapefruit, which excel further north.

PROTECTION FROM WIND

All citrus are shallow-rooted, so can easily be wind damaged. The fact that they are evergreen means the leaf foliage has a habit of catching the wind in the blowier times of the year, uprooting the shallowest roots and affecting their health. Always protect your trees from the prevailing winds and, when young, stake them so there's support.

TIMELINE						
	Plant in-ground, in either good quality potting mix or with plenty of compost in the soil. Carefully stake the tree – do not damage the young roots. Feed with slow-release organic fertiliser and then mulch.	Apply liquid seaweed fertiliser every month.	The new growth on young plants is susceptible to gall wasp, so using a sticky yellow trap will help to mitigate this risk.	Don't over-fertilise once flowers and fruit begin to appear, as they will drop from the oversupply of nitrogen. Add liquid potassium to assist.	Fruiting happens over a prolonged period and often twice a year. The end of fruiting is the best time to prune the plant into a healthy shape, something akin to an upside-down pear. This is the time to cut out any new gall wasp on the plant. Feed with slow-release organic fertiliser and re-mulch.	
WEEK	0	4	8	28	32	48 52
GROWTH						
WATER	Daily			3–4 times a week		

FREE-DRAINING SOIL

'Don't like wet feet' is an interesting gardening term. It means that they don't like to sit in water, but in my mind it seems to imply that they don't like water. Incorrect! All plants love water – and lots of it. What plants don't like is sitting in stagnant water, so your soil needs to be free draining. You will need to water your plants regularly, like any other.

DROPPING ITS FLOWERS

A common problem with citrus, particularly new plants, is the dropping of flowers, which means that the fruit does not set. This is part and parcel of establishing a tree, as they are notoriously slow to adapt to their new environment. Even when you have ticked all the boxes, citrus are particularly tricky to transplant and will take a few warm seasons to really find their feet. Sometimes the problem can be caused by overfeeding when the plants are producing flowers. Too much nitrogen will focus the plant's efforts on producing foliage rather than flowers and fruit, and consequently they will drop. Fertilise your plants just after they have fruited, rather than during.

YELLOWING OFF

Without fail, all citrus will lose their vibrancy throughout the cool season, particularly if you live somewhere cold. Without fail, citrus owners will rush into a garden centre concerned about their dying plants and buy up an array of citrus fertilisers to address the problem. Don't be concerned by a winter yellowing off. Plants will be a little exhausted from their production of fruit, and colder temperatures will also restrict the flow of water through the plants' systems. As soon as spring arrives, the flow of water increases and plants regain vibrancy.

FRUITING

Timing of fruit will depend on the variety you are growing, but as many varieties fruit more than once a year and develop their fruit over an extended period, it is common to see fruit on trees in the depths of winter. For the kitchen gardener this is a real indulgence as citrus is so intertwined with warm-climate Asian or Mediterranean cooking. It can really boost our spirits.

I NEED HOT STUFF
I WANT SOME HOT STUFF

NONNO'S TIP Make sure to stake directly after planting as citrus have shallow roots and can be damaged by winds.

KITCHEN TIP Loosen the juices of the fruit by rolling it on your kitchen bench before squeezing.

PLANTING A DWARF CITRUS TREE

Planting a dwarf citrus tree is all about knowing your limits. With space at a premium, these smaller trees are made for small-space gardening, but they also produce a more manageable yield of fruit, which doesn't end up fermenting on the ground of hot concrete laneways. It also means that rather than limiting yourself to one large tree and a lot of the same fruit, you can diversify your tree stock and the fruit they grow.

All dwarf fruit trees are grafted, meaning that there are two distinguishable parts: the leaf stock on which the fruit will grow; and the rootstock, which is chosen for its ability to grow in small spaces. Dwarf rootstocks make the foliage of the plant more compact – usually 25–50% of its normal size – producing less fruit. It doesn't, however, mean you're producing dwarf fruit!

Even the smallest of spaces has the potential to grow a number of dwarf fruit trees. Here are the basics of how to choose and then plant one.

1. Choose a healthy plant that has signs of new growth, and choose a shape that is similar to what you're after.

2. Focus on plants with good foliage. You may get some bonus fruit on your plant, but it's best to cut these free and focus energy on foliage growth initially. We know that's a hard thing to do, but the fruit will come later.

3. Pot size is key for any plant. For a dwarf citrus, choose a pot that is at least 50 cm (1 ft 7 in) wide and 40 cm (1 ft 3 in) deep. Because citrus have shallow root zones, favour width over depth. When choosing a pot for deciduous fruit trees, depth is more important to accommodate the long tap root.

4. Use good-quality organic potting mix when planting, but also some organic compost. Use a ratio of 3:1 for potting mix to compost. Potting mix is designed to drain perfectly well by itself, making scoria or crushed rock superfluous.

5. Clear any excess soil from the base of the tree to avoid stem rot.

6. Water in with liquid seaweed solution and repeat this dosage every month as a tonic. Because you are growing in pots, the plant will need daily watering at warm times of the year, regulated depending on how mild/cold/wet your cooled times are.

7. Staking is critical. No young plant likes to be uprooted, particularly young fruit trees, so stake your trees and use soft twine to attach to them (as it won't damage the stems). This is most important with citrus that have a shallow root zone. Being evergreens, they'll have foliage that will catch the wind given the chance.

8. Pruning is a necessary job for all fruit trees to promote new growth on which most fruit forms. For deciduous fruit trees, we generally cut back once in winter and then feed once in early spring. For citrus, we prune and feed once in early spring.

9. Fruit setting can take a while. All fruit trees will need to find their feet before producing meaningful fruit. You may get small amounts of fruit early on, but as the plant settles in and becomes more comfortable with its new environment, the rate at which it produces fruit will increase. You need to be patient, Daniel son.

CORIANDER (CILANTRO)

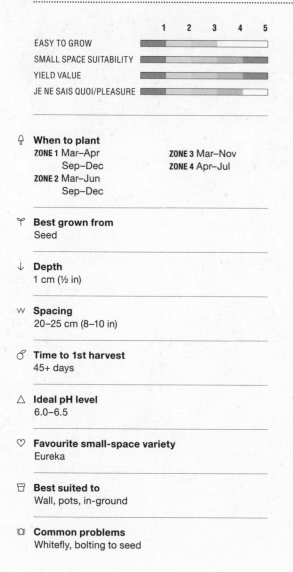

	1	2	3	4	5
EASY TO GROW					
SMALL SPACE SUITABILITY					
YIELD VALUE					
JE NE SAIS QUOI/PLEASURE					

When to plant
ZONE 1 Mar–Apr
        Sep–Dec
ZONE 2 Mar–Jun
        Sep–Dec
ZONE 3 Mar–Nov
ZONE 4 Apr–Jul

Best grown from
Seed

Depth
1 cm (½ in)

Spacing
20–25 cm (8–10 in)

Time to 1st harvest
45+ days

Ideal pH level
6.0–6.5

Favourite small-space variety
Eureka

Best suited to
Wall, pots, in-ground

Common problems
Whitefly, bolting to seed

Foodies and gardeners alike often find coriander to be among the most polarising plants in the patch, eliciting equally passionate responses of both love and hatred. While there is nothing that we can offer to change your taste, gardening haters may need to accept some responsibility for their difficulties with the plant.

Coriander can sometimes feel like a tumultuous relationship that you keep going back to. But have you ever considered that maybe coriander is not the difficult partner we make it out to be? Rather, it always seems to be dating absolute duds. That's right, we need to stop trying to change coriander, and rather try to understand it better. Appreciate it for what it has to offer. After all, it has so much – leaves, stems, roots and seeds are all edible, making it a true object of desire.

The most important thing to learn about coriander is when to plant it. Despite some marketing attempts to promote 'slow bolting' varieties, the fact is that when you plant it in summer and the warmer parts of spring, all varieties will want to bolt to seed. Planting in the cool of autumn or early winter is a better fit for this herb. During the warmer months, we have great success growing coriander in a bright but shaded courtyard, where it gets lots of indirect light but little heat.

NONNO'S TIP Coriander always grows best in the cool season and will get stressed from lack of water or from the hot afternoon sun.

KITCHEN TIP This is a multifaceted plant with many culinary uses. While the foliage seems to be favoured, there is also the stem, root, flower and seed.

TIMELINE

Prepare the patch with compost and slow-release organic fertiliser and plant seeds directly into the patch.

Thin out the seedlings if overcrowded. However, they won't mind being grown in close quarters. Coriander will appreciate a monthly feed of a liquid seaweed solution and regular watering.

Begin to harvest in moderation, ensuring that the plants have consistent moisture to reduce stress. Mulch to a depth of 3 cm (1¼ in) using pea straw, lucerne hay or sugar cane mulch.

The length of harvest will depend on the availability of moisture and nutrition, and the temperature. Plants tend to bolt in warmer conditions. Even when the foliage gives way to flowers and seed heads, don't waste any part of this multi-faceted edible plant.

WEEK	0	4	8	16
GROWTH				
WATER			Daily	

ROOT TO BLOOM EATING

When it comes to fruit, vegetables and herbs, we desperately need to update our perspective of edibility. As growers and consumers, many people are still locked into the idea that food is what we get at the supermarket, which is to say limited and uniform. Thinking of coriander as a leaf is like thinking of a pig as bacon. We are missing all of the other delicious 'cuts' that have only recently come to be regarded as waste. Therefore, we are championing what we call 'root to bloom' eating. There are so many edible parts of common plants that we needlessly discard that we should be eating.

It's easy to be so focused on the primary growth of our plants at the expense of everything else that is on offer. Thus, a small shift in perspective can open up so many more culinary possibilities. Many lesser 'cuts' present an opportunity to utilise more of the plant, and harvest before and after the primary growth.

OUR FAVOURITES

Coriander (cilantro) and parsley are our root to bloom pin-ups, possessing edible leaves, stems, roots and flowers. Yet we rarely use more than the leaves and often toss the rest. When we have put so much effort into growing a plant we should not let any of it go to waste.

Broccoli stalks are perfectly edible, yet commonly discarded. The brilliant, yellow flowers add colour and flavour to any dish.

Rocket (arugula) goes to seed when it gets too hot and dry, but seed heads should be added to everyone's repertoire, offering strong bitter flavours similar to endive.

Broad bean leaves have a comforting, mellow broad bean flavour and could be mixed into any fresh salad.

Celery greens have a strong, almost herbal celery taste and much more nutrition than the stalk. A great substitute for parsley.

Basil stems pack just as much flavour as the leaves and nobody can tell when you use them to bulk up your pesto.

Squash and pumpkin leaves offer a wealth of nutrients and are commonly used in many African cuisines. Young leaves are the most prized and can be steamed/sautéed to reveal a taste similar to rich greens like broccoli and asparagus. Something to keep you full while waiting for that giant pumpkin!

Beetroot (beet) greens and, in fact, most root vegetable greens are nutritionally dense with an earthy, green flavour. While the root may take time to mature, greens can be picked leaf by leaf throughout development.

As we patiently wait the 9 months for garlic bulbs to develop, **garlic greens** are like an endless baby shower of sweet, punchy produce. Harvest these like spring onions and serve to taste.

BROAD BEAN LEAVES

BROCCOLI STALKS

PUMPKIN LEAVES

CORIANDER (CILANTRO)

PARSLEY

CELERY

ROCKET (ARUGULA)

BASIL STEMS

GARLIC GREENS

CUCUMBER

	1	2	3	4	5
EASY TO GROW					
SMALL SPACE SUITABILITY					
YIELD VALUE					
JE NE SAIS QUOI/PLEASURE					

When to plant
ZONE 1 Oct–Dec   ZONE 3 Aug–Mar
ZONE 2 Sep–Jan   ZONE 4 Mar–Aug

Best grown from
Seed

Depth
1–2 cm (½–¾ in)

Spacing
50 cm (1 ft 7 in)

Time to 1st harvest
60–90 days

Ideal pH level
6.5–7.0

Favourite small-space variety
Mexican

Best suited to
Pots, in-ground

Common problems
Powdery mildew

Everything changes as spring approaches – wardrobes, ideology, even the pasty tone of your skin – and, of course, the veggie patch sees revitalisation too. This is most pronounced when an early spring classic, the cucumber, comes back on the planting agenda. It's a vegetable whose presence makes the light shine a little brighter.

For us, cucumber is an essential component of any warm-season veggie patch. Thrown in salads, tzatziki, pickled, infused in a more cultured G&T, pulled straight off the vine and munched, it is a vegetable that sets off the spring ideology and gets the ball rolling on the good times that lie ahead.

Once flowering and fruit start to form, it's worth curtailing new growth by pruning vine tips so that energy can be redirected to producing world-class cucumbers. For those short on space, plant cucumbers on the edge of the patch or in pots and encourage them to sprawl away from the garden.

NONNO'S TIP As a vegetable with the ability to climb, grow it up a trellis to conserve ground level real estate for those that absolutely need it.

KITCHEN TIP Pick when young and tender. They're best enjoyed straight off the vine, accompanied by a crack of salt and pepper and a drizzle of good quality olive oil.

TIMELINE						
WEEK	0	4	8	12	14	20
GROWTH						
WATER		Daily		3–4 times a week		Daily

Add slow-release organic fertiliser and sow seeds in mounds of compost after the last frost. Cucumbers are cold sensitive and susceptible to rodents, so protect young seedlings with open-ended plastic bottles.

Give monthly applications of liquid seaweed solution and mulch to a depth of 3–5 cm (1¼–2 in) using pea straw, lucerne hay or sugar cane mulch.

Grow the vines vertically and attach them to a trellis that conserves ground-level real estate for other plantings.

Apply liquid potassium to encourage flower growth and fruit development. As cucumbers begin to develop, keep the watering up.

Fruiting plants will begin to die back and will be overcome by powdery mildew. Prune off affected leaves and use a milk spray to help control its spread.

EGGPLANT (AUBERGINE)

	1	2	3	4	5
EASY TO GROW					
SMALL SPACE SUITABILITY					
YIELD VALUE					
JE NE SAIS QUOI/PLEASURE					

When to plant
ZONE 1 Nov–Jan   ZONE 3 Sep–Feb
ZONE 2 Oct–Feb   ZONE 4 Apr–Jul

Best grown from
Seeds – propagate in trays and transplant into the patch.

Depth
1 cm (½ in)

Spacing
50 cm (1 ft 8 in)

Time to 1st harvest
90 days

Ideal pH level
6.0–7.0

Favourite small-space variety
Lebanese

Best suited to
Pots, in-ground

Common problems
Root rot

Eggplant is a vegetable that really knows how to get its groove on in the summer heat.

Sometimes just by looking at a plant you can tell it copes well under duress, and the eggplant is a formidable looking vegetable – shiny and curvy in all of the right places. The plant's tough leaves grow broadly, in effect shielding the soil beneath against overheating. The fruit itself has a dark, leathery skin with annoying spikes on its neck – as if announcing inedibility. Surely when the first human ate an eggplant, their situation must have been quite bleak.

When selecting a variety of eggplant to grow, let the timing of the season help you choose. Thinner varieties, such as Lebanese, develop earlier than larger fruit and also cope better earlier in the season.

NONNO'S TIP Don't be rash when harvesting, as the necks of eggplants are built to withstand people like you taking them off the plant.

KITCHEN TIP Salt the eggplant before cooking to sweat out its bitterness, a process known as degorging.

	Propagate seeds in a seed tray and prepare the patch with plenty of compost and slow-release organic fertiliser. Apply rock minerals for trace elements.	Transplant the seedlings into the patch long after the last frosts, at half the spacing of mature plants. Then mulch to a depth of 3–5 cm (1¼–2 in) with pea straw or lucerne hay.		If all seedlings have taken, thin out to the required spacing of approximately 50 cm (20 in)	Apply liquid potassium to encourage flower growth and development of the eggplants. Stake plants now before they become heavily laden with fruit.	Begin harvesting. Size is the real consideration with an eggplant, as the taste doesn't alter much between a small and large fruit. Don't leave them on the vine until skin toughens and turns yellow, as the inside will become porous and chalky.	Eggplants can be cut back to a bare skeleton and left dormant in the ground to reshoot the following warm season. This only works in more temperate areas, so in colder climates, incubation will be necessary.
WEEK	-4	0		8	12	16	24
GROWTH							
WATER		Daily			3–4 times a week		

TIMELINE

FENNEL

	1	2	3	4	5
EASY TO GROW					
SMALL SPACE SUITABILITY					
YIELD VALUE					
JE NE SAIS QUOI/PLEASURE					

When to plant
ZONE 1 Mar–May
       Sep–Nov
ZONE 2 Mar–Jun
       Sep–Dec

ZONE 3 Mar–Sep
ZONE 4 Apr–Jul

Best grown from
Seedling

Depth
1 cm (½ in)

Spacing
30 cm (12 in)

Time to 1st harvest
60–90 days

Ideal pH level
6.5–7.5

Favourite small-space variety
Bronze

Best suited to
Pots, in-ground

Common problems
The naysayers

We admire fennel because in the vegetable world it's often made out to be an outcast and the underdog.

If there's one vegetable that comes up time and time again as the one to avoid planting next to others, it's fennel. But that rap is unfounded in the small-space garden, with this mild-mannered, anise-flavoured, quasi–root vegetable/herb getting on well with its fellow tenants.

Fennel is known for its digestive qualities – balancing out the 'windy vegetables', such as cabbage and Jerusalem artichoke – but is better known as being another swear word in Italian (this time not so mild). See what we mean by the underdog?

Fennel is a hardy, sun-worshipping plant known for its vigorous growth. Because it often reaches heights of around 1.5 m (4 ft 11 in), fennel tends to shade out other plants. With this in mind, a good idea is to play matchmaker and plant shade-tolerant varieties in its shadow, especially in an exposed garden. While harvesting the root bulbs of this vegetable is the ultimate goal, and can be done with relative ease, don't ignore the abundant fronds, which can be continuously harvested for a sweet herbal flavour.

NONNO'S TIP If you don't have space to grow this vegetable, you will find it growing wild in sunny positions just about everywhere. We see it near rivers, along railway lines, and even on the shoulder of the freeway.

KITCHEN TIP The sharp anise-flavoured fronds can be used as a substitute for chervil and tarragon. It's great with fish.

Add compost to the patch and plant seedlings at half the recommended spacing.

Mulch to a depth of 3–5 cm (1¼–2 in) and apply a monthly dose of liquid seaweed solution to give them a tonic.

Thin out the plants, harvesting some as young fennel and allowing the remaining plants to reach maturity. Fronds can be harvested sparingly during their growth and used as a herb.

Harvest by loosening the soil with a hand fork and gently pulling on the fronds to free them from the soil.

TIMELINE	WEEK	0	4	8	12	16	20
	GROWTH						
	WATER		Daily		3–4 times a week		

FLOWERS

	1	2	3	4	5
EASY TO GROW					
SMALL SPACE SUITABILITY					
YIELD VALUE					
JE NE SAIS QUOI/PLEASURE					

For us, the emergence of spring is inextricably tied to aromatic herbs and flowers. Providing much more than just decoration, flowers fill a key companion planting role in the veggie patch and offer a range of subtle tastes, textures and colours to mealtime. Furthermore, compared to some more demanding edible plants, flowers are a piece of cake to grow, maybe even a piece of cake with a scattering of edible flower petals thrown over the top.

Planting a floral and herbaceous perimeter will help to attract friendly predators and pollinators into the veggie patch. This isn't the kind of wall that keeps things out. Rather, it is an invitation to foster diversity and prosperity in your patch. Creating a balanced ecosystem helps plants get on with their jobs, because if trouble strikes, there's extra support to get things back on track.

It also should come as no surprise that flowers have always had a place in the human diet. When you think about the evolution of our eating habits, it makes perfect sense that something as fragrant and colourful as a flower would be one of the first things consumed. Flowers present a much better case than a potato, for example, which needs to be dug from the ground, boiled and then preferably mixed with butter before becoming palatable. Considering that our sense of smell is so closely aligned to that of our taste, and our palates are so often tempted by the sight of food, a flower has a gravitational pull towards nearly any dish.

Though flowers such as borage, viola and nasturtium will thrive during the long spring/summer growing season, once established they will self-seed and continue growing through cooler parts of the year in temperate and warmer climates.

NOT ALL FLOWERS ARE EDIBLE!

BORAGE

When to plant
Spring, after the last frost through to summer.

Best grown from
Seedling

Depth
1 cm (½ in)

Spacing
50 cm (1 ft 7 in)

Time to 1st harvest
75–90 days

Ideal pH level
5.0–8.0

Favourite small-space variety
Common

Best suited to
Pots, in-ground

Common problems
Rarely affected

NONNO'S TIP
One of the best plants for attracting bees. Furry foliage also deters snails/slugs.

KITCHEN TIP
Flowers have a subtle, sweet cucumber taste.

CHAMOMILE

When to plant
Spring, after the last frost through to summer.

Best grown from
Seedling

Depth
1 cm (½ in)

Spacing
30 cm (12 in)

Time to 1st harvest
60–75 days

Ideal pH level
5.5–7.5

Favourite small-space variety
German

Best suited to
Wall, pots, in-ground

Common problems
Aphids

NONNO'S TIP
Has a strongly perfumed flower that helps repel a multitude of pests and when completely desperate can be used as a green, raw deodorant.

KITCHEN TIP
Tea time, lovelies!

CORNFLOWER

When to plant
Spring, after the last frost through to summer.

Best grown from
Seed

Depth
1 cm (½ in)

Spacing
30–40 cm (12 in–1 ft 3 in)

Time to 1st harvest
75–90 days

Ideal pH level
6.5–7.5

Favourite small-space variety
Polka dot

Best suited to
Pots, in ground

Common problems
Rust

NONNO'S TIP
Plants can grow tall and whimsically, so some staking may be required.

KITCHEN TIP
With a sweet to almost spicy flavour, cornflower petals are great in salads.

HYSSOP

⚘ **When to plant**
Spring, after the last frost through
to summer.

⚘ **Best grown from**
Seedling

↓ **Depth**
1 cm (½ in)

〜 **Spacing**
40 cm (1 ft 3 in)

♂ **Time to 1st harvest**
75–90 days

△ **Ideal pH level**
6.5–7.0

♡ **Favourite small-space variety**
Anise

⊡ **Best suited to**
Pots, in-ground

☼ **Common problems**
Birds

NONNO'S TIP
This is a tall plant that is closer to a small
shrub than a flower so you will need to
allocate space in the veggie patch.

KITCHEN TIP
Compared to the flavour of its foliage,
the flowers are a little tasteless.

LAVENDER

⚘ **When to plant**
Spring, after the last frost through
to summer.

⚘ **Best grown from**
Cutting

↓ **Depth**
1 cm (½ in)

〜 **Spacing**
30–40 cm (12 in–1 ft 3 in)

♂ **Time to 1st harvest**
60–75 days

△ **Ideal pH level**
6.5–7.5

♡ **Favourite small-space variety**
Munstead

⊡ **Best suited to**
Pots, in-ground

☼ **Common problems**
Whitefly

NONNO'S TIP
Prune the plant in winter to encourage
new spring growth and maintain shape.

KITCHEN TIP
Mix with thyme and salt to make a great
rub. Make sure to plant culinary lavender.

MARIGOLD

⚘ **When to plant**
Spring, after the last frost through
to summer.

⚘ **Best grown from**
Seed

↓ **Depth**
1 cm (½ in)

〜 **Spacing**
20 cm (8 in)

♂ **Time to 1st harvest**
75–90 days

△ **Ideal pH level**
5.5–7.5

♡ **Favourite small-space variety**
Safari red

⊡ **Best suited to**
Wall, pots, in-ground

☼ **Common problems**
Aphids, mildew

NONNO'S TIP
Helps to deter aphids, beetles, leaf
hoppers and nematodes. Plant it as
a border around your veggie patch.

KITCHEN TIP
Break off its petals and sprinkle liberally
over desserts, cakes or salads.

SUNFLOWER

VIOLA

**NASTURTIUM
SEE PAGE 208**

When to plant
Spring, after the last frost through to summer.

Best grown from
Seed

Depth
2–3 cm (¾–1¼ in)

Spacing
50 cm (1 ft 7 in)

Time to 1st harvest
75–90 days

Ideal pH level
6.0–7.5

Favourite small-space variety
Bronze

Best suited to
Pots, in-ground

Common problems
Rust

NONNO'S TIP
These are used to help provide shade and a windbreak for some summer plants.

KITCHEN TIP
Roasted and shelled seeds should be sprinkled on all salads and muesli with reckless abandon.

When to plant
Spring, after the last frost through to summer.

Best grown from
Seedling

Depth
1 cm (½ in)

Spacing
20–30 cm (8–12 in)

Time to 1st harvest
75–90 days

Ideal pH level
5.5–6.5

Favourite small-space variety
Johnny jump up

Best suited to
Wall, pots, in-ground

Common problems
Aphids

NONNO'S TIP
A regular self seeder, this shallow-rooted plant will keep coming back each year.

KITCHEN TIP
The most prolific of the edible flowers, it has edible foliage too.

COMPANION PLANTING IN SMALL SPACES

The rise of (or return to) organic farming and companion planting in the 1970s was a reaction to the habits of large commercial growing operations that sprung up in the decades before. Large-scale growing often relies on the practice of growing one crop over a vast plot of land, called monoculture growing, which in turn relies on seasonal pesticides and fungicides to control the inevitable outbreaks of pests and diseases. However, organic farmers found that by interplanting crops with companions, it negated the need for these harmful chemicals, benefitted soil health, reduced the risk of food contamination, and increased productivity over time.

This movement gave rise to our modern concept of companion planting and from it emerged a catalogue of matchmaking data to rival any dating website. The legacy of this method can be found in any garden around the world; from our experience, the first assessment in any garden design is determining the good and bad companions and organising accordingly.

In a small-space garden, however, we're not growing acres of the one crop, so pest and disease doesn't act in the same way. For example, in a small space we've found that even fennel – the pin up for bad-ass and unsociable growing – will get along with all its neighbours. The key to small-space gardening is diversity. By interplanting herbs, salads, vegetables and flowers, we strike a natural balance of pests, predators and pollinators, and your garden party will be a raging success.

Flowers, of course, play a pivotal role in luring beneficial insects for pest control and pollination. By splashing some colour through the patch, not only do you add an interesting food source, but to your insect friends it's like putting a red flag in front of a bull. If you're planting gourds in spring, having a horde of insects about (in particular, the industrious bee) will vastly improve the chances of natural pollination of the fruit.

OH, I GET BY WITH A LITTLE HELP FROM MY FRIENDS

FRUIT TREES

Every garden deserves a fruit tree. In fact, most gardens are designed around them because fruit trees are some of the most productive food plants that exist. If we break down the amount of fruit required in our diets, it sits almost on par with vegetables, so why are fruit trees becoming extinct in the garden? The answer may be space, or more accurately the perceived space.

Our childhood memories are littered with images and scents of the more unforgettable fruit trees – those that you could climb up to find the ripened fruit the others missed, or others that pumped out so much produce that if you added a little sugar and citric acid to the laneway where they sat fermenting, a year of jam wasn't far away. None of our memories had any sitting in a pot in the courtyard, particularly not the deciduous varieties that could commit the ultimate sin of dropping leaves on the clean concrete.

Space constraints have changed the dynamic of the edible garden, but then again fruit trees have, too. They've had to change in order to be considered in our gardening plans and now dwarf varieties are available in almost every type of fruit that exists. In case you're wondering, that doesn't mean a small plant that produces small dwarf-sized fruit. Rather, it's a compact plant that produces a smaller and more manageable regular supply of sweet, fruity treasures.

Other than the great produce they supply, fruit trees are also magnets for pollinators and predators that help us create a balanced ecosystem. And yes, they can even balance out the mini ecosystem in your courtyard or on your balcony.

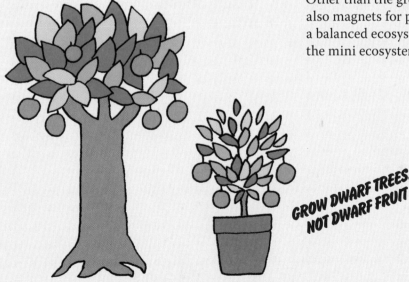

GROW DWARF TREES, NOT DWARF FRUIT

CITRUS
SEE PAGE 158

APPLE

Our genetic makeup as humans means that if we want to perpetuate our bloodline we require a partner. In the fruit tree world – in this case, that of the apple – some varieties jump this prerequisite and can self-pollinate. However, the majority will need a matching partner to make apple babies. Make sure you're aware of what variety you're growing and what it'll need to produce fruit.

An apple tree can be a large investment in space, but thanks to selective breeding there are also dwarf varieties that will be little more than a compact, upright stem.

When to plant
ZONE 1 Apr–Dec
ZONE 2 Apr–Nov
ZONE 3 May–Nov
ZONE 4 Not suitable

Best grown from
Adolescent tree

Pollination
Some self-pollinate, but partners are often required to improve production.

Spacing
4–5 m (approx 13–16 ft)

Ideal pH level
5.5–6.5

Favourite small-space variety
Gala dwarf

Best suited to
Pots, in-ground

Common problems
Birds, bats

NONNO'S TIP
In order to have good quality, edible fruit, some culling of apples is essential to redirect growing energy to those that remain.

KITCHEN TIP
Apples keep extraordinarily well. Store them in a cool, dark place and enjoy them at your leisure.

CHERRY

Some of music's finest moments have been inspired by the cherry tree – The National's 2004 EP, for example – and without doubt some of life's best moments have, too. The cherry is a highly sought-after commodity, and growing any ornamental variety that doesn't fruit is like visiting a football stadium when there's no game playing.

Like all deciduous fruit trees, it will require a certain number of chilling hours in order to set fruit. This means they will only grow in cool, temperate and some milder subtropical environments, but that suits us just fine.

When to plant
ZONE 1 Mar–Nov
ZONE 2 Mar–Nov
ZONE 3 May–Oct
ZONE 4 Not suitable

Best grown from
Adolescent tree

Pollination
Some self-pollinate, but partners are often required to improve production.

Spacing
3–4 m (approx 10–13 ft)

Ideal pH level
6.0–6.5

Favourite small-space variety
Stella (self-pollinating)

Best suited to
Pots, in-ground

Common problems
Birds, children

NONNO'S TIP
Cherries are probably the most prized of all fruit. Netting is essential to protect the fruit and deter stealthy neighbours.

KITCHEN TIP
Cherry pie, of course. Reduce sugar and add a little lemon to bring out the natural tartness.

FIG

If there's one tree you're likely to inherit on your inner-city block it would be a wise old fig, stretching out and leaning over the laneways and fence lines. They're the legacy of European migration in the 1950s and '60s, when quite possibly the first act of home settlement was to plant a tree.

The fig is an abundant treasure in late summer when it seems to grab the attention of every creature that passes by. This includes bats, possums, rodents, kids and even local neighbours looking for overhanging fruit. While the trees are strong, hardy and largely resistant to pests and disease, the figs themselves are not. They will demand netting to protect the ripening fruit.

⚲ **When to plant**
ZONE 1 Mar–Nov   ZONE 3 May–Oct
ZONE 2 Mar–Nov   ZONE 4 Apr–Jul

⚕ **Best grown from**
Adolescent tree

⸰ₒ **Pollination**
Self-pollinating

ᴡ **Spacing**
5–7 m (approx 16–23 ft)

△ **Ideal pH level**
6.5–7.5

♡ **Favourite small-space variety**
Black genoa

⊟ **Best suited to**
Pots, in-ground

☼ **Common problems**
Birds

NONNO'S TIP
Figs are perhaps the second most prized fruit of all, and many pests have a sixth sense to the ripening of the fruit. It's best to net well before the first bird digs its beak in.

KITCHEN TIP
Halved figs with a blob of mascarpone cheese are like an arrow from Cupid's bow.

OLIVE

There's a reason Mediterranean immigrants made their home so easily in Australia. Olives grew so well that the newcomers could be forgiven for thinking they were still on Mykonos. Drought-resistant and largely pest-free, the olive is the toughest of fruit trees, an evergreen that produces an abundance of fruit to either cure or turn into olive oil.

Trees will flower and fruit at the same time, and are only able to hold their limit. So, in the year you get a large glut of fruit you will get fewer flowers, meaning the following year you will have fewer olives and plenty of flowers. The peaks and troughs of olive production seem to flow in sync with the highs and lows of Mediterranean life.

⚲ **When to plant**
ZONE 1 Sep–Apr   ZONE 3 Mar–Nov
ZONE 2 Sep–May   ZONE 4 Apr–Jul

⚕ **Best grown from**
Adolescent tree

⸰ₒ **Pollination**
Self-pollinating

ᴡ **Spacing**
4–5 m (approx 13–16 ft)

△ **Ideal pH level**
7.0–8.0

♡ **Favourite small-space variety**
Manzanillo

⊟ **Best suited to**
Pots, in-ground

☼ **Common problems**
Lace bug

NONNO'S TIP
Olive trees fruit and flower at the same time, meaning your tree will alternate from a bountiful crop one year to a lower harvest the following. Swings and roundabouts.

KITCHEN TIP
Fully ripened olives are not useful for curing (as they turn mushy) or for making olive oil (as their oil content is much lower than younger olives).

POMEGRANATE

Native to the region around Iran, the pomegranate is a deciduous (and evergreen) tree that produces unique hard-shelled fruit that hide hundreds of gem-coloured seeds.

This is another drought-tolerant fruit tree that copes best in a dry, Mediterranean-style climate, and is prone to root rot in wetter conditions.

When to plant
ZONE 1 Oct–Jan
ZONE 2 Sep–Jan
ZONE 3 Aug–Dec
ZONE 4 Not suitable

Best grown from
Adolescent tree

Pollination
Self-pollinating

Spacing
3–4 m (approx 10–13 ft)

Ideal pH level
5.5–7.0

Favourite small-space variety
Sirenevyi

Best suited to
Pots, in-ground

Common problems
Aphids

NONNO'S TIP
The pomegranate comes from the Middle East, meaning they love dry, hot weather. A free-draining soil is imperative.

KITCHEN TIP
Pomegranate can be used to add a depth of flavour and texture to savoury dishes. Try a lamb tagine using pomegranate juice and then top with fresh seeds.

STONE FRUIT
(PEACH, NECTARINE, PLUM)

All stone fruit trees follow a similar order in the way they grow and produce fruit. Deciduous in nature, they often need a partner for flower pollination and require chilling hours to produce fruit, so they are best suited to cooler and more temperate climates. Just before spring, they splash out their blossoms, which signal the imminent arrival of better times. Falling in sync with the order of these trees as they flower and fruit is all part of becoming a hardcore gardener.

Full-sized growing varieties demand a level of space that is usually not available in the small-space garden, so one option is to plant compatible partners together in the same root hole. This will effectively stunt their growth – moderating size – while planting proximity ensures excellent pollination. Otherwise, look for dwarf varieties that self-pollinate or, even better, get a multi-grafted tree that can have two or three varieties on the one plant.

When to plant
ZONE 1 Mar–Nov
ZONE 2 Mar–Nov
ZONE 3 May–Sep
ZONE 4 Not suitable

Best grown from
Adolescent tree

Pollination
Some self-pollinate but partners are often required to improve production.

Spacing
3–4 m (approx 10–13 ft)

Ideal pH level
6.0–7.0

Favourite small-space variety
Blenheim apricot

Best suited to
Pots, in-ground

Common problems
Leaf curl

NONNO'S TIP
Try your hand at a multi-grafted plant, which is basically limbs of different varieties grafted onto one tree. This can only be done with compatible partners, one of which is the cherry tree.

KITCHEN TIP
So many crumbles and cobblers, so little time. Anything topped with a mix of oats, brown sugar and butter would be great. But peach, nectarine and apricot rise above the rest. Mix them all together if the opportunity presents itself.

GARLIC

	1	2	3	4	5
EASY TO GROW					
SMALL SPACE SUITABILITY					
YIELD VALUE					
JE NE SAIS QUOI/PLEASURE					

When to plant
ZONE 1 Feb–Apr
Oct–Nov
ZONE 2 Feb–Apr
Oct–Nov
ZONE 3 Apr–Jun
ZONE 4 Apr–Jun

Best grown from
Cloves (see page 108)

Depth
3–4 cm (1¼–1½ in)

Spacing
15–20 cm (6–8 in)

Time to 1st harvest
45–60 days for scapes (stalks) or 180–270 days for bulbs.

Ideal pH level
6.5–7.5

Favourite small-space variety
Melbourne market, of course

Best suited to
Pots, in-ground

Common problems
Rotting

There's something special about garlic that makes it more than just a vegetable. It's more like a cultural building block. Used liberally in just about every homemade remedy that rids the common cold, its antibacterial and antiviral qualities are well documented and equally well celebrated. While a mouth full of garlic serves us well to deter the advances of an over-enthusiastic, unwanted love interest, garlic grown throughout the garden is equally effective as a natural fungicide and aphid deterrent.

In the kitchen, garlic shouldn't only be thought of in terms of heads and cloves. The foliage of the plant offers a subtle garlic chive–like flavour and can be harvested continuously while waiting for bulbs to mature. Sauté them in a stir-fry or add to your morning eggs for a real treat.

Plant a single clove in well-composted soil and watch a whole bulb grow over the next 9 months. As it is a growing adventure that transpires over many months, you will have plenty of time to sit by the fire with a glass of pinot – and the anticipation at harvest time builds to one of the ultimate lotteries. Shoots will start to brown off when bulbs are ready to be harvested. However, double-check bulb size by digging down or even exhuming one or two plants. Homegrown garlic rarely reaches the colossal sizes of its supermarket cousins, but there is no match for the satisfaction and potency of fresh garlic.

NONNO'S TIP At about the 6-month mark, tie the foliage up in knots. This is thought to divert growth from the foliage to the bulbs. Even if it doesn't, it looks totally legit.

KITCHEN TIP The foliage, or scapes, are a bonus harvest along the way and should be used in salads and stir-fries. Don't take too many from a single plant or it will affect the growth of the ultimate prize.

TIMELINE

Prepare the soil with compost and blood and bone, then plant cloves into the patch, ensuring the thinner tip (from which it sprouts) is pointing skywards. Firm down the soil.

Cloves will have sprouted. Mulch to a depth of 3–5 cm (1¼–2 in) with pea straw, lucerne hay or sugar cane. Garlic will also benefit from a monthly application of liquid seaweed solution.

Apply compost around the base of the garlic and reapply mulch. If the plants are too close together, thin them out and use as scapes.

Foliage often begins to die back. Lessen the amount of water on the patch to allow bulbs to mature and harden.

Harvest by pulling on the foliage while loosening the soil with a hand fork. Cut off the foliage to be used as a milder garlic substitute, shake off the soil and hang up to dry for storage.

WEEK	0	4	8	18	24	28	36
GROWTH							
WATER	Daily		3–4 times a week		1–2 times a week		

	1	2	3	4	5
EASY TO GROW					
SMALL SPACE SUITABILITY					
YIELD VALUE					
JE NE SAIS QUOI/PLEASURE					

Herbs are an absolute no-brainer and one of the few plants or groups of plants aces the veggie patch rating. If you are planting for value, herbs will provide it in spades. To leave them out of the patch is like leaving your 8-year-old son, Kevin, home alone while you go on holiday to France. Sure, the consequences are outrageous and hilarious, but who forgets their son and catches a plane to Paris? Probably the same kind of people who don't plant herbs in the veggie patch.

Nothing breaks our heart more than having to buy herbs from the supermarket. They are so easy to grow and most will produce year-round. Paying $4 for a sprig of rosemary that lasts you one roast would be much better spent at the nursery, which will satisfy your rosemary needs for life.

Rather than head to the supermarket with heads bowed – shaming ourselves into buying fresh herbs for the meal that wouldn't be the same without them – we prefer to scout the neighbourhood and find some legal tender. Using rosemary as our case in point, we know there are entire nature strips full of it less than a block away. Parsley protrudes from our next-door neighbour's fence, as does sage. Get to know what is on offer in your local area while cultivating your own supply.

Not only will planting herbs reduce unwanted trips to the supermarket, they will also provide a range of scents and colours when in flower that attract beneficial insects into the patch. If you build a mini ecosystem of plants and insects, the veggie patch will operate at greater efficiency.

CHERVIL

CHIVES

DILL

CHERVIL

♧ **When to plant**
ZONE 1 Mar–Apr
Oct–Nov
ZONE 2 Mar–Jun
Sep–Oct

ZONE 3 Apr–Sep
ZONE 4 Jun–Jul

♈ **Best grown from**
Seed

↓ **Depth**
1 cm (½ in)

ω **Spacing**
30 cm (12 in)

♂ **Time to 1st harvest**
30 days (sensibly)–75 days
(more feverishly)

△ **Ideal pH level**
5.5–7.0

♡ **Favourite small-space variety**
Plain

⊟ **Best suited to**
Wall, pots, in-ground

☼ **Common problems**
Heat and cold stress

NONNO'S TIP
The timing is crucial when planting chervil.
They are very delicate and easily get frost
and heat damage.

KITCHEN TIP
Add to mayonnaise, butter, soft cheese
or thickened cream for a delightful
herbal spread.

CHIVES

♧ **When to plant**
ZONE 1 Sep–Apr
ZONE 2 Sep–May

ZONE 3 Anytime
ZONE 4 Anytime

♈ **Best grown from**
Seedling

↓ **Depth**
1 cm (½ in)

ω **Spacing**
20 cm (8 in)

♂ **Time to 1st harvest**
30 days (sensibly)–75 days
(more feverishly)

△ **Ideal pH level**
6.0–7.0

♡ **Favourite small-space variety**
Garlic

⊟ **Best suited to**
Wall, pots, in-ground

☼ **Common problems**
Aphids

NONNO'S TIP
When chives go to seed, pull out the
flowers and hard stems on which
they grow to free up energy for more
production.

KITCHEN TIP
One flower head produces hundreds of
lilac-coloured petals that can be used
liberally in salads.

DILL

♧ **When to plant**
ZONE 1 Mar–Apr
Oct–Nov
ZONE 2 Mar–Jun
Sep–Oct

ZONE 3 Apr–Sep
ZONE 4 Jun–Jul

♈ **Best grown from**
Seed

↓ **Depth**
1 cm (½ in)

ω **Spacing**
40 cm (1 ft 3 in)

♂ **Time to 1st harvest**
30 days (sensibly)–75 days
(more feverishly)

△ **Ideal pH level**
5.5–6.5

♡ **Favourite small-space variety**
Mammoth

⊟ **Best suited to**
Pots, in-ground

☼ **Common problems**
Heat stress, aphids

NONNO'S TIP
As most dill plants mature, they become
quite tall and clumsy, so staking is
advised to prevent them from falling over.

KITCHEN TIP
Though dill is prone to bolt to seed, don't
become despondent, as the flowers are
incredibly tasty. Perfect in your zucchini
(courgette) fritters.

OREGANO

♀ **When to plant**
ZONE 1 Sep–Apr   ZONE 3 Apr–Sep
ZONE 2 Sep–May   ZONE 4 Jun–Jul

⚘ **Best grown from**
Seedling

↓ **Depth**
1 cm (½ in)

〰 **Spacing**
40 cm (1 ft 3 in)

♂ **Time to 1st harvest**
30 days (sensibly)–75 days
(more feverishly)

△ **Ideal pH level**
6.5–7.0

♡ **Favourite small-space variety**
Greek

⊔ **Best suited to**
Wall, pots, in-ground

☼ **Common problems**
Root rot through overwatering

NONNO'S TIP
The plant can become thickly matted with
roots and will benefit from division in early
spring to encourage new growth.

KITCHEN TIP
Use its beautiful flowers to garnish any
savoury dish.

ROSEMARY

♀ **When to plant**
ZONE 1 Oct–Feb   ZONE 3 Anytime
ZONE 2 Oct–Mar   ZONE 4 Anytime

⚘ **Best grown from**
Cutting

↓ **Depth**
1 cm (½ in)

〰 **Spacing**
50 cm (1 ft 7 in)

♂ **Time to 1st harvest**
30 days (sensibly)–75 days
(more feverishly)

△ **Ideal pH level**
5.0–6.0

♡ **Favourite small-space variety**
Majorca pink

⊔ **Best suited to**
Pots, in-ground

☼ **Common problems**
Fungal disease

NONNO'S TIP
It's prone to fungal disease early,
which will cause your rosemary to
mysteriously dry out and die. However,
once established this is a plant for life.

KITCHEN TIP
Infuse a few sprigs in your olive oil
so it's more than ready to coat your
roast vegetables.

SAGE

♀ **When to plant**
ZONE 1 Oct–Feb   ZONE 3 Anytime
ZONE 2 Oct–Mar   ZONE 4 Anytime

⚘ **Best grown from**
Cutting

↓ **Depth**
1 cm (½ in)

〰 **Spacing**
40 cm (1 ft 3 in)

♂ **Time to 1st harvest**
30 days (sensibly)–75 days
(more feverishly)

△ **Ideal pH level**
5.5–6.5

♡ **Favourite small-space variety**
Purple

⊔ **Best suited to**
Wall, pots, in-ground

☼ **Common problems**
Rust

NONNO'S TIP
Becomes very woody in winter and
needs pruning to invigorate the plant
and encourage new growth. Be brutal.

KITCHEN TIP
Dry the sage from your late winter
cutback and then combine it with salt
to make a delicious rub.

TARRAGON

When to plant
ZONE 1 Oct–Feb ZONE 3 Anytime
ZONE 2 Oct–Mar ZONE 4 Anytime

Best grown from
Cutting

Depth
1 cm (½ in)

Spacing
50 cm (1 ft 7 in)

Time to 1st harvest
30 days (sensibly)–75 days
(more feverishly)

Ideal pH level
6.5–7.5

Favourite small-space variety
French

Best suited to
Pots, in-ground

Common problems
Rust

NONNO'S TIP
Divide plants every few years.

KITCHEN TIP
Tarragon-flavoured butter is ideal
for baking fish.

THYME

When to plant
ZONE 1 Sep–Apr ZONE 3 Anytime
ZONE 2 Sep–May ZONE 4 Anytime

Best grown from
Seedling

Depth
1 cm (½ in)

Spacing
40 cm (1 ft 3 in)

Time to 1st harvest
30 days (sensibly)–75 days
(more feverishly)

Ideal pH level
5.5–7.0

Favourite small-space variety
Orange creeping

Best suited to
Wall, pots, in-ground

Common problems
Root rot through overwatering

NONNO'S TIP
The plant can become thickly matted
with roots and will benefit from division
in early spring to invigorate the plant
and encourage new growth.

KITCHEN TIP
Not just for roasted chickens. Try using
thyme to infuse oil and coat soft cheeses.
We make a thyme za'atar by grinding
dried thyme with salt, pepper and
sesame seeds.

BASIL
SEE PAGE 132

**CORIANDER
(CILANTRO)**
SEE PAGE 162

MINT SEE PAGE 202

PARSLEY
SEE PAGE 212

KALE

	1	2	3	4	5
EASY TO GROW					
SMALL SPACE SUITABILITY					
YIELD VALUE					
JE NE SAIS QUOI/PLEASURE					

When to plant
ZONE 1 Mar–Jun
Sep–Dec
ZONE 2 Mar–Jun
Sep–Nov
ZONE 3 Mar–Oct
ZONE 4 Apr–Jul

Best grown from
Seed – propagate in trays and transplant into the patch.

Depth
1 cm (½ in)

Spacing
50 cm (1 ft 7 in)

Time to 1st harvest
60+ days

Ideal pH level
5.5–7.0

Favourite small-space variety
Dwarf blue curled

Best suited to
Pots, in-ground

Common problems
White cabbage moth

Love it or hate it (is there no room for ambivalence anymore?), the feelings you harbour for kale seem to hinge on how long you've known it, the relationship you've shared, or how much you enjoy butter and garlic. I grew up knowing it by a much sexier alias, cavolo nero, and that may very well explain my fondness. If you have lived in the UK and tried your hand at allotment gardening, for example, you'd know that kale is about the only thing that survives during the winter. In these cases, it may trigger memories of cold and wet semi-darkness, infused with the scent of boiled kale seasoned with silent tears. Or so we imagine.

For many of us, however, kale probably emerged on the scene along with acai and goji berries, riding a superfood wave of adoration straight to our hearts. Whatever your experience, there is no denying its abundance of nutrients, reliability and hardiness. Kale is a productive winter staple.

As a member of the brassica family, it is especially hungry for nitrogen, so try to plant in a site previously occupied by beans or peas. Similarly watch out for the white cabbage moth and consider netting plants early in the season when the moths are active laying their larvae.

NONNO'S TIP
Net your kale during the peak times of the cabbage moth, that being late spring and early autumn.

KITCHEN TIP
Kale chips, of course.

TIMELINE

WEEK	-4	0	4	8	10	16	20+
GROWTH							
WATER			Daily			3–4 times a week	

-4: Propagate in a seed tray and prepare the patch with plenty of compost and high-nitrogen manures.

0: Transplant into the patch on a day that is not too hot and space out at half of that required for mature plants. Net the plants to prevent damage from the white cabbage moth.

4: Thin out seedlings to required spacing and mulch with pea straw, lucerne hay or sugar cane to a depth of 3–5 cm (1¼–2 in).

10: Begin to harvest leaf by leaf in moderation, ensuring you leave enough foliage on the plant so it can reproduce. If conditions are now suitably cold, netting can be removed as the white cabbage moth won't be as active.

16: Production gets into full swing – continue to take leaf by leaf but on a more regular basis. Plants can be picked for over a year, and will grow long and tall stems that become bare through picking. Aphids and other sucking pests, as well as the moths, will eventually return to decimate the crop, signalling its end.

KOHLRABI

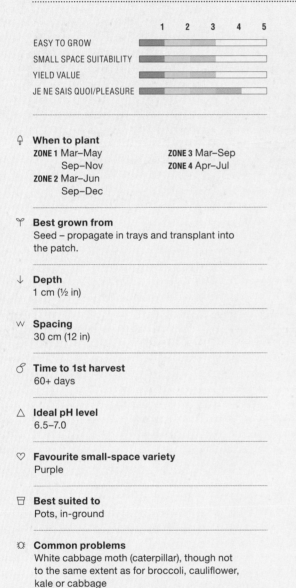

	1	2	3	4	5
EASY TO GROW					
SMALL SPACE SUITABILITY					
YIELD VALUE					
JE NE SAIS QUOI/PLEASURE					

♀ When to plant
ZONE 1 Mar–May
        Sep–Nov
ZONE 2 Mar–Jun
        Sep–Dec

ZONE 3 Mar–Sep
ZONE 4 Apr–Jul

⚘ Best grown from
Seed – propagate in trays and transplant into the patch.

↓ Depth
1 cm (½ in)

⋈ Spacing
30 cm (12 in)

⚲ Time to 1st harvest
60+ days

△ Ideal pH level
6.5–7.0

♡ Favourite small-space variety
Purple

⊟ Best suited to
Pots, in-ground

☼ Common problems
White cabbage moth (caterpillar), though not to the same extent as for broccoli, cauliflower, kale or cabbage

The common misconception is that kohlrabi, German for 'cabbage turnip', is a vegetable heralding from those parts. While that could be true, we have also heard that it is a crashed alien vessel that has not only embedded itself in the garden, but has firmly lodged itself in the European diet. Indeed, the rich purple heirloom variety and ability to weather colder conditions speaks to an extraterrestrial origin. Its growth is certainly otherworldly as well, not forming a root or a head, but rather an enlarged stem (no doubt concealing tiny, spying aliens).

Whatever its origins, kohlrabi wins many accolades. A member of the brassica family, it is a versatile, fast-growing, low-maintenance, pest-resistant, hardy crop, extraordinarily healthy yet with a slightly milder and sweeter taste than its cohorts. While the stem is the main prize, harvesting young leaves will greatly extend the lifetime of the plant and provide a bounty of nutritionally dense greens, much like kale or silverbeet (Swiss chard).

This is a beloved, reliable cold-climate crop and established plants are frost tolerant. However, be sure to cultivate seedlings well before the first frost so that they are strong enough to handle a sudden drop in temperature. A thick layer of mulch is particularly important to help insulate kohlrabi's shallow roots. Temperate and warmer climate regions can get away with growing at any time outside summer.

NONNO'S TIP The seed can be grown as a micro green.

KITCHEN TIP Use the leaves as a kale substitute and fried as chips.

TIMELINE						
	Propagate in a seed tray and prepare the patch with plenty of compost and slow-release nitrogen-rich fertiliser, such as pelletised chook manure.	Transplant into the patch spaced out at half the required distance for mature plants. Netting for white cabbage moth is optional.	Thin out seedlings to required spacing and mulch with pea straw, lucerne hay or sugar cane to a depth of 3–5 cm (1¼–2 in).		As the foliage develops you can begin to harvest leaves as salad greens, ensuring you leave enough for the stems to fully swell.	Swelling of the stem accelerates. Pick when you're satisfied with the size. They keep well in-ground in cooler conditions, but can get tough and fibrous when it's warmer.
WEEK	-4	0	4	8	10	16
GROWTH						
WATER			Daily		3–4 times a week	

LEEK

	1	2	3	4	5
EASY TO GROW					
SMALL SPACE SUITABILITY					
YIELD VALUE					
JE NE SAIS QUOI/PLEASURE					

When to plant
ZONE 1 Oct–Nov &
Feb–Apr
ZONE 2 Sep–Nov &
Feb–May
ZONE 3 Feb–Apr
ZONE 4 Mar–Apr

Best grown from
Seed – propagate in trays and transplant into
the patch.

Depth
1 cm (½ in)

Spacing
10–15 cm (4–6 in)

Time to 1st harvest
150–180 days

Ideal pH level
6.5–7.5

Favourite small-space variety
American flag

Best suited to
Pots, in-ground

Common problems
Mostly pest-free, but slugs can find a way inside
the leaves.

It's hard to get into the cool-season spirit during the peak of summer, but certain things are worth the mental shift, such as booking a family ski holiday or propagating seeds. From the allium family – which includes onion and garlic – leek is a slow-burn, easy-to-grow vegetable that we have on our minds when the weather is hot.

Patient gardeners are best suited to growing leek, as these veggies have a lifespan of up to 9 months in the veggie patch. However, from around the second month, they're also well suited to forgetful, lazy, oblivious gardeners. After they are set, they can be 'put to sleep' in the patch. For those familiar with horse racing, leek sits three back on the inside rail collecting cover and a nice trail from the leader. Come the final straight, about 3–6 months later, leek pull out and steamroll home.

Hardy, tough and relatively pest-free, leek store well in-ground and will happily stay in the patch until you find the perfect quiche recipe. Everyone who grows leek will be a winner.

NONNO'S TIP Rather than discard the roots, replant in the patch for a much quicker round two.

KITCHEN TIP While all parts of the leek are edible, it's the sweeter and tenderer lower section of the plant that is favoured. 'Blanching' is the process of starving this part of sunlight by building up a thick layer of mulch around it. Keeping the stem away from the sun's rays makes a larger part of the leek more suitable for cooking.

TIMELINE

Propagate in a seed tray.

Prepare soil with compost but don't over-fertilise, as this will make them susceptible to frost damage. Transplant into the patch at the required spacing.

Mulch to a depth of 3–5 cm (1¼–2 in) using pea straw, lucerne hay or sugar cane mulch.

Apply some liquid seaweed solution every couple of months but otherwise, don't feed.

As the leeks begin to develop, build up soil or mulch around their bases to blanch the stems by mounding mulch extra high, making them sweeter and more tender.

Harvest using a hand fork, gently pulling on the foliage. They have intensive root zones so loosening up the soil is essential. They keep well in-ground during the cooler times of the year, so let the others rest until required.

WEEK	-6	0	4	8	16	24
GROWTH						
WATER			Daily		3–4 times a week	

LETTUCE

	1	2	3	4	5
EASY TO GROW					
SMALL SPACE SUITABILITY					
YIELD VALUE					
JE NE SAIS QUOI/PLEASURE					

When to plant
ZONE 1 Sep–Jun
ZONE 2 Aug–Jun
ZONE 3 Anytime
ZONE 4 Anytime

Best grown from
Seed

Depth
1 cm (½ in)

Spacing
20–30 cm (8–12 in)

Time to 1st harvest
45+ days

Ideal pH level
6.0–7.0

Favourite small-space variety
Red mizuna

Best suited to
Wall, pots, in-ground

Common problems
Bolting to seed, snails and slugs

Lettuce is the golden retriever of the vegetable world: simple, loyal and easy to satisfy. Throw any season at a lettuce and you're bound to get some produce in return.

We categorise lettuce as any leafy green that hasn't had a life as a superfood on Oprah – this excludes kale, spinach and silverbeet (Swiss chard). It seems to thrive best in early autumn and spring conditions but, like your retriever, will be happy with most seasons. Lettuces are not especially hungry for nutrients, but do require a steady supply of nitrogen. Scatter pelletised chook manure through the garden at the beginning of the growing season and water with seaweed solution every 2 weeks for optimal leaf quality.

If you're told to fetch a head of lettuce from the supermarket you have roughly three or four choices. Go to a good nursery, such as The Little Veggie Patch Co, and there are enough varieties to start a leafy green cult – from red mizuna to speckled mignonette, sweet rocket (arugula) to a personal favourite, wasabi greens. There's a lettuce for every occasion.

Lettuces can be broken down as either hearting (iceberg, for example) or non-hearting (mignonette), and this gives you an indication of how they should be harvested. Hearting varieties should be taken as whole heads, while non-hearting varieties can be harvested in our favoured leaf-by-leaf manner. However, if you harvest all types of lettuce leaf by leaf, it helps to achieve a perpetual harvest and more output from the patch.

		Thin seedlings so that remaining plants have the room to mature and then mulch to a depth of 3–5 cm (1¼–2 in) using pea straw, lucerne hay or sugar cane mulch. Lettuce are sweet and desired by a number of night-time critters, including snails and slugs, so set up adequate defences.	Leaf-by-leaf harvesting is encouraged for a perpetual harvest. Take more mature outer leaves and work your way in, leaving enough foliage on each plant to properly reproduce.	
	Add compost to the patch and plant seeds directly into the soil.	All leafy greens will appreciate a fortnightly application of liquid seaweed solution.		Continue in the same fashion until the plant bolts to seed.

TIMELINE

WEEK	0	2	8	10	12	16+
GROWTH						
WATER			Daily			

HEY-HO! LETTUCE GO!

BUTTERHEAD

The retriever of all retrievers, butterhead is an easy-to-please pleasure-to-grow type of lettuce. Its soft, delicate, almost buttery foliage is something that can bulk up a green salad without a confronting taste.

COS (ROMAINE)

Since the height of its popularity in a 1990s caesar salad, the cos (like the iceberg) has experienced a sharp decline and is only now making its resurgence. Texture is its main attribute and, like butterhead, it is without the bitterness that can turn off some salad eaters.

ENDIVE

Endive, pronounced 'on-dive', is a mildly bitter, textured leafy green belonging to the same family as radicchio and chicory. The almost white inner stems are highly sought after and are a Veggie Patch Co favourite.

MIZUNA

Mizuna is a solid leafy green with an interesting jagged foliage, nice texture and subtle bitterness. But it's red mizuna that really brings this vegetable to life. Spicy and delightfully bitter, red mizuna is outstanding and performs well in the cooler seasons.

RADICCHIO

The tough, bitter outer leaves of a radicchio are largely a waste of time but their true value is in protecting the dense hearts. These are highly sought after, so are often difficult to obtain. Look for them at the markets. They're totally worth the effort.

SORREL

Sorrel is a zesty leafy green, with each bite reminding us of opening a can of lemonade. The leaves are best when young as they become tougher and tarter when mature. Cook them only if you are fond of tangy mush.

NONNO'S TIP

If you notice your lettuce bolting to seed, pick off the flower heads to redirect energy back to more productive foliage growth. Flowers that stem from mizuna and rocket (arugula) are edible themselves and quite delicious. However, other varieties such as cos (romaine) and butterhead will begin to spiral skywards from the main stem and quickly turn bitter. It's best to catch the seedling early to redirect energy back to foliage production, but the key is to pick leaves often to keep them young and fresh.

KITCHEN TIP

Hearting varieties such as iceberg, cos (romaine) and radicchio are fantastic when cut in half and charred on the barbecue.

MELONS

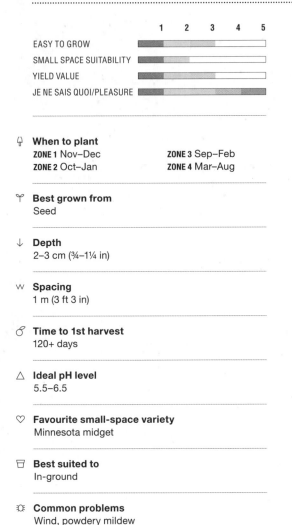

	1	2	3	4	5
EASY TO GROW					
SMALL SPACE SUITABILITY					
YIELD VALUE					
JE NE SAIS QUOI/PLEASURE					

⚲ **When to plant**
ZONE 1 Nov–Dec   ZONE 3 Sep–Feb
ZONE 2 Oct–Jan   ZONE 4 Mar–Aug

⚘ **Best grown from**
Seed

↓ **Depth**
2–3 cm (¾–1¼ in)

⚖ **Spacing**
1 m (3 ft 3 in)

♂ **Time to 1st harvest**
120+ days

△ **Ideal pH level**
5.5–6.5

♡ **Favourite small-space variety**
Minnesota midget

🪣 **Best suited to**
In-ground

☼ **Common problems**
Wind, powdery mildew

If we lived further north, in the tropics, our gardens would always be full of melons. We would completely let ourselves go, fawning about in cut-off denim shorts, our long beards clutching seeds and dripping with melon juice. Unfortunately, we live in a cooler, more temperate part of the country. While rockmelon, watermelon and honeydew are heat-loving varieties that perform best in warmer climates, our commitment to them has never wavered. When battling less than ideal conditions, timing and position become critical choices to ensuring success.

Propagating and then planting young seedlings needs to be one of the final acts of warm-season planting. Given that melons won't tolerate any cold remnants of spring, but need a substantial growing period to produce fruit, it is best to propagate seeds indoors or in a greenhouse in early spring and then transplant in a warm position once conditions suit.

Melons grow extensive plant matter, so the key to successful growth is in the preparation of the soil. Loading the patch full of nitrogen with manure and compost will ensure the plant has plenty of power to fuel its growth. We like to plant them in pots or on the corner of our veggie patch, so that the vines creep out of the garden. Likewise, melon vines can also be trained to grow vertically, but ensure that the trellis is strong enough to support the expected fruit size.

NONNO'S **TIP** The plants need ample hydration while growing, but once the fruit begins to form and is the size of a fist, cut back to allow its flavour to develop.

KITCHEN **TIP** The difference between a ripe melon and an immature one is a significant amount of sweetness. Ripe melons will start to yellow where they are in contact with the ground and should almost fall off the vine (or at least pull very easily).

TIMELINE						
		Integrate the patch with slow-release nitrogen-rich fertiliser and sow seeds in small mounds of compost well after the last frost. Incubate seedlings with plastic bottles when planting in cooler areas.	Give monthly applications of liquid seaweed solution and mulch to a depth of 3–5 cm (1¼–2 in) using pea straw, lucerne hay or sugar cane mulch.	Grow the vines vertically and attach them to a trellis that conserves ground-level real estate.	Apply liquid potassium to encourage flower growth and development of the fruit. The process of fruit production is an exciting, but slow journey.	Prune off the growth tips of the vine to help redirect energy into the developing fruit. Use milk spray to control any powdery mildew. The melon is ready once it can break free from the vine with minimal effort.
WEEK	0		4	8	14	20
GROWTH						
WATER		Daily			3–4 times a week	

MICRO GREENS

	1	2	3	4	5
EASY TO GROW					
SMALL SPACE SUITABILITY					
YIELD VALUE					
JE NE SAIS QUOI/PLEASURE					

When to plant (indoors)
ZONES 1–4 Anytime

Best grown from
Seed

Depth
1 cm (½ in)

Spacing
Not important

Time to 1st harvest
As soon as 7–10 days, depending on the variety

Ideal pH level
6.5–7.5

Favourite small-space variety
Cherry belle radish

Best suited to
Wall, pots, in-ground

Common problems
No pest is quick enough to realise
you've grown them

If you want something tiny, nutritious, delicious and incredibly cute, get a micro pig. However, if cuteness isn't on the menu, try micro greens. Long revered by chefs for their subtle flavours and delicate texture, they are very easy to grow and will add some extra street cred to any kitchen. Serve them up and let the compliments start rolling in, or keep them all to yourself for the world's tiniest salad.

Anything and everything that has edible shoots or leaves can be grown as a micro green. However, it is best to choose varieties that are quick to germinate and easy to raise. Radish, beetroot (beets), mustard, kale, peas, basil and spinach are most commonly used, but that shouldn't prevent you from looking left field and trying out some lesser-known varieties.

Because plants are not grown to full maturity, we don't have to worry about a lot of common challenges like spacing, light, pests and disease. Instead, growing is an all-out sprint with a high-density of seeds placed in a tray and watered daily. Only a little bit of light is necessary, which makes these a popular option for people who want to grow indoors.

NONNO'S TIP Use a mini-greenhouse to incubate and to prevent the growing medium from drying out. This will mean less frequent watering.

KITCHEN TIP Once the seedling develops its first true set of leaves (the initial leaves are essentially baby leaves that then drop off), a micro green becomes just a green. From that point on, the flavour and texture of the green toughens.

TIMELINE

Plant seeds in a seed tray using seed-raising mix and make sure to keep them incubated for the duration of their lives. Give fortnightly applications of liquid seaweed solution.

Depending on the type of seed, they could be ready to harvest within 2 weeks. Cut at the base of the stems or pull free from the soil, whichever you prefer.

WEEK	0	2	6
GROWTH			
WATER		Daily	

GROWING MICRO GREENS

The all-out sprint of growing micro greens can be done in a cost-effective way, with the main expenditure on the seed you're growing. This really flips the traditional approach to growing on its head. Usually the cost lies in your pot and soil and space. However, when growing micro greens the investment in infrastructure is minimal.

1 Grab a selection of seeds. We like a variety of colour and flavour. Fill the propagation tray with seed-raising mix. This is light and free-draining, but also has nourishing organic matter that holds moisture.

2 Sow the seeds into a shallow growing tray to about 5 mm (¼ in) depth and don't worry about density. These plants will never be big enough to compete with one another! Use a spray bottle or watering can with a gentle fan spray to water; a powerful flow could dislodge seeds or prevent germination.

3 Place the tray on a brightly lit windowsill and keep moist. Dim lighting is no problem, as the young shoots will elongate in an attempt to find light; leggy micro greens are as useful to chefs as baby oil to a body-building competition.

4 Once germinated, seeds will take a couple more weeks to be considered micro greens. First leaves will appear to be very similar on all plants, but will soon be replaced by distinct 'true leaves'. It is best to harvest before these appear. Harvest mature micro greens with sharp scissors and micro appetite. For a continual harvest, try planting different varieties in the same tray and also having multiple trays going at one time.

MINT

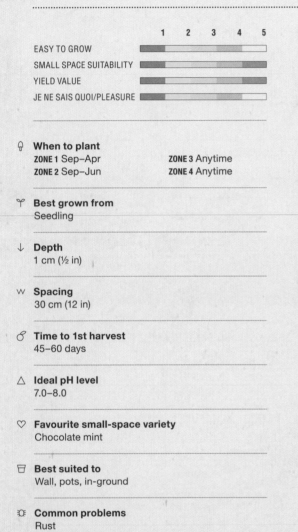

	1	2	3	4	5
EASY TO GROW					
SMALL SPACE SUITABILITY					
YIELD VALUE					
JE NE SAIS QUOI/PLEASURE					

When to plant
ZONE 1 Sep–Apr   ZONE 3 Anytime
ZONE 2 Sep–Jun   ZONE 4 Anytime

Best grown from
Seedling

Depth
1 cm (½ in)

Spacing
30 cm (12 in)

Time to 1st harvest
45–60 days

Ideal pH level
7.0–8.0

Favourite small-space variety
Chocolate mint

Best suited to
Wall, pots, in-ground

Common problems
Rust

The best soils for mint are those that can hold a steady reservoir of moisture without becoming waterlogged. Building up organic matter through the soil, such as compost and manures, effectively covers two bases for the mint: it improves your soil's water-retaining ability, while at the same time providing the plant with plenty of nitrogen to sprawl.

For many plants, mint is not a great companion. In gardening circles it is bitterly referred to as the kikuyu of the edible world, as it will quickly bully your other plants when competing for space. For this reason it's best to grow mints in their own private spot – pots are recommended – so they can be contained.

When planting mint varieties in pots, make sure you use a decent-sized vessel that the plant can grow into. Like buying your child shoes three sizes too big, there is better value in buying a larger-sized pot for your mints.

Many of us will know the basic varieties of mint – common, spear, pepper – but there are many more types, and so much potential for spicing and sweetening up your summer entertaining. Here are a few of our favourites.

TIMELINE

WEEK	0	4	8	12	16+
GROWTH					
WATER			Daily		

Prepare the soil with plenty of compost and plant as a seedling in its own pot or a specially dedicated part of the garden. Semi-shaded spots are acceptable.

Mulch with a 3–5 cm (1¼–2 in) layer of pea straw, lucerne hay or sugar cane mulch and give monthly feeds with a liquid seaweed solution.

Sometimes mint finds it difficult to get established, but at this stage you should be able to start picking junctions of leaves.

As the roots spread through the soil, growth becomes prolific and the plant seems impossible to kill.

Potted mint will inevitably become rootbound and stop growing. Harshly cut back the foliage to encourage fresh growth or dig out badly affected pots and replant runners that will quickly sprout.

EAU DE COLOGNE

No, not part of Armani's latest fragrance collection. However, it would make a great substitute if you're running low on grooming products. Simply grab a bunch of leaves, twist and then rub all over your naked body for the most organic and fresh eau de toilette on the market. One of the most fragrant mints, it is used as garnish on desserts or fruit salads.

CHOCOLATE

An immediate eye-catcher, this is a match made in food heaven, teaming up everyone's favourite vice with one of our most loved herbs. Don't deny it, you want it – it's simply irresistible! A rigorous grower with dark-green, purplish leaves and stems, this mint has an incredible scent. Yes, it's comparable to chocolate. As such, it's often used as a dessert garnish or a healthy alternative to substitute chocolate.

EGYPTIAN

A tall, upright plant that reaches nearly 1 m (3 ft 3 in) in height, this is an ancient culinary mint that has been used since the time of the pharaohs, thus the name. The leaves are large, serrated and covered in a fine hair, giving them a silvery sheen. Having a more subtle flavour than common mint and its counterparts, Egyptian mint is favoured in Middle Eastern cooking.

NONNO'S TIP Mint has a domineering attitude to neighbouring plants that get in its way, so it's best to keep it solo in a pot or its own patch of earth.

KITCHEN TIP So versatile in so many types of cuisine and beverages, you'd be foolish not to explore mint's full repertoire.

MUSHROOM

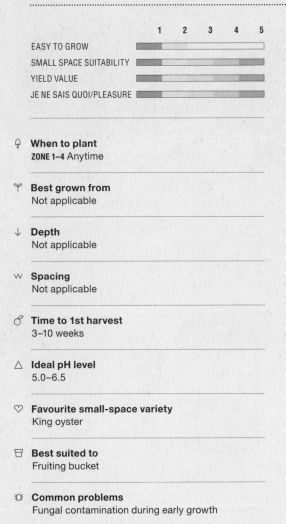

	1	2	3	4	5
EASY TO GROW					
SMALL SPACE SUITABILITY					
YIELD VALUE					
JE NE SAIS QUOI/PLEASURE					

When to plant
ZONE 1–4 Anytime

Best grown from
Not applicable

Depth
Not applicable

Spacing
Not applicable

Time to 1st harvest
3–10 weeks

Ideal pH level
5.0–6.5

Favourite small-space variety
King oyster

Best suited to
Fruiting bucket

Common problems
Fungal contamination during early growth

We use the term 'vegetable' loosely when describing a lot of varieties, but in particular when talking about the mushroom. A mushroom is actually the fruiting part of a fungal organism called mycelium (plural: mycelia). They live in the soil, wood and many other substrates, and are primarily involved in the decomposition of plant material. You may not have heard, but mycelia are a big deal. They are superstars of the growing world, with a devoted subculture around the world.

Growing mushrooms is a great practice for those with limited space because many varieties can be grown indoors with minimal light. Gourmet mushrooms such as oyster and shiitake offer extraordinary value, as they are very costly to buy, yet inexpensive and easy to grow. The key to growing is to understand and imitate mycelium's natural life cycle (see page 204). At its heart, mushroom cultivation is about propagating a very small amount of mycelium into larger and larger vessels. Just like a sourdough starter, we start with a tiny amount of live culture and grow it. It is a process of continual dividing and colonising. Once we get to a large enough vessel, we stop dividing and allow the mycelium to colonise and consume the entire substrate. This triggers fruit production and we get to wow our friends with a tiny forest of mushrooms growing under the couch!

NONNO'S TIP Start with a premade kit and work your way back as you get comfortable with each stage of cultivation.

KITCHEN TIP Compared to common field mushrooms, such as button and portobello, homegrown shiitake and other gourmet varieties will add a much greater dimension of texture and flavour to any dish.

UNDERSTANDING GOURMET MUSHROOM CULTIVATION

This is not an exact how-to, but rather a conceptual overview of gourmet mushroom cultivation. Different mushrooms have distinct environmental needs, but the progression is generally quite similar. Serious growers and those with a penchant for precision will choose to grow from the earliest possible stages (stages 1 and 2), which requires a great duty of care, sterile conditions, and lots of patience. While perfectly achievable at home, a comprehensive guide to mushroom production is beyond the scope of this book. We recommend starting your mushroom adventure at later stages (3 and beyond) and working your way back as you get more confident with each step. As production can span months, it is important to label every stage with name and date.

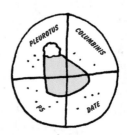

1–3 WEEKS: GROW MYCELIAL INOCULANT

Add starter culture (order online or from local mushroom supplier) to sterilised nutrient water or agar tray (agar is a gelatine-like food product). Keep in a dark, room-temperature environment, such as a linen cupboard or pantry. Mycelium will grow through and colonise the substrate. The risk of contamination during this stage is very high and the sample should be discarded if growth appears in any colour other than white.

2–3 WEEKS: CULTIVATE GRAIN SPAWN

Transfer the liquid inoculant or divided agar tray to a number of sterilised grain containers (we like organic rye). Risk of contamination is again high, so be sure to work under sterile conditions and discard if any coloured growth appears. White mycelia will grow through the grains and colonise the jar to create 'grain spawn'. When it is about 25% colonised, the jar should be shaken once to help distribute myceliated grains throughout and speed up colonisation.

TIMELINE									
	Add starter culture to liquid or agar substrate and store in a dark place at room temperature – 20°C (68°F).	White mycelial growth will start to spread through the substrate. Discard if any colours appear.	Transfer liquid inoculant or agar to a jar full of sterilised grain.	Shake jar once when mycelium has colonised about 25% of the grain. Discard if any colours appear.	Once grain is 100% colonised, prepare a fruiting substrate and divide into buckets.	Incubate fruiting buckets in a dark place until they are fully colonised with knots of white mycelium.	Move fruiting buckets to a warm, humid place with indirect light and fresh air. Fruiting will now begin in earnest.	Harvest mushrooms with a clean knife by cutting them away near the base. Expect two to three regrowths of decreasing yield.	
WEEK	0	1	4	5	7	8	12	14	16
GROWTH									
WATER						Mist with spray bottle every 3–4 days			

COUPLE OF HOURS:
PREPARE FRUITING SUBSTRATE

Once the mycelium has completely colonised the grain, it is time to prepare the final fruiting substrate. We use sugar cane mulch because we have access to a lot of it, but oyster mushrooms grow well on anything from pea straw and hardwood shavings to coffee grounds. This is a great place for many people to start their mushroom production, as it doesn't require sterile conditions. Grain spawn can be ordered online or sourced from a reputable mushroom supplier.

1   Fill a large esky (cooler) with boiling water and allow it to cool to 77°C (170°F). Fill a pillowcase with sugar cane mulch (substrate) and immerse in the water to pasteurise. Place a brick on top to ensure that it remains completely submerged.

2   Keep the material submerged for 75 minutes. Use a kitchen thermometer to ensure that temperature stays between 60°C–77°C (140°F–170°F). Additional hot water can be added as required.

3   Carefully remove the filled pillowcase (it will be bloody hot) and hang so that it can drip dry and cool. Meanwhile, find a couple of plastic 5–10 litre (170–340 fl oz) buckets with lids (hospitality yoghurt containers work well) and drill 2–6 holes around the sides. These will be the growing containers.

4   Sanitise hands, table and buckets with rubbing alcohol or disinfectant. Seal the bucket holes with breathable paper tape (found at most pharmacies).

5   Spread the cooled sugar cane mulch across the table and sprinkle with half a handful of gypsum.

6   Remove the grain spawn from its container and break it apart with your hands. We typically add at least 1 cup per fruiting bucket, but adding more will speed colonisation.

7   Spread the pieces through the mulch and gypsum mixture, breaking up any large clumps and lightly pack into a plastic bucket. Repeat the above steps until all buckets are filled.

8   Write the mushroom name and date on each bucket. Set to incubate in a dark, stable environment like a linen closet or on top of a wardrobe.

2–8 WEEKS: INCUBATION

Place buckets in a dark location. Like the previous stages, white mycelium will slowly overtake the mulch, forming little knots of tissue. Once the mycelium has fully colonised the substrate it will enter the fruiting stage. Move the buckets to a warm, humid place with plenty of fresh air. The bathroom, laundry room and under the couch are all good for this.

FRUITING

This is what you get when you buy a mushroom kit. With light and air, fruit production will begin in earnest and you can remove the paper tape from the holes and allow growth to push out of the bucket.

HARVEST

Mushroom caps will progress from downturned to upturned, but the best time to harvest is while they are flat. This usually occurs between 5–8 days after the caps appear. Harvest mushrooms at their base with a sharp knife. Most varieties will fruit multiple times, but each batch will yield less than the one before. Spent substrate can be composted.

NASTURTIUM

	1	2	3	4	5
EASY TO GROW					
SMALL SPACE SUITABILITY					
YIELD VALUE					
JE NE SAIS QUOI/PLEASURE					

When to plant
ZONE 1 Oct–Apr   **ZONE 3** Anytime
ZONE 2 Sep–May   **ZONE 4** Anytime

Best grown from
Seed

Depth
2–3 cm (¾–1¼ in)

Spacing
25 cm (10 in)

Time to 1st harvest
45+ days for leaves and 75–90 days for flowers

Ideal pH level
5.5–7.5

Favourite small-space variety
Dwarf jewel

Best suited to
Wall, pots, in-ground

Common problems
Aphids, snails and slugs, whitefly

Nasturtium is a fast-growing, self-seeding and multi-purpose edible flower that should not only get a place on everyone's plate, it should be a constant companion in the patch. After all, companionship is nasturtium's strong suit. It is low-maintenance, gets along well with others, and provides plenty of value in small spaces.

Nasturtium's good looks and easy-going personality make it the perennial diplomat, naturally attracting useful predators and pollinators. Bees are particularly drawn to its charm and, once in the garden, will pollinate on your behalf. Another frequent visitor and ally is the ladybird, the sworn enemy of parasitic pests. It is also an effective decoy plant, diverting pest attention from other plants to itself.

The plant is relatively shallow rooted, so can be planted close to others without competing for resources. It does very well in pots and wall gardens, where foliage can cascade down the side without monopolising precious garden real estate.

NONNO'S TIP   Soak seeds overnight in water prior to planting. Remove old and fading flowers to redirect energy to new growth.

KITCHEN TIP   Fresh, green seeds are produced in excess and can be picked to make nasturtium capers.

TIMELINE

| WEEK | 0 | 4 | 8 | 12 | 20 | 24 |

Soak seeds overnight prior to planting and then plant directly into the patch. Make sure the soil has compost and a slow-release nitrogen-rich fertiliser worked through it.

Thin out any overcrowded seedlings and apply a monthly dose of liquid seaweed fertiliser. Mulch to a depth of 3–5 cm (1¼–2 in) using pea straw, lucerne hay or sugar cane mulch.

As the plants begin to grow, their leaves become the first harvesting opportunity. Pick younger leaves, which are milder and tenderer.

Apply some liquid potassium that will help with the development of flowers. These present the second harvesting opportunity.

Plants begin to explode in size at the beginning of autumn, where they become a great hiding place for slugs and snails. As more flowers are produced, the plant also produces pods – the third opportunity for a harvest – which will continually self-seed.

GROWTH

WATER   Daily   3–4 times a week

ONION

	1	2	3	4	5
EASY TO GROW					
SMALL SPACE SUITABILITY					
YIELD VALUE					
JE NE SAIS QUOI/PLEASURE					

When to plant
ZONE 1 Feb–Jun   ZONE 3 Feb–May
ZONE 2 Feb–Jun   ZONE 4 Apr–May

Best grown from
Seed – propagate in trays and transplant into
the patch.

Depth
1 cm (½ in)

Spacing
10–15 cm (4–6 in)

Time to 1st harvest
45–60 days as spring onions, 180+ days as bulbs

Ideal pH level
6.5

Favourite small-space variety
Crimson forest bunching onion

Best suited to
Pots, in-ground

Common problems
Aphids and fungal disease

Humans are specially programmed to love the smell of sautéed onion. It triggers a signal like a series of dominoes cascading up our spine and straight into our reptilian brain, crossing our eyes and causing involuntary drooling. At least, that's what happens to me.

In the garden, onions are the classic cold-season crop, trusted for their hardiness and ease of growing. When well mulched, plants (though not young seedlings) will withstand light freezes and even prolonged snow. So long as temperatures don't drop below about -5°C (20°F), cold weather can actually enhance an onion's flavour by causing it to produce more sugars.

Like any plant that takes a while to mature, onions will do best in nutrient-rich soil, so don't hold back on that extra shovel of compost and wood ash when preparing the bed. They have shallow roots and will require a steady supply of water; however, be aware that onion bulbs suffer from fungal disease and rot in boggy soil. This is yet another good case for well-draining soil or even growing in pots.

Harvest early to get spring onions or wait for the bulb to push up to the surface for the big show. Foliage will start to brown off when nearly ready to harvest. We typically pull onions from the ground on a dry spring day and leave them on top of the bed to cure for a few days if no rain is predicted. Hang in a cool dry place to store.

NONNO'S TIP If you don't have the appetite for the full growing season, you can harvest the younger shoots as spring onions. However, for those with the perseverance, make sure that once onion bulbs begin to push to the surface, don't fertilise and don't cover the bulbs.

KITCHEN TIP Onion flowers have a potent but sweet onion flavour and should be a part of everyone's culinary repertoire.

TIMELINE									
		Propagate in a seed tray.	Prepare the soil with compost but don't over-fertilise with nitrogen. Rather, add liquid potassium just prior to planting. Transplant into the patch at the required spacing.	Mulch to a depth of 3–5 cm (1¼–2 in) using pea straw, lucerne hay or sugar cane mulch.	Apply some liquid seaweed solution every couple of months.	If the onions are pushing up out of the ground, mound up some soil around their bases.		Once the foliage begins to die back, tie it in knots – this is said (by our nonna's uncle's cousin's nephew) to transfer energy to the bulb growth.	Harvest using a hand fork, gently pulling on the foliage. So that they store properly, hang them up to dry in a cool, dry place.
WEEK		-6	0	4	8	12	16	18	24
GROWTH									
WATER				Daily		3–4 times a week		Twice a week	

PARSNIP

	1	2	3	4	5
EASY TO GROW					
SMALL SPACE SUITABILITY					
YIELD VALUE					
JE NE SAIS QUOI/PLEASURE					

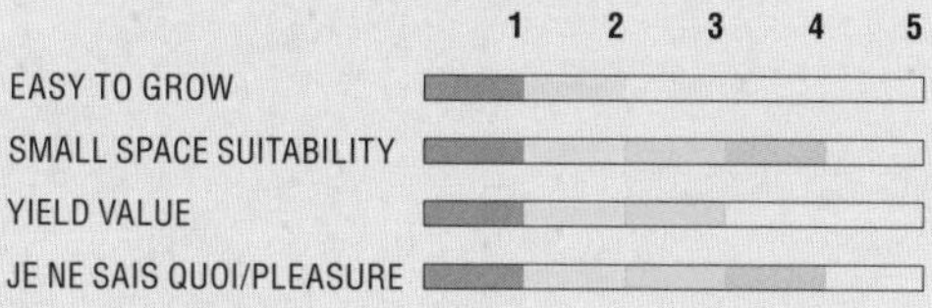

⚲ **When to plant**
ZONE 1 Sep–Nov &
Mar–May
ZONE 2 Mar–May
ZONE 3 May–Aug
ZONE 4 Jun–Jul

⅄ **Best grown from**
Seed – propagate in trays and transplant into
the patch.

↓ **Depth**
1 cm (½ in)

�w **Spacing**
15–20 cm (6–8 in)

♂ **Time to 1st harvest**
60–75 days

△ **Ideal pH level**
6.5–7.0

♡ **Favourite small-space variety**
Harris model

🖻 **Best suited to**
Pots, in-ground

☼ **Common problems**
Splitting roots, root rot

Not one for the training wheels gardener, the parsnip is
a challenging root to grow, but a sweet addition to the table
once conquered. Exuding characteristics of potatoes, carrots,
turnips, swedes (rutabagas), kohlrabi, pumpkins (winter
squash) and carrots, it's the ultimate blind taste test wild card.

A relative of the carrot, the parsnip has a similar shape,
with a thick top that quickly tapers to a wispy, rooty point.
Best grown in cooler climates throughout the cooler parts of
the year, the frosts help turn the vegetable's starch into sugar,
enhancing its flavour. Consistent moisture in the soil will also
help with developing long, straight roots rather than forked
and strangely shaped vegetable prototypes.

**NONNO'S
TIP**
Once you find good, viable seed, stick to it,
as it can often be hard to come by.

**KITCHEN
TIP**
Use them swiftly as they quickly turn limp after harvest.
Best roasted.

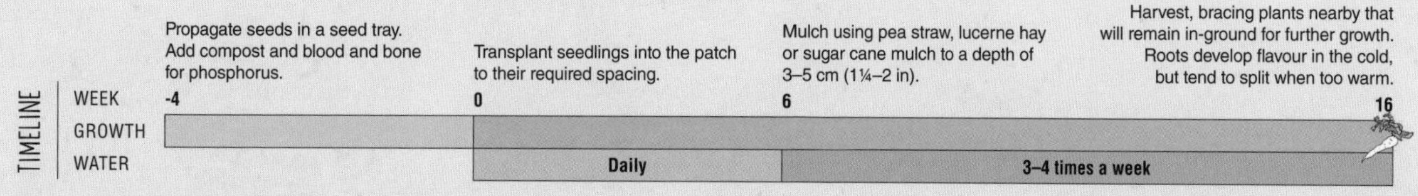

TIMELINE					
		Propagate seeds in a seed tray. Add compost and blood and bone for phosphorus.	Transplant seedlings into the patch to their required spacing.	Mulch using pea straw, lucerne hay or sugar cane mulch to a depth of 3–5 cm (1¼–2 in).	Harvest, bracing plants nearby that will remain in-ground for further growth. Roots develop flavour in the cold, but tend to split when too warm.
	WEEK	-4	0	6	16
	GROWTH				
	WATER		Daily	3–4 times a week	

PARSLEY

	1	2	3	4	5
EASY TO GROW					
SMALL SPACE SUITABILITY					
YIELD VALUE					
JE NE SAIS QUOI/PLEASURE					

When to plant
ZONE 1 Sep–Apr   ZONE 3 Anytime
ZONE 2 Sep–May   ZONE 4 Anytime

Best grown from
Seedling

Depth
1 cm (½ in)

Spacing
40–50 cm (1 ft 4 in–1 ft 8 in)

Time to 1st harvest
30–45 days

Ideal pH level
6.0–7.0

Favourite small-space variety
Italian (flat-leaf)

Best suited to
Wall, pots, in-ground

Common problems
Whitefly, rats

To put it simply, parsley invented globalisation. It is a staple of many culinary traditions, spanning cultures and climates in a way that would make the most ardent free-trade advocates drool. From tabbouleh to chimichurri, parsley butter to salsa verde, it has a way of fitting in with anything, yet can also be eaten on its own as a breath freshener.

Rich in vitamin C and iron, parsley is a robust, self-seeding herb. It has a long tap root, which allows the plant to access deep water in drier conditions. In the absence of frost, we are able to grow it year-round, but a single plant is only good for about 6 months before it gets exhausted and begins to seed. Parsley foliage will benefit greatly from a fortnightly water with liquid seaweed solution, which will quickly replenish nutrients.

For those choosing between flat-leaf (Italian) or curly leaf, we have found that the curly varieties tend to take the heat better but flat-leaf is more palatable. On the other hand, as our friend Sam likes to say, 'the curls get the girls'. Too many choices cause stress, so you may as well grow both!

NONNO'S TIP
Parsley seeds are incredibly small and hard, making them difficult to propagate. If you're intent on earning your veggie patch stripes, soak them in warm water with a dash of dishwashing liquid for a few hours to help break down the coating and encourage more success in propagation.

KITCHEN TIP
Cut stalks and leaves will survive a long time on a benchtop or in the fridge when placed in a cup of water.

TIMELINE

Prepare soil with compost and slow-release all-round fertiliser and plant seedlings directly to the patch. Choose a planting time that is neither extremely hot or cold. Mulch with pea straw, lucerne hay or sugar cane mulch to a depth of 3–5 cm (1¼–2 in).

Feed monthly with liquid seaweed solution and pick off any yellowing leaves that can develop early on.

Begin harvesting in moderation, taking from the more mature outer stems, allowing the younger inner growth to develop.

Production becomes so prolific you wonder if you'll ever be without it, but this is followed by seed heads that need to be continually cut back to refocus growth. Eventually it'll give in and you'll need to replant.

WEEK	0	4	6	16
GROWTH				
WATER	Daily		3–4 times a week	

PASSIONFRUIT

	1	2	3	4	5
EASY TO GROW					
SMALL SPACE SUITABILITY					
YIELD VALUE					
JE NE SAIS QUOI/PLEASURE					

When to plant
ZONE 1 Nov–Feb   ZONE 3 Aug–Apr
ZONE 2 Sep–Mar   ZONE 4 Anytime

Best grown from
Grafted seedling

Depth
To the base of the roots

Spacing
2 m (6 ft 6 in)

Time to 1st harvest
6–12 months

Ideal pH level
5.5–6.5

Favourite small-space variety
Nellie Kelly

Best suited to
Pots, in-ground

Common problems
Excessive sucker growth from its roots

My first share house had a dusty old passionfruit along the back fence and, although it sometimes produced tempting fruit, most of us were too afraid to go near it. The overgrown plant served as a spider den of sin as well as a decorative wall covering. Who were we to disrupt this important business? Nevertheless, our plant emphasised two important passionfruit qualities: its relentless vigour and the importance of pruning.

Anything that grows quickly has high nutrient and water needs, and passionfruit is no exception. During the summer, a monthly feed with seaweed extract will fuel it to produce new growth, while an application of liquid potash will help towards fruit production. Passionfruit originated in the Amazon and therefore does best in warm/tropical conditions. However, hybrids/grafted varieties have been developed to tolerate cooler climates. Its love of heat is equally matched by its intolerance of wind, so be sure to plant in a warm, protected location.

The vine can be trained up trellises and along walls. All it needs is a little bit of wire and encouragement. Fruit only sets on new growth, so we give our own vines a hard, lavender-like pruning to a third of their original size at the end of winter. Light pruning during the summer will allow more light to reach/ripen fruit and discourage fungal disease. When planted in spring, vines should bear fruit within about 6 months and continue to be productive over the next 5 years.

NONNO'S TIP Choose a well-grafted variety that has both male and female parts for pollination and beware of suckers shooting from the root zone.

KITCHEN TIP Fruit keeps well long after a harvest and even the most shrivelled dog scrotum of a fruit can have sweet flesh inside.

TIMELINE

WEEK	-2	0	4	8	26	52

Prepare your best A-grade space with plenty of compost and chicken manure that is high in nitrogen. **(-2)**

Plant seedling, preferably a grafted variety that will flower and fruit off the same vine, or plant both a female and male plant. Make sure you have an extensive trellising system set up from the outset. Mulch with 3–5 cm (1¼–2 in) of pea straw or lucerne hay. **(0)**

A heavy feeder, the passionfruit will appreciate a monthly feed with a liquid seaweed solution. **(4)**

Attach the vine to a trellis as it grows. Remove any sucker growth that flares from the root zone. Anything below the graft point will need to be cut off. **(8)**

Give another application of compost and some slow-release nitrogen-rich fertiliser and re-mulch around its base. **(26)**

First-year fruiting is not often prolific, but in ideal conditions the plant will quickly increase its output. Fruit is ready when it begins to dry and hollow out. **(52)**

GROWTH

WATER   Daily   3–4 times a week

PEAS

	1	2	3	4	5
EASY TO GROW					
SMALL SPACE SUITABILITY					
YIELD VALUE					
JE NE SAIS QUOI/PLEASURE					

When to plant
ZONE 1 Mar–May
      Sep–Dec
ZONE 2 Mar–Jun
      Sep–Nov

ZONE 3 Mar–Aug
ZONE 4 Apr–Jun

Best grown from
Seed

Depth
2–3 cm (¾–1¼ in)

Spacing
20–30 cm (8–12 in)

Time to 1st harvest
60–75 days

Ideal pH level
6.0–7.0

Favourite small-space variety
Sugar snap pea

Best suited to
Pots, in-ground

Common problems
Rats, stem rot, powdery mildew

We all have our Achilles heel. Zoolander's was turning left. Mine is growing peas any larger than a bite-sized pod – and that's because peas provide the ultimate vegetable snack-age. There are few tastier times in the patch than when peas are in season and those sweet, crunchy snacks litter the foliage.

Their bounty aside, peas also provide benefit to the garden as a whole, injecting the soil with nitrogen as they grow. After those greedy summer vegetables – such as tomatoes, sweet corn, zucchini (courgettes), etc. – your soil will be depleted of that essential element and in need of replenishment. Planting peas in the spaces that these crops once occupied will help redress the imbalance because, along with broad beans and other legumes, peas produce their own nitrogen.

The difference between a tiny bite-sized pod or a proper mouthful is about 2 weeks and a lot of willpower. Given that pods are sweetest when young, it's that difficult compromise between taste and yield. Remember that harvesting frees up your plants for more production, so it's in everyone's best interest to keep the good times rolling.

NONNO'S TIP
Soaking the seed overnight prior to planting gives the pea a full body of water. This will help break down the tough exterior coating and then can be used by the seed over the first 3-4 days leading up to germination. Try not to overwater them during the first few days after planting as they can become susceptible to rat attack.

KITCHEN TIP
While the pods are the prized harvest, the entire plant is edible, from the stem to the leaves and, of course, the flowers. Pea shoots are a fantastic addition to any green salad.

TIMELINE					
	Prepare the soil with compost and ensure it is free draining. Don't over-fertilise with nitrogen. Soak seeds in water overnight and sow directly into the patch at the required spacing. Set up a trellis to enable pea tendrils to grab hold.	Thin out any extra seedlings and use in your salads. Mulch to a depth of 3–5 cm (1¼–2 in) using sugar cane mulch. If seedlings are disappearing overnight, you may have a possum or rodent problem, so act if necessary.	Apply liquid potassium to encourage flower development and setting of pods.	Picking pods will encourage more to develop, so harvest accordingly. Use milk spray to control powdery mildew.	For those growing in-ground, chop up plants and integrate through the soil post-harvest. This will fix the soil with more nitrogen for the next lot of hungry feeders.
WEEK	0	4	12	14	20
GROWTH					
WATER		3–4 times a week			

POTATO

	1	2	3	4	5
EASY TO GROW					
SMALL SPACE SUITABILITY					
YIELD VALUE					
JE NE SAIS QUOI/PLEASURE					

When to plant
ZONE 1 Sep–Jan
ZONE 2 Sep–Dec
ZONE 3 Aug–Oct
ZONE 4 Apr–May

Best grown from
Seed potatoes (they're like normal potatoes, but sold at nurseries or online and guaranteed to be disease-free).

Depth
10–20 cm (4–8 in)

Spacing
30–40 cm (1 ft–1ft 4 in)

Time to 1st harvest
75–130 days

Ideal pH level
4.8–6.5

Favourite small-space variety
All blue (indeterminant)

Best suited to
In-ground, large pot (try a potato tower)

Common problems
Potato blight

There are few plants more comforting than a potato. Whether you have it fried, baked, boiled, puréed, scalloped, or as latkes or gnocchi, potatoes rule the kitchen and our hearts. Potatoes are also valuable for their ability to break up soil in the patch.

Ideal growing conditions are cool and overcast with consistent moisture – basically, the UK. Of the thousands of varieties, representing a diversity of climates, pest/disease resistance, shapes, colours and taste, we have limited our diet to a bare few. To broaden your repertoire, source some weird and wonderful seed potatoes from a local nursery. Expose them to indirect light until they produce shoots and choose a site not previously occupied by tomato, eggplant, onion or chilli. Now, you are ready to plant (see Tubers, page 105).

The practice of 'earthing' is to repeatedly cover shoots with 20 cm (8 in) of soil/manure as they push through to the surface. **DETERMINANT** or short-season potatoes can be covered once and then shoots are allowed to turn to leaves. These tubers will mature to harvest in about 70–100 days. **INDETERMINANT** varieties will yield a bigger, albeit later harvest (110–140 days). The shoots of these varieties can be repeatedly earthed to increase the yield (three cycles is about enough). Each time the shoots are covered, a new level of tubers will form.

Harvesting is always a surprise party, as we never know what quantities of edible treasure we will discover under the surface.

NONNO'S TIP If growing an indeterminant variety, consider growing in a spud tower or a felt pot for the best results.

KITCHEN TIP Washing potatoes shortens their storage life, so leave them caked with soil until just before cooking.

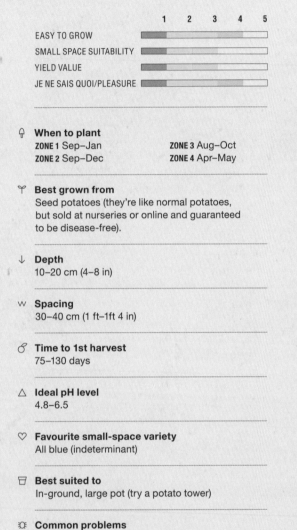

TIMELINE

WEEK / GROWTH / WATER

-2: Integrate plenty of compost and nitrogen-rich fertiliser in the soil, and dig through some lucerne hay or pea straw.

0: Plant the sprouting potatoes, making sure each piece has one or two eyelets. Cover with 10–20 cm (4–8 in) of soil and water in with liquid seaweed solution, which you can reapply every fortnight. For indeterminant varieties, we like using a separate pot or making a potato tower, as they are easy to empty out upon harvesting. Mulch with a 5 cm (2 in) layer of lucerne hay or pea straw.

8: If growing indeterminant varieties, cover over the foliage with a 10–15 cm (4–6 in) layer of compost, encouraging another level of potatoes to develop. Mulch with a 5 cm (2 in) layer of lucerne hay or pea straw.

12: Repeat the process of covering over the growth with compost. Mulch with a 5 cm (2 in) layer of lucerne hay or pea straw.

16: Harvest time. This is the most fun when you can empty out your pot or tower and easily hunt for the treasure. Potatoes store well in-ground when conditions are cool and dry.

20

3–4 times a week

PUMPKIN (WINTER SQUASH)

	1	2	3	4	5
EASY TO GROW					
SMALL SPACE SUITABILITY					
YIELD VALUE					
JE NE SAIS QUOI/PLEASURE					

When to plant
ZONE 1 Oct–Dec   ZONE 3 Aug–Jan
ZONE 2 Sep–Dec   ZONE 4 Mar–Sep

Best grown from
Seed

Depth
2–3 cm (¾–1¼ in)

Spacing
1 m (3 ft 3 in)

Time to 1st harvest
90+ days

Ideal pH level
6.5–7.0

Favourite small-space variety
Small sugar

Best suited to
In-ground

Common problems
Whitefly, powdery mildew

Sometimes there's no space for the big boys and girls of the vegetable world in a small-space garden. Shrinking property sizes go hand in hand with smaller patches to weave our green magic. And when we do get around to waving our wand, something as bold as a pumpkin rarely eventuates.

A sprawling mess of vine punctuated by burgeoning jack-o-lanterns can feel more like a scene out of an off-the-grid organic Halloween gardening magazine than our cluttered urban reality. But even when real estate is at an absolute premium there will be ways to accommodate all that the gardening gods have to offer, and it'd be rude to turn your nose up at the pumpkin.

While there are some varieties that love to go on and on and on – much like a Bollywood movie – there are also those that grow large enough to house a border collie. Thus, your choice of variety has never been a more important decision. If, for example, you have a bad back, you probably shouldn't consider growing an Atlantic giant or any other jumbo pumpkins. Alternatively, if you have a point to prove, or need to compensate for your gardening inadequacies, by all means go jumbo.

NONNO'S TIP
There's nothing more frustrating than a whole lot of vine hoo-ha occupying your real estate and few female flowers being fertilised to produce fruit. See Hand Pollination (page 244).

KITCHEN TIP
When harvesting pumpkins, make sure to cut the stem 3–5 cm (1¼–2 in) from the fruit to make sure it keeps properly. This is important because pumpkins will develop more flavour when allowed to mature for a number of months off the vine.

Integrate the patch with slow-release nitrogen-rich fertiliser and sow seeds in small mounds of compost after the last frost. Incubate seedlings with plastic bottles and choose an open space where the plant's vine can roam, or climb vertically. The trellis will need to be strong to hold the sizeable fruit.

Give monthly applications of liquid seaweed solution and mulch to a depth of 3–5 cm (1¼–2 in) using pea straw, lucerne hay or sugar cane mulch.

If growing vertically, make sure that as the vines grow you attach them properly to the trellis. Those sprawling at ground level will shoot secondary roots into soil that helps ground them and provide further energy for the plant.

Apply liquid potassium to encourage flower growth and development of the fruit. If you notice fruit forming and then quickly dying, it's a sign you need to hand pollinate.

Prune off the growth tips of the vine to help redirect energy into the developing fruit. Use milk spray to control any powdery mildew.

TIMELINE	WEEK	0	4	8	12	14	20
	GROWTH						
	WATER	Daily			3–4 times a week		

RADISH

	1	2	3	4	5
EASY TO GROW					
SMALL SPACE SUITABILITY					
YIELD VALUE					
JE NE SAIS QUOI/PLEASURE					

When to plant
ZONE 1 Sep–Jun ZONE 3 Anytime
ZONE 2 Anytime ZONE 4 Anytime

Best grown from
Seed

Depth
1 cm (½ in)

Spacing
5 cm (2 in)

Time to 1st harvest
30–45 days

Ideal pH level
6.5–7.0

Favourite small-space variety
Cherry belle

Best suited to
Pots, wall, in-ground

Common problems
Slugs, poor seed quality

The radish is one of those vegetables that constantly surprises as you begin to explore the heirloom varieties available to the home grower. Rainbow, watermelon, white icicle, rat's tail, purple plum ... the list of fanciful names and unusually shaped, coloured and textured varieties makes the radish the tomato of the root world.

The ultimate confidence booster, the radish is the perfect introduction to gardening newbies or those who haven't yet mastered the art. A small-space specialist that gives almost instant gratification, it gets close to top marks in our rating system. And speaking from the perspective of a generation that is often defined by our short attention spans and love for instant gratification, the radish may just be our champion.

Sourcing good quality seed is paramount to your success, so always purchase from a reputable supplier and store excess seed properly – in a cool, dry place. If you want to introduce your kids to the biology of food, grow radish with them. It's a journey that takes you from sowing to germination and finally to harvesting, sometimes within the space of a month.

NONNO'S **TIP** Most of the troubleshooting with radishes begins if they are left to mature too long in the veggie patch. So catch them early before the slugs, and before splitting, which can occur when watering practices are less than ideal.

KITCHEN **TIP** Radishes are best eaten fresh, though try pickling excess radish to have them keep longer and to change their flavour dimension.

TIMELINE

WEEK	0		4		8		12
GROWTH							
WATER				Daily			

Add compost and blood and bone for phosphorus. Sow seeds directly to the patch.

Thin out seedlings to a spacing of 10–15 cm (4–6 in) and mulch using pea straw, lucerne hay or sugar cane mulch to a depth of 3–5 cm (1¼–2 in). For staggered and successive harvest, plant the next batch of seeds now.

Begin harvesting leaves as salad greens, but distribute among the plants evenly so as not to affect their growth. Beware of snails and slugs leaving holes in your developing roots and act accordingly.

Harvest roots, bracing plants nearby that will remain in-ground for further growth. We prefer to take them when they are young and bitey, as they tend to become aerated and fibrous when left to overcook in the ground.

RHUBARB

	1	2	3	4	5
EASY TO GROW					
SMALL SPACE SUITABILITY					
YIELD VALUE					
JE NE SAIS QUOI/PLEASURE					

When to plant
ZONE 1 Oct–Dec   ZONE 3 Aug–Oct
ZONE 2 Sep–Dec   ZONE 4 Not suitable

Best grown from
Crown (rhizome)

Depth
Top of the rhizome covered with a few centimetres of soil.

Spacing
1 m (3 ft 3 in)

Time to 1st harvest
150+ days

Ideal pH level
6.0–6.8

Favourite small-space variety
Lilibarber

Best suited to
Pots, in-ground

Common problems
Snails and slugs

The thought of rhubarb conjures fond memories of Greek yoghurt with stewed rhubarb on top, or sweet fruit crumbles packed with scarlet stems. The flavour is like no other, offering a unique tart sweetness. Rhubarb has also been credited for curing everything from stuttering to gambling addictions. After all, anything that is this colour has got to be either great for you or toxic. Rhubarb is both.

Unlike most leafy plants, we prize rhubarb for its stems alone. Leaves are toxic and are unfit for human and animal consumption. No doubt there were more than a few stomach aches going around as early humans worked this one out.

Rhubarb is a hardy, resilient perennial rhizome (see Rhizomes, page 104) that can survive even the hardest freezes when covered in a layer of compost and mulch. It's best planted with the cuttings from another crown and shouldn't really be harvested until well established. Plants will produce for around 10 years, but every few years the stems will become visibly crowded and thin. You'll need to divide the root bulb (best to do this in late autumn). Share your divided rhubarb around to become the most popular gardener on the block.

NONNO'S TIP
Don't be precious with your plant. At the end of the growing season, cut back stems right to the ground and cover with 10 cm (4 in) of compost. Divide the plant by cutting through the crown, ensuring you have sprouting 'eyes' on the pieces you pull apart. These can then be planted directly into the veggie patch.

KITCHEN TIP
Nearly all rhubarb leaves are toxic to eat due to the level of oxalic acid they contain. However, the leaves of the Lilibarber variety are edible. So, unless growing this variety, use only the stalks. Try oven-roasting the stalks for about 5–10 minutes (prepared by sprinkling some sugar over them) and then mix them through a garden salad.

TIMELINE

	WEEK							
	-2	0	4	12	16		30	48

Prepare the soil with plenty of compost and chook manure. **(-2)**

Plant as a crown, covering the top with a few centimetres of compost. **(0)**

The plant begins to shoot new growth. Mulch to a depth of 3–5 cm (1¼–2 in) using pea straw, lucerne hay or sugar cane mulch. **(4)**

Feed with compost. **(12)**

Begin to harvest, taking from the more mature outer stems and working in. The leaves are inedible, so these should be composted. **(16)**

Any extra plants that shoot from the root zone can be carefully taken from the plant and grown elsewhere in the garden. **(30)**

Cut back prior to the break of spring and feed again with compost and chook manure. Plants are productive for a number of years. **(48)**

GROWTH

WATER — 3–4 times a week

ROCKET (ARUGULA)

	1	2	3	4	5
EASY TO GROW					
SMALL SPACE SUITABILITY					
YIELD VALUE					
JE NE SAIS QUOI/PLEASURE					

When to plant
ZONE 1 Sep–May
ZONE 2 Sep–Jun
ZONE 3 Anytime
ZONE 4 Mar–Sep

Best grown from
Seed

Depth
1 cm (½ in)

Spacing
20 cm (8 in)

Time to 1st harvest
45+ days

Ideal pH level
6.5–7.0

Favourite small-space variety
Astro

Best suited to
Wall, pots, in-ground

Common problems
White cabbage moth, bolting to seed

A job, home and Radiohead's *OK Computer* are all basic requirements of living, and without one of them life would quickly begin to hollow out. The same could be said in relation to the garden. There are some needs so basic that without them it starts to feel a little empty. Having rocket in your veggie patch is one of those.

Perhaps it is my Italian heritage, but a veggie patch without rocket is just not a veggie patch. Rocket, or arugula as it is also known, is the evergreen, ever-ready leafy green that fills the patch at any time of the year in almost all regions of our country. Perhaps the most challenging thing about this perennial performer is keeping up with production. A rocket plant loaded with leaf matter will quickly bolt to seed when ignored for picking. But on the upside, this produces perfectly edible, peppery flowers, and the very good chance of self-seeding plants to follow.

NONNO'S TIP
It's a constant battle to stay on top of seeding, so pick regularly to prevent bolting. In the case that it does, cut flower heads to the stem base of the plants and pick the flowers to use in your next garden salad.

KITCHEN TIP
The light and peppery foliage is the perfect accompaniment to a heavy Sunday pasta ragu.

TIMELINE

	WEEK	0	2		6	8	12	16
	GROWTH							
	WATER				Daily			

Add compost to the patch and plant seeds directly into the soil.

Apply a fortnightly application of liquid seaweed solution.

Thin seedlings so that remaining plants have the room to mature and then mulch to a depth of 3–5 cm (1¼–2 in) using pea straw, lucerne hay or sugar cane mulch.

Leaf by leaf harvesting is encouraged for a perpetual harvest. Take more mature outer leaves and work your way in, leaving enough foliage on each plant to properly reproduce. Pick any seed heads that prematurely develop.

Continue in the same fashion until the rocket becomes too bitter, or the foliage toughens up.

SILVERBEET (SWISS CHARD)

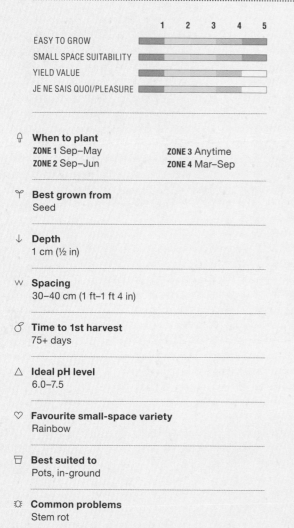

	1	2	3	4	5
EASY TO GROW					
SMALL SPACE SUITABILITY					
YIELD VALUE					
JE NE SAIS QUOI/PLEASURE					

When to plant
ZONE 1 Sep–May
ZONE 2 Sep–Jun
ZONE 3 Anytime
ZONE 4 Mar–Sep

Best grown from
Seed

Depth
1 cm (½ in)

Spacing
30–40 cm (1 ft–1 ft 4 in)

Time to 1st harvest
75+ days

Ideal pH level
6.0–7.5

Favourite small-space variety
Rainbow

Best suited to
Pots, in-ground

Common problems
Stem rot

There comes a time when we need to boost our confidence a little bit. A small success is often all we need to get into a rhythm and, once again, reach our own high standards. Fortunately for edible gardeners, there is a plant called silverbeet – the ultimate gardening rebound.

Silverbeet, known in North America as Swiss chard, is a robust and diplomatic leafy green that is decisively neutral to the seasons. It can be planted all-year-round, provided the environment isn't extremely hot or cold, so it's a ready tenant whenever new garden real estate becomes available. For us, however, we like to use all our available space for summer veggies during the hot months, so at the Little Veggie Patch Co silverbeet has become a de facto winter crop.

Although it is part of the beet family, silverbeet does not have an edible root bulb (or any root bulb for that matter), but does come in a variety of colours that would suitably impress the fussiest of peacocks. Rainbow chard has stalks so colourful you will wonder if you haven't stepped out of your garden and into Chagall's studio. A single plant should steadily produce for 12 months or more. It's so safe and reliable ... so Swiss.

NONNO'S TIP
Silverbeet is one of the enduring and everlasting leafy greens. Try to harvest often to maintain more tender leaves. However, even when the plant goes to seed, the leaves do not turn bitter like others. The main issue with seeding silverbeet is the size they grow and the space they begin to occupy, though this may take 12 months to happen.

KITCHEN TIP
Great as a substitute for spinach in a spanikopita, silverbeet can also be used liberally in the frying pan to bulk up breakfasts (we like it accompanied with olive oil and garlic).

TIMELINE

	WEEK	-4	0	8	10	16	20
	GROWTH						
	WATER		Daily		3–4 times a week		

Propagate in a seed tray and prepare the patch with plenty of compost.

Transplant into the patch on a day that is not too hot or too cold and space out at half of that required for mature plants.

Thin out seedlings to required spacing and mulch with pea straw, lucerne hay or sugar cane to a depth of 3–5 cm (1¼–2 in).

Begin to harvest leaf by leaf in moderation, picking from the more mature outer leaves and then working your way in.

Production is in full swing. Continue to take leaf by leaf, but more regularly. Plants can be picked for over a year and will become the powerhouse of the patch. They are indestructible now. Even when they go to seed, the flavour of the foliage stays consistent.

SPINACH

	1	2	3	4	5
EASY TO GROW					
SMALL SPACE SUITABILITY					
YIELD VALUE					
JE NE SAIS QUOI/PLEASURE					

When to plant
ZONE 1 Sep–May   ZONE 3 Anytime
ZONE 2 Sep–Jan   ZONE 4 Mar–Sep

Best grown from
Seed

Depth
1 cm (½ in)

Spacing
20 cm (8 in)

Time to 1st harvest
40–60 days

Ideal pH level
6.0 7.0

Favourite small-space variety
Bloomsdale

Best suited to
Pots, wall, in-ground

Common problems
Snails and slugs, possums

I once went through a period of dating girls with challenging dietary restrictions.* One was raw and vegan, but mostly ate cashews and turmeric. The other was vegetarian, gluten-free, dairy-free and fructose-free. I wish I was joking. Needless to say, we went our separate ways. But in both cases we did find common ground in spinach. Raw or cooked. Dressed or undressed. Spinach doesn't mind. Spinach is an easy-going plant that gets along with everyone.

Spinach is a must in any garden, as it is fast growing and less delicate than other lettuces. In mild climates like our own, spinach will grow year-round. However, we are always moving it around to match the current conditions. We grow spinach in full sun during the cooler months and then find a protected aspect when the seasons heat up.

A good way to keep spinach, and most leafy greens, from bolting to seed is to maintain a steady harvest and water daily. A little bit of neglect will send them packing.

NONNO'S TIP
While in more temperate climates spinach can grow at most times of the year, it does become heat stressed when exposed to afternoon sun. Do your best to keep it on the morning sun side of the patch, and protect it early on when it is most susceptible to pest attack (use something as simple as a plastic bottle cover).

KITCHEN TIP
Pick young leaves frequently to encourage perpetual harvesting and to experience leaves when they are at their most flavoursome.

* Not to say that there is anything wrong with dietary requirements. However, in this case the diets in question were dramatically incompatible with my cheese-loving, salami-bingeing and carb-loading ways.

Propagate in a seed tray and prepare the patch with plenty of compost.

Transplant into the patch on a day that is not too hot or too cold and space out at half of that required for mature plants.

Thin out seedlings to required spacing and mulch with pea straw, lucerne hay or sugar cane to a depth of 3–5 cm (1¼–2 in). Young seedlings are susceptible to overnight patch raids, so provide some protection. Spinach will appreciate monthly applications of a liquid seaweed solution.

Begin to harvest leaf by leaf in moderation, picking from the more mature outer leaves and then working your way in.

Production intensifies and you will need to keep picking with regularity to prevent the plants from bolting to seed. Foliage is best when young and sweet.

TIMELINE	WEEK	-4	0	4	8	12	16
	GROWTH						
	WATER			Daily			

SPRING ONION (SCALLION)

THE LITTLE
VEGGIE PATCH CO
RATING
4.0

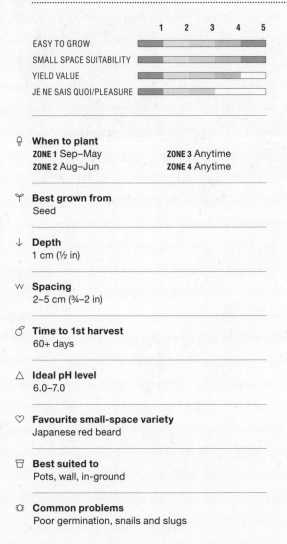

	1	2	3	4	5
EASY TO GROW					
SMALL SPACE SUITABILITY					
YIELD VALUE					
JE NE SAIS QUOI/PLEASURE					

When to plant
ZONE 1 Sep–May   ZONE 3 Anytime
ZONE 2 Aug–Jun   ZONE 4 Anytime

Best grown from
Seed

Depth
1 cm (½ in)

Spacing
2–5 cm (¾–2 in)

Time to 1st harvest
60+ days

Ideal pH level
6.0–7.0

Favourite small-space variety
Japanese red beard

Best suited to
Pots, wall, in-ground

Common problems
Poor germination, snails and slugs

Growing bulbing onions is a slow, steady and space-consuming process. It's the ultimate relationship vegetable – the love of your life, perhaps – but only when you're ready for it. Sometimes we just want to cut loose and party. Let's enjoy the precious moments that we have, but c'mon, you spring onion babe, we don't have long.

The spring onion is a bunching variety that is hardy, fast growing and ideally suited to the home gardener. If you find yourself looking for a confidence booster in the veggie patch, the spring onion is always happy to partner up, whether in spring, or any other time of the year in our parts. In fact, despite its name, the spring onion could easily be the autumn, winter and summer onion, too.

Where our classic, slow-burning, bulbing onion is destined for French cooking, the spring onion finds its natural environment in fast-paced salads and Asian cuisine. Quick and punchy stir fries and fresh on-the-go salads are the perfect partners for this swiftly growing vegetable.

NONNO'S TIP
Rather than harvest the entire onion once ready, cut down at the base of the stem and the shoot will quickly regenerate. This will mean you can have two, three or even four flushes of the same spring onion and a greater yield of produce. Onions left to mature for too long in the ground tend to develop a slimy inner coating. Make sure you don't overcook your onions – whether in the kitchen or in the garden.

KITCHEN TIP
Harvest spring onion flowers for an unexpected and effective ingredient in any meal. Flowers contain thousands of tiny seed blossoms, each with a concentrated onion flavour. Use them fresh or dried.

		Prepare the soil with compost but don't over-fertilise with nitrogen. Rather, add an application of liquid potassium just prior to planting. Transplant into the patch at the required spacing.	Mulch to a depth of 3–5 cm (1¼–2 in) using pea straw, lucerne hay or sugar cane mulch. Apply a monthly dose of liquid seaweed solution.	If onions are too closely bunched together, harvest entire plants to free up space for those that remain.	Cut at the base of the stem to allow the remaining root zone to resprout and provide a perpetual harvest. This can be done until the plants begin to go to seed or turn slimy.
	Propagate in a seed tray.				

TIMELINE

WEEK	-4	0	4	8	12	16
GROWTH						
WATER			Daily		3–4 times a week	

SQUASH

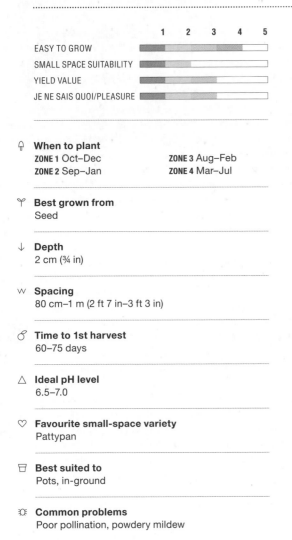

	1	2	3	4	5
EASY TO GROW					
SMALL SPACE SUITABILITY					
YIELD VALUE					
JE NE SAIS QUOI/PLEASURE					

When to plant
ZONE 1 Oct–Dec   ZONE 3 Aug–Feb
ZONE 2 Sep–Jan   ZONE 4 Mar–Jul

Best grown from
Seed

Depth
2 cm (¾ in)

Spacing
80 cm–1 m (2 ft 7 in–3 ft 3 in)

Time to 1st harvest
60–75 days

Ideal pH level
6.5–7.0

Favourite small-space variety
Pattypan

Best suited to
Pots, in-ground

Common problems
Poor pollination, powdery mildew

We love growing squash almost as much as we love eating it – especially the soft-skinned summer squash that comes in an endless selection of shapes, sizes and colours. The lumpier and more irregular they are, the better. They are a true summer vegetable, and few plants look or taste better with grill marks.

Like those perfect summer days, squash comes and goes faster than you would like. Plants grow very quickly and require a lot of nutrients to sustain their pace. Foliage gets large and bushy, but they tend to have relatively shallow and delicate root systems, which means a little extra care should be taken to grow the best possible produce. Consistent watering practices and mulch will go a long way. It's not unusual for leaves to wilt on very hot days, but they will bounce back overnight. We find that our plants grow well when planted among sunflowers and sweet corn. Both companions offer a little extra shade, and sunflowers help to attract much-needed bees to assist with pollination.

Harvest fruit frequently to encourage more production. There is nothing worse than an overcooked, engorged squash sucking the energy out of your plant. It's better to harvest small and even take a few flowers before they fruit.

NONNO'S TIP
Squash and pumpkin (winter squash) are often less productive than they could be, due to poor pollination. Plant with herbs and flowers to encourage more pollinators. Don't be afraid to do it by hand (see page 244).

KITCHEN TIP
Slice into thick pieces, coat in salt and pepper and extra-virgin olive oil and grill on the barbecue. Summer perfection.

Integrate the patch with slow-release nitrogen-rich fertiliser and sow seeds in small mounds of compost after the last frost. In cooler areas it's best to incubate the young seedlings – using open-ended plastic bottles – which will also keep pests at bay.

Give monthly applications of liquid seaweed solution and mulch to a depth of 3–5 cm (1¼–2 in) using pea straw, lucerne hay or sugar cane mulch.

While not typically a vertical climber, they will grow out in a particular direction, which you can manipulate to suit the rest of your garden. Apply liquid potassium to encourage flower and fruit growth. As squash begin to develop, keep watering. Hand pollination may be necessary if fruit sets and then quickly dies off.

Fruiting plants will begin to die back and will be overcome by powdery mildew. Prune off affected leaves and use a milk spray to help control its spread.

TIMELINE	WEEK	0	4	8	12	14	20
	GROWTH						
	WATER		Daily		3–4 times a week		

STRAWBERRY

	1	2	3	4	5
EASY TO GROW					
SMALL SPACE SUITABILITY					
YIELD VALUE					
JE NE SAIS QUOI/PLEASURE					

⚲ **When to plant**
ZONE 1 Oct–Mar   ZONE 3 Anytime
ZONE 2 Sep–Apr   ZONE 4 Anytime

⚑ **Best grown from**
Seedling

↓ **Depth**
1 cm (½ in)

〰 **Spacing**
30–40 cm (1 ft–1 ft 4 in)

♂ **Time to 1st harvest**
120+ days

△ **Ideal pH level**
5.0–6.0

♡ **Favourite small-space variety**
White soul

🏺 **Best suited to**
Pots, wall, in-ground

☼ **Common problems**
Snails and slugs, rats, birds, possums, kids, pet dogs, guests at your house, next-door neighbour …

To say that a strawberry is a fruit is to call Jimmy Hendrix a guitar player. Sure, it's true, but it also misses the point entirely. The strawberry is the ace of the garden and the king of the plate. It is an object of desire equally welcomed in Eros's private bathhouse and in a child's lunchbox. But it's not just daiquiri makers who covet this sweet flesh – rats, slugs, birds and bats are similarly enamoured. Like looking at a campfire, the strawberry stirs some primal longing within all of us.

Although we are all very familiar with the summer-bearing supermarket strawberry, few people realise that there are hundreds of weird and wonderful varieties that you can grow yourself. As is often the case, what we see on the shelves has been selected for commercial characteristics, such as size, yield and disease resistance, often at the expense of taste. There are red, white, blue, black, green and even purple strawberries. Consider the pineberry: a white strawberry with red seeds and a pineapple-like taste. Hands up if you'd like to grow this? Thought so.

Strawberries are also a great small-space variety and prime candidate for growing in a pot or wall garden unit.

NONNO'S TIP Most pests can be avoided by growing the plants off the ground. Because the strawberry is rather shallow rooted, your growing infrastructure doesn't need to be a feat of engineering.

KITCHEN TIP Getting them in the kitchen is more than half the challenge, but once there you don't have to do much. To pull out the flavour in relatively tasteless supermarket fruit, we would dump a bucketload of sugar over them (when no parent was looking). But if you allow the fruit to ripen on the plant, or alongside members of the allium family, you shouldn't have to. That's easier said than done when every garden pest is waiting for them, too.

TIMELINE							
	Add compost and slow-release nitrogen-rich fertiliser. Plant seedlings or runners near any alliums. Mulch with 3–5 cm (1¼–2 in) of pea straw or sugar cane mulch.	Apply a monthly dose of liquid seaweed solution.	Avoid overwetting the foliage during watering, as this makes it more susceptible to fungal diseases.	As the strawberries begin to develop, they become the target of every pest around. Netting is advisable, as well as good snail and slug defences. Growing off the ground is a great way to overcome pests. If you notice runners forming, break them free to refocus energy on fruit production. These can be planted elsewhere in the patch.	Depending on where you live, strawberries can produce over extended periods, particularly in temperate and warmer conditions. However, once winter sets in the older foliage will begin to die back and should be freed up from the plant.	Feed the plants with compost and a slow-release nitrogen-rich fertiliser.	The strawberry plant will produce for a number of years. However, production will peak and then begin to decline after its third year.
WEEK	0	4	8	12	36	48	52
GROWTH							
WATER		Daily			3–4 times a week		

SWEDE (RUTABAGA)

	1	2	3	4	5
EASY TO GROW					
SMALL SPACE SUITABILITY					
YIELD VALUE					
JE NE SAIS QUOI/PLEASURE					

When to plant
ZONE 1 Sep–Nov
Mar–May
ZONE 2 Sep–Nov
Apr–Jun
ZONE 3 Apr–Oct
ZONE 4 May–Jun

Best grown from
Seed

Depth
1 cm (½ in)

Spacing
30–40 cm (11–15 in)

Time to 1st harvest
75–90 days

Ideal pH level
6.0–7.0

Favourite small-space variety
Champion purple

Best suited to
Pots, in-ground, wall (if only growing for foliage)

Common problems
Snails and slugs

There is still some confusion as to the proper scientific difference between a swede and a turnip. Just to create extra confusion, the swede is also commonly referred to as the Swedish turnip. However, the majority view is that a swede is larger and yellow/orange fleshed, while the turnip is smaller and white fleshed. Believed to be a naturally occurring hybrid of the cabbage and turnip, the swede is a cool-climate, frost-tolerant vegetable that is happy to occupy the lesser grade parts of your veggie patch.

Not overly fussy or demanding of either nutrition or sunlight, it will keep well in the ground for long periods of time. This means a long window of opportunity while you harvest its edible greens and decide on a suitable use for it. We suggest slow-cooking the root – roasting, for example – which will intensify its colour and flavour.

NONNO'S TIP
Doesn't require a lot of nitrogen or sunlight, so perfectly suited to your B-grade space.

KITCHEN TIP
They store far better in-ground than in the refrigerator, so only harvest when required.

TIMELINE	WEEK	0	6	12	16
	GROWTH				
	WATER	Daily	3–4 times a week		

Add compost and blood and bone and then sow seeds directly to the patch. They don't demand full sun, so will tolerate a B-grade patch space.

Thin out seedlings to a spacing of approximately 30 cm (12 in) and mulch using pea straw, lucerne hay or sugar cane mulch to a depth of 3–5 cm (1¼–2 in).

Harvest some foliage for salad greens, but do so in moderation.

Harvest roots, bracing plants nearby that will remain in-ground for further growth. Roots keep well in the ground, particularly when the soil temperature is cool, so only harvest as required.

SWEET CORN

THE LITTLE
VEGGIE PATCH CO
RATING
2.9

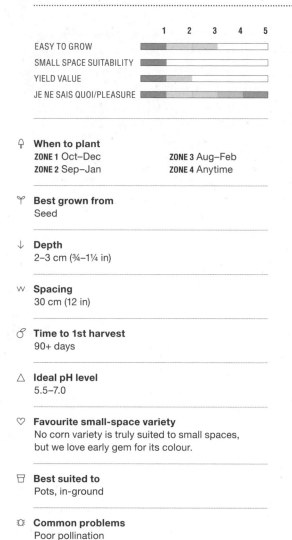

	1	2	3	4	5
EASY TO GROW					
SMALL SPACE SUITABILITY					
YIELD VALUE					
JE NE SAIS QUOI/PLEASURE					

When to plant
ZONE 1 Oct–Dec
ZONE 2 Sep–Jan
ZONE 3 Aug–Feb
ZONE 4 Anytime

Best grown from
Seed

Depth
2–3 cm (¾–1¼ in)

Spacing
30 cm (12 in)

Time to 1st harvest
90+ days

Ideal pH level
5.5–7.0

Favourite small-space variety
No corn variety is truly suited to small spaces,
but we love early gem for its colour.

Best suited to
Pots, in-ground

Common problems
Poor pollination

Whole societies have been built on and continue to be fuelled by corn. Our feeling is that half the world would fall apart and turn to dust if corn suddenly ceased to exist. It is more than just a crop, it is a critical food commodity – and in the home garden, nothing is more impressive than a patch bursting with its lanky stems swaying in the summer sun. Corn goes with scarecrows and veggie patches much like butter goes with toast in the morning. One without the other leaves a dry and unsatisfied feeling.

Growing corn on a commercial scale is entirely different to growing it in a small-space garden. As cobs rely on each other to pollinate properly, planting in a grid of at least 12–16 plants is advised. Any less will have you gambling on the cobs. Some may be fully kernelled while others will look more like your grandfather's teeth if he decided to remove his dentures.

Of course, not many of us have the space to grow 16 corn plants on our balconies, but that's ok. There is a way to hand pollinate (see Nonno's Tip) that will ensure its dentures are fully capped with succulent, juicy kernels.

NONNO'S TIP In small-space gardens where only a few corn plants are growing, hand-pollinate by breaking off the tips of the plant (that carry the pollen) and dust the silks of the developing cobs. Even on commercial-scale farms, this practice is used along the outer perimeter where full development of the kernels can also be problematic.

KITCHEN TIP Char on the barbecue and then coat in butter, dust in smoky paprika and finish off with grated parmesan cheese.

TIMELINE

	WEEK	-2	0	4	8	12	16	20
	GROWTH							
	WATER				3–4 times a week			

Prepare soil with plenty of compost and nitrogen-rich chook manure.

Sow seeds directly into the patch at the required spacing, sowing two seeds per hole. Sow cucumber at the same time (if doing the three sisters companion planting).

Thin seedlings if both seeds have germinated and mulch with 3–5 cm (1¼–2 in) of lucerne hay or pea straw. Feed fortnightly with liquid seaweed solution. Sow climbing beans if doing the three sisters companion planting.

Apply compost around the base of the plants for an extra mid-season feed and to help them form stronger roots.

As the tassels form on top of the plant, and the cobs and silks below, routinely shake the plant to help transfer the pollen from the male to the female parts. This helps fuller cobs set.

When growing just a few corn plants, it is advisable to hand pollinate the silks by brushing the tassel along it. When the silks have browned off, they are ready for picking. To harvest, twist by hand and pull down.

TOMATO

	1	2	3	4	5
EASY TO GROW					
SMALL SPACE SUITABILITY					
YIELD VALUE					
JE NE SAIS QUOI/PLEASURE					

When to plant
ZONE 1 Oct–Dec   ZONE 3 Aug–Jan
ZONE 2 Sep–Jan   ZONE 4 Mar–Jul

Best grown from
Seed – propagate in trays and transplant into the patch.

Depth
1 cm (½ in)

Spacing
60 cm (2 ft)

Time to 1st harvest
75–90 days

Ideal pH level
5.5–7.0

Favourite small-space variety
Tumbling tom

Best suited to
Pots, in-ground

Common problems
Aphids, blight

With more than 3000 varieties, there is one for everyone and the tomato you fall in love with could as easily be red and round, as it could be purple and brain-shaped.

There is no more important fruit anywhere in the world, so despite the challenging nature of the tomato, anyone who's anyone will rush out and plant one in spring. Beginners, intermediates and the pros – everyone wants a piece of this A-lister. There is no such thing as an expert here. Even those who have grown plants, saved seeds and perpetuated the strongest genes for decades still harbour a level of unease at what the season will throw at them.

All styles differ, whether that's the variety you choose (cherry, staking, bush), the infrastructure or maintenance – to pinch or not to pinch is one of life's enduring questions. There are so many variables you won't find the same two set-ups anywhere.

The key to a successful tilt is timing. While every bone in your body seeks the soft touch of its fruit and the smell of the foliage on your skin, patience is a virtue. Once the dodgy weather has passed and the soil temperature is nudging 20°C (68°F), you will again be reunited with your favourite fruit.

NONNO'S TIP
There are few companion planting partnerships as strong as tomato and basil, so make sure to plant basil around the base of the plants. Prune the tomato's lower branches as it begins to grow, allowing more airflow for the initial clusters of fruit that develop.

KITCHEN TIP
Vine-ripened fruit is the ultimate goal, but early on it can be a race between you and the caterpillars, possums or rats. If you notice fruit being spoiled once the skin turns to the third hue of red, pick at the second and then let it ripen further in the fruit bowl.

	Propagate seeds in a tray, making sure they are well-incubated. Meanwhile, prepare the soil with plenty of compost and nitrogen-rich chook manure.	Plant seedlings once the last frost is long gone, spacing at half the distance for a mature plant. Establish a trellising system if growing varieties that require it. Plant basil. Mulch with a 3–5 cm (1¼–2 in) of lucerne hay or pea straw.	Give a fortnightly feed with liquid seaweed solution and pinch out bilateral growth tips to encourage a strong, well-shaped plant.	Make sure to routinely attach the plant's foliage to the trellis or it can quickly get out of control. Use soft twine and tie to the stake first, and then around the plant. Continue to pinch out bilateral growth tips.	Apply liquid potassium to help with flower development and setting of fruit. Over-fertilising with nitrogen will inhibit flower development or cause them to drop at the expense of foliage.	As the plant produces fruit, it naturally begins to die back. Snip off as you notice them. If you notice blossom end rot, don't panic. It generally abates with later fruit. If you notice caterpillars, apply dipel to control.
WEEK	-4	0	4	8	12	14 20
GROWTH						
WATER		Daily			3–4 times a week	

TIMELINE

TOMATO LIFE CYCLE

1 PROPAGATING

Seeds can be propagated during the end of winter and beginning of spring. Don't be stressed about getting young seedlings into the ground at the earliest possible moment. You need to be patient as young seedlings are intolerant of the cold. A mini greenhouse is always recommended for germinating seeds as they incubate your little babies at night and help retain moisture in the soil. Without the greenhouse effect, your small pots will dry faster than a towel in the Atacama Desert.

2 PREPARING SOIL

Tomatoes are hungry nitrogen feeders, so it's best to plant them where you have just grown broad beans or peas in the cool season. In addition to the help those previous plants provided – flooding the soil with nitrogen as they grew – some solid soil preparation is needed. A few weeks prior to planting, mix in compost and well-rotted/pelletised chook poo, loading it with the nutrition required for sustained tomato growth.

3 TRANSPLANTING

Timing is everything here. Don't transplant your babies on a severe weather day – that means, not too hot or too cold – and do it in the morning. Water seedlings 30 minutes before transplant, and have stakes at the ready (if not in place already). Have basil at the ready too. These two friends are a constant inspiration to each other.

4 PROTECTING

Tomatoes have little tolerance for frost or cool weather, so those with an early start on the growing season should protect young, delicate seedlings from any cool changes. It's easy to make an improvised greenhouse using a soft drink bottle with the base cut off. Just be sure to remove the lid.

5 STAKING

Unless you're planting tumbling/bush varieties, tomatoes will need staking immediately. A central stake will be crucial early on, keeping your clumsy seedlings upright and preventing them from getting wind damaged. Drive the stakes in early, when the soil isn't full of delicate tomato roots.

6 MULCHING

This is such an important part of growing tomatoes. Mulching the soil with a 3–4 cm (1¼–2 in) layer of pea straw, sugar cane or lucerne hay will help suppress weeds, retain moisture, keep a consistent soil temperature and feed your hungry plants. Do I need to say more?

7 PINCHING

To pinch or not to pinch? One of life's enduring questions. I sit on the pinch side of the fence and routinely pinch out the bilateral growth tips. This allows better airflow and helps shape a stronger, more defined plant, one that is better able to cope with fruit production.

8 KEEPING IT TIDY

The garden should be your happy place, but keeping it untidy makes it the happy place for a lot of pests and diseases. Keep the patch tidy and in order, meaning free of weeds, mulched well and well hydrated (consistent watering helps prevent blossom end rot and reduces plant stress). A hygienic patch is particularly important once fruiting commences and all parties want in on the action.

9 MORE STAKING

As the plants grow, they'll need to be attached to the trellising framework to help support their own weight – not only their current weight, but the weight they'll be when they're producing lovely precious fruit. Some varieties have tomatoes that grow up to 1 kg (2 lb 3 oz) per fruit, and while they won't break free from the vine, they will bring the entire plant crashing to the ground.

10 ADDING POTASSIUM

With all the compost and poo in your soil, there can often be an imbalance that means you grow monster tomato plants with insufficient flowering and fruiting. A mid-season hit of potassium will turn things in your favour, helping the plant develop and then set flowers into fruit.

11 HARVESTING

Though the first tomatoes of the season will always be a gamble, consider harvesting the early ones when they're a touch green. Birds, caterpillars, rats, possums and next-door neighbours all have a sixth sense about ripening tomatoes, so pick early and ripen them in the bowl.

TUBERS (TURMERIC, GINGER, HORSERADISH, WASABI)

	1	2	3	4	5
EASY TO GROW					
SMALL SPACE SUITABILITY					
YIELD VALUE					
JE NE SAIS QUOI/PLEASURE					

When to plant
ZONE 1 Oct–Dec   ZONE 3 Aug–Dec
ZONE 2 Sep–Jan   ZONE 4 Mar–Oct

Best grown from
Tuber

Depth
The top of the tuber covered over with a few centimetres of soil.

Spacing
30–50 cm (1 ft–1 ft 8 in)

Time to 1st harvest
90+ days

Ideal pH level
5.5–7.0

Favourite small-space variety
Turmeric

Best suited to
Pots, in-ground

Common problems
Rotting

Potatoes aren't the only tuber in the garden, though they do seem to steal all of the headlines. Turmeric, ginger, horseradish and wasabi are all part of this group of mysterious subterranean dwellers. Although they are not prolifically planted in the home garden, they are relatively straightforward to grow and perfectly suited to pots.

All tubers love a loose and friable soil that allows easier passage of the roots. You need to ensure it is free draining and won't become boggy or waterlogged, as that can cause rotting. This is achieved in a good quality potting mix, but when planting in the ground make sure to loosen the surface and incorporate plenty of organic matter.

The break of spring is the best time for planting and division of roots, and most prefer a warmer climate to thrive; however, ideal conditions do vary from plant to plant. Wasabi, for example, loves the temperate regions, while ginger prefers more tropical climes. All, however, are sun-smart and prefer part shade. This means that B-grade spaces of the patch are now up for grabs. Make sure you help them out and protect them from hot afternoon sun.

NONNO'S TIP
You can keep perpetuating plants by breaking off segments – keeping the bulk for your harvest – and then using the remaining pieces for replanting. The preference is to replant those that are already sprouting.

KITCHEN TIP
While the roots are the prized possession, the stems and leaves are also edible. In particular, the lower stem is the most tender and flavoursome and shouldn't be ignored.

ZUCCHINI (COURGETTE)

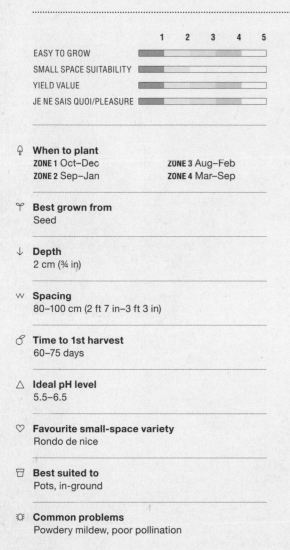

	1	2	3	4	5
EASY TO GROW					
SMALL SPACE SUITABILITY					
YIELD VALUE					
JE NE SAIS QUOI/PLEASURE					

When to plant
ZONE 1 Oct–Dec
ZONE 2 Sep–Jan
ZONE 3 Aug–Feb
ZONE 4 Mar–Sep

Best grown from
Seed

Depth
2 cm (¾ in)

Spacing
80–100 cm (2 ft 7 in–3 ft 3 in)

Time to 1st harvest
60–75 days

Ideal pH level
5.5–6.5

Favourite small-space variety
Rondo de nice

Best suited to
Pots, in-ground

Common problems
Powdery mildew, poor pollination

Whenever there's zucchini growing in the garden, it feels like I have options in the kitchen. This is a veggie that's useful for breakfast, lunch or dinner. Zucchini never wakes up grumpy and is happy to go to bed late. Sure, it's a bit of a guts when it comes to eating up your garden space, but with one plant able to produce a prolific amount of produce, it can satisfy even the gutsiest zucchini eaters. Scrambled eggs, salads and ratatouille, all day, any day.

When growing the plant, zucchini has a less-is-more approach to the veggie patch. Allowing one plant to grow properly and realise all its hopes and fritters is always better than keeping a couple that are breathing all over each other. It will appreciate airflow to control pests and diseases, as well as a clear landing path for pollinating insects, primarily the bee.

A common problem is when fruit begins to form but quickly turns into shrivelled prunes – a sign of poor pollination – so good old-fashioned hand pollination may be required (see page 244). If your kids haven't yet had the birds and the bees conversation, take them out to the garden, hand pollinate a zucchini flower and kill two birds with one stone.

NONNO'S TIP
Don't cram your patch with plants, as it will only end in tears. Give them space and plant directly into a small mound of compost at the beginning of spring for the best results.

KITCHEN TIP
Zucchini is one fruit that is best when young, and can be used from the earliest of stages with flowers still attached. You can cook the flowers in olive oil and garlic, scrambled in egg – it's a pungent start to any day.

Integrate the patch with slow-release nitrogen-rich fertiliser and sow seeds in small mounds of compost after the last frost. In cooler areas it's best to incubate the young seedlings using open-ended plastic bottles, which will also keep pests at bay.

Give monthly applications of liquid seaweed solution and mulch to a depth of 3–5 cm (1¼–2 in) using pea straw, lucerne hay or sugar cane mulch.

While not a vertical climber, they will grow out in a particular direction, which you can manipulate to suit the rest of your garden. Apply liquid potassium to encourage flower and fruit growth. As zucchinis begin to develop, keep watering at a good level.

Fruiting plants will begin to die back and will be overcome by powdery mildew. Prune off affected leaves and use a milk spray to help control its spread.

TIMELINE	WEEK	0	4	8	12	14	20
	GROWTH						
	WATER		Daily		3–4 times a week		Daily

HAND POLLINATION

Sometimes gourds and melons can have difficulty attracting the right partner. In these cases, canny gardeners take matters into their own hands. Hand pollination is standard practice in the horticultural world and is one way to pick up the slack when the birds and the bees just aren't doing their job.

As always, you want to get the mood right. Maybe you want to invite your friend Marvin Gaye over for a bottle of pinot, or perhaps it's more of a Guns 'N' Roses kind of affair. No matter your taste, you will want to get down to business quickly and that means getting to know the anatomy of your plants.

1. Inspect your plant for different flower genders.

SORRY, I'VE GOT A HEADACHE

2. While both flowers are superficially very similar, a closer examination will reveal that female flowers have a longer and thicker stem than the male flowers on your plant. Fruit grows from the base of female flowers and even before pollination has occurred, the stem should be slightly engorged. Male flowers, on the other hand, will have thin stems and tend to bloom earlier and in greater abundance.

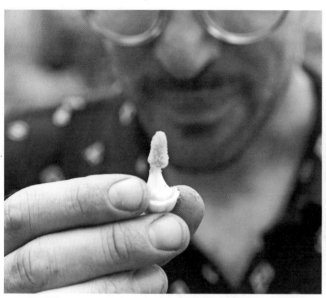

3. Pluck a couple of the males by the stem. Peel back their petals to expose the plant's stamen, a phallic structure at the centre of the blossom.

4. Male flower in hand and stamen ready, begin to move about your patch like a dutiful honey bee. Carefully spread the petals of the female flowers and carefully push the stamen inside. No rush.

5. Yes, it may feel a bit naughty, but before you know it you will be a seasoned pro, ready to pollinate any flower that crosses your path. It's not possible to over pollinate, so go crazy.

6. With your plants pollinated and the garden yielding abundant fruit, there is nothing left to do but sit back and relax. Cheers to gardening.

PESTS & DISE

Ants
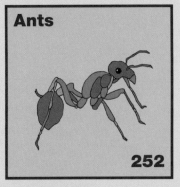
252

Aphids
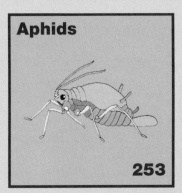
253

Birds

254

Child
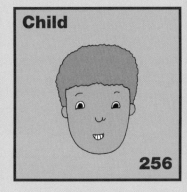
256

Slaters

259

Leaf miner

262

Possum/Racoon/ Squirrel

263

Rodent

264

Snails/Slugs

270

Thrip
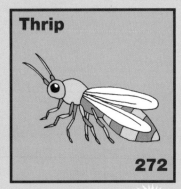
272

Whitefly
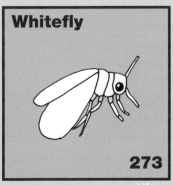
273

White cabbage moth
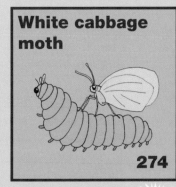
274

Leaf roll/curl
DISEASE!

278

Magnesium deficiency
DISEASE!
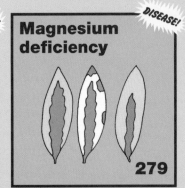
279

Powdery mildew
DISEASE!

280

Root rot/ stem rot
DISEASE!
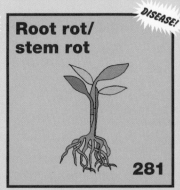
281

...ASES TO KNOW

Earwig

257

Fruit fly

258

Root-knot nematodes
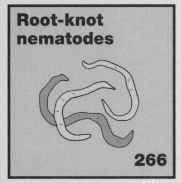
266

Scale
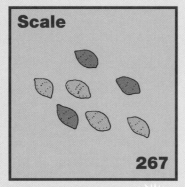
267

Blossom end rot

276

Leaf blight

277

Rust

282

HOW TO BEAT THEM

Netting
255

Controlling Rats
265

How to Make Multipurpose Organic Sprays
268

Ultimate Snail/Slug Defence
271

Dummy Butterfly
275

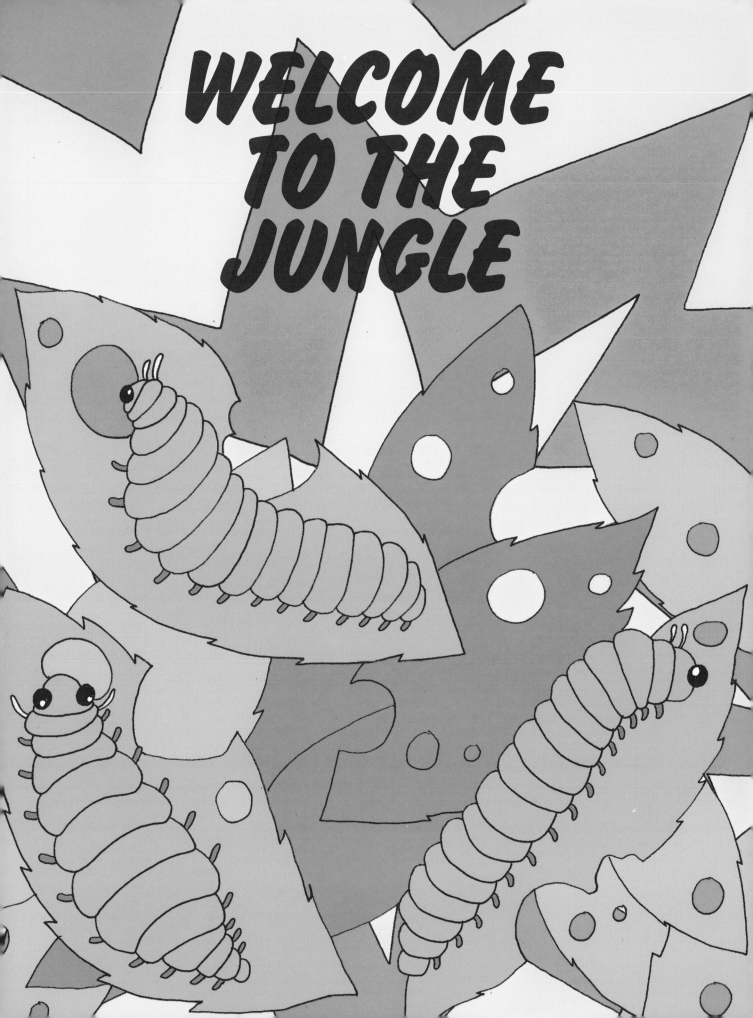

PESTS & DISEASES TO KNOW

No garden is complete without a few pests. They are inevitable, often accompanying each new season and providing a creeping source of tension. However, when growing on a personal or family scale, pests are seldom catastrophic. In fact, they're more of a nuisance than a problem. Many of us don't have to worry about a swarm of locusts carrying away our livelihood overnight. Rather, pests challenge us to be better, more attentive gardeners.

Diseases, too, can be thought of in a similar vein. Rarely terminal and often controllable, some diseases – such as powdery mildew – are just part and parcel of growing particular varieties. In a way they are almost expected, and part of becoming a good gardener is understanding when a pest or disease is more likely to strike, and accepting that they are often seasonal or simply part of a plant's life cycle.

Unlike commercial production, when growing in small spaces it is easier to notice subtle changes and react quickly. Tending to the needs of a few afflicted plants often requires only a few minutes, and some simple practices and concepts will help to ensure that the impact of any pest or disease is kept to a minimum. This will give your garden the best possible chance to thrive.

DON'T PANIC ...
IT'S JUST A BUG

THE ORGANIC APPROACH

Try organic for simple practicality if not for ideological reasons. Whatever you put on your food will inevitably end up inside your body. The same goes for your soil. And you know what? We love your body. Have you been working out? I seriously thought you were only 25 ... At any rate, a chemical that kills the 'bad insects' will also kill the 'good insects', which can leave the garden even more susceptible to outbreaks.

DIVERSIFY THE GARDEN

Just like us, pests (and diseases) have their plant of choice and by fostering diversity in the patch we ensure that at least some crops will escape unwanted attention. If you are not relying on a single source for all of your food, then other plants can help to fill in the gaps. Some plants, such as nasturtium, act as decoys, focusing unwanted attention to one place. Others, such as chives, may have properties to actively repel certain pests. To this purpose, flowers and herbs are essential in every edible garden, as they often attract allies and pollinators to promote a healthy garden on your behalf.

NOT ALL INSECTS ARE EVIL

In fact, some will be your new best friends. Ladybirds are your top ally and have a rapacious appetite for sucking pests like aphids and thrips. Praying mantises may not make the best lovers (watch out boys!), but they're merciless in their pursuit of flies, moths and caterpillars. Spiders love all things that fly and flutter. Bees, of course, are the essential pollinators that make the world go 'round.

EVEN THE BADDIES AREN'T ALL BAD

Every pest has its predator and sometimes a pest is also a predator. Birds will eat caterpillars and slaters (roly polys) from the garden as surely as they will nibble your strawberries. Possums and raccoons dined on escargot long before it was fashionable. We've been told that even children aren't pure destruction.

LEAVES WITH HOLES ARE STILL EDIBLE

Sometimes all we have to do is adjust our expectations. It's okay to eat forked carrots, split tomatoes and lumpy apples. Rather than deformed, we prefer words like 'unique' and 'distinguished'. After all, aren't we all a little distinguished?

RATINGS EXPLAINED

Scale of destruction

We've decided to rate the pests and diseases in this section, so you can get a snapshot of what you are up against. Not all pests are created equal, so we've assessed a few of their traits to help understand which ones are worth careful planning and maybe a pre-emptive strike, and which to feel comfortable turning your back on (to continue growing prize-winning pumpkins).

The characteristics and ratings roughly translate to the following:

DAMAGE
Amount of physical (not emotional) harm to your plants

1	5

Purely cosmetic   **Biblical plague**

PROBABILITY
Likeliness that your garden will experience this problem

1	5

Passing comprehensive climate change policy   **Tax breaks for the wealthy**

PERSISTENCE
The level of sophistication and resilience of your foe

1	5

Donkey Kong   **King Kong**

THE LITTLE VEGGIE PATCH CO RATING
Very sophisticated gardening stuff. The result of a complicated formula taking into consideration the combination of damage + probability + cleverness + our own biased emotional responses. Total divided by how much we like the plant affected.

☼ SEASON
The time of year that pest/disease is most likely to appear.

⌂ OPTIMAL CONDITIONS
Perfect combination of environmental factors that favour an outbreak.

⚘ FAVOURED PLANTS
Most commonly affected plants.

◯ SIGNATURE
Real junior detective and crime scene investigation kind of stuff. Unique damage or evidence that indicates their presence. Their calling card.

✕ PREVENTION
Proactive steps that you can take to prepare the garden and avoid problems before any damage has even occurred.

⚗ COPING
Palliative care for a garden that has already been affected by pests/disease. It may not solve the problem, but with any luck you can continue growing the food that you love.

⚡ ERADICATING
An all out declaration of war and a strategy to completely eliminate the pest/disease in question. Nothing like a real war, more like mixing some organic substances in a spray bottle and gently misting your plants. Feeding snails to chooks is about as tough as we get.

ANTS

THE LITTLE
VEGGIE PATCH CO
RATING
2.5

	1	2	3	4	5
DAMAGE					
PROBABILITY					
PERSISTENCE					

☼ **Season**
Summer and autumn

⌂ **Optimal conditions**
Warm, dry conditions after rainfall.
That is when sucking pests are active,
and the ant will usually follow.

⚘ **Favoured plants**
Any plant that attracts sucking pests,
in particular citrus and most gourds.

○ **Signature**
Black powdery substance – honeydew –
on the plant.

✕ **Prevention**
Keep your garden hygienic, properly watered
and properly spaced.

⚲ **Coping**
Sucking pests are seasonal and so are ants.
Direct damage by ants is rare, so again don't panic,
but keep the sucking pests in check to prevent
it snowballing.

⚡ **Eradicating**
Clean the affected plants of the honeydew using
a soapy spray or soapy sponge for tougher staining.
Then apply an organic white oil – two applications
a few days apart in dry/mild conditions – to curb the
sucking pests.

There are thousands of ant species in our country, but the most common one that people encounter worldwide in the home and garden is the black house ant. Of course, spotting some ants floating around the garden is next to a certainty, but encountering a problem that is caused by these ants is very rare.

Rather than thinking of the ant as a pest itself, think of it as an indicator of the existence of others. More often than not an ant is cleaning up the mess left by another. Sucking insects, such as whitefly, aphids and thrip, leave behind a black, sugary residue – honeydew – that the ants feed on and clean up. Of course, it's not all good news. Ants are smart and organised and acutely aware of their sugar mommies and daddies, and how to protect them from natural predators.

When you notice an outbreak of ants, don't panic (like my mum always does), but rather inspect for more information. The first part of the eradication process is cleaning the plant of its food – a soapy spray or sponge usually suffices – and then dealing with those who are actually responsible.

APHIDS

	1	2	3	4	5
DAMAGE					
PROBABILITY					
PERSISTENCE					

☼ **Season**
Spring

⬠ **Optimal conditions**
Early spring weather – warm and wet –
is its breeding ground.

⚜ **Favoured plants**
Roses, tomatoes, garlic, onions, nasturtiums

◯ **Signature**
Clusters of small black or green dots on the
stems of your plants and underside of the leaves.
They turn the leaves yellow by sucking out their
sap and then leave behind a sugary residue (called
honeydew), which ants feed on. An abundance of
ants, which then protect the aphids, is a telltale
sign of a problem.

✕ **Prevention**
Keep the plants well spaced and consistently
watered. Don't overfeed with nitrogen, which
tends to make plants more susceptible.

⏳ **Coping**
Accept that it's seasonal and apply a soapy spray
to clean the leaves of aphids, the honeydew and
the ants. Don't use chemical fixers, which will
discourage predators to come in and help.

⚡ **Eradicating**
White oil (or eco oil), applied on a dry day in the
morning and then reapplied in similar conditions
a few days apart to compound its effectiveness.
You should also introduce the aphids' number
one predator, the ladybird. Go get 'em guys!

In the world of pests, the aphid is a top dog. It belongs to the superfamily of pests known as the Aphidoidea and is a small, flying sucking insect that feeds on the sap of your edible plants. But its bark is worse than its bite, if you know how to handle it.

Aphids are semi-microscopic pests – seen with regular eyes or better with a microscope – that come as predictably as the change of season. Each spring, as the weather warms up and rains fall in greater volumes, the aphid population rises faster than your pumpkin seedlings. In a blink of an eye, many hundreds of aphids take up cover and a feeding spot on your plants, eating them from the inside out.

When eating they create a sugary substance called honeydew, which then feeds their number one ally, the ant. If you happen to notice ants scampering up and down your plants, it is usually an indication of another problem, perhaps aphids.

BIRDS

	1	2	3	4	5
DAMAGE					
PROBABILITY					
PERSISTENCE					

☼ **Season**
Spring through to summer when birds are feeding

⌂ **Optimal conditions**
Freshly mulched garden beds

⚘ **Favoured plants**
Fruit trees, strawberries, tomatoes –
however, they tend to scratch around in
a garden bed rather than target individual plants.

○ **Signature**
Pecked but not entirely eaten fruit plus random
holes and mess in the veggie patch – as though
your toddler has been digging around.

✕ **Prevention**
Banging on a window or yelling or other erratic
behaviour tends to have a good effect. Otherwise,
keeping an active pet, such as a cat, will scare the
life out of most birds. What seemed like a fun place
to hang out will quickly lose its appeal.

⚲ **Coping**
City birds tend to be too busy to spend time
hassling you and eating out of your veggie patch,
but if you're living regionally, birds are much more
sinister and destructive. Try a scarecrow or a
structure that creates noise and/or reflections when
moved by a gentle breeze. Your old AC/DC albums
should suffice.

⚡ **Eradicating**
Netting is a 100% guarantee (or your money back)
form of eradicating bird damage.

The bird often gets a bad rap in the veggie patch, yet it's an animal that rarely targets your crops in the city. In fact, most of its damage is a result of its own clumsiness. With such little intent, it's hard to hold a grudge.

It reminds us of an ex-colleague, Bobby, who kept breaking things while he worked with us at The Little Veggie Patch Co Pots, windows, the clutch on our 4WDs ... It was still so difficult to be upset with him because, as he explained it: 'My limbs have grown at a faster rate than my brain knows how to control them!' And he was right.

But that's not to say every bird is as innocent as Bobby. Birds often target our ripening fruit and nut trees. And they are guilty of the two greatest crimes against our veggie patches – the random pecking of our ripening tomatoes and strawberries – so you would be naive to ignore them.

NETTING

Netting is the only true protection against the most destructive pests in the veggie patch. Without a barrier between the (insert possum, bird, moth, rat, child) and your plants you are only gambling on the outcome, and unfortunately this is one gamble when the odds are truly stacked against you.

A soundly constructed net is the only way to tell pests 'not on my watch'. It is an important message to send out while your patch seedlings are young and most vulnerable, because this is a stage when a stealthy overnight mission can end the season.

The security of a net is often overlooked only because of vanity; if there is one way to make a veggie patch look like a complete mess, with a net thrown on top, then it's this. So, while netting can sometimes look cumbersome, we have evolved our setup to be as low impact as possible while still maintaining functionality.

You can buy all the infrastructure you need from a hardware store. Electrical conduit as the frame, u-brackets and screws to attach it to the raised bed or crate, good quality bird netting and some hooks to hold it taught.

Attach two u-brackets (one at the top and one at the bottom) on either side of your raised bed where each length of conduit will slot – making up the framework. Each frame should be no more than 1 m (3 ft 3 in) apart, so if your bed is 3 m (9 ft 10 in) long, you'll need four lengths of conduit and four sets of the u-brackets to hold the framework.

Slot the conduit in one side and then arch over and place in the opposing side. The length of the conduit will determine the height of your netting frame. Ideally, you'll need 1 m (3 ft 3 in) of clearance for most salads, herbs and vegetables. The framework is now ready to hold the net.

Attach hooks at each corner of the raised bed and at regular internals – every 30–40 cm (1 ft–1 ft 3 in) – around the perimeter so you can secure the net and make it taut.

Place the net over the frame and attach it to the hooks to make it tight. 'Not on my watch.' Say it: 'NOT ON MY WATCH!'

CHILD

	1	2	3	4	5
DAMAGE					
PROBABILITY					
PERSISTENCE					

☀ **Season**
All year round

⌂ **Optimal conditions**
Early afternoon, post–midday nap

⚘ **Favoured plants**
Strawberries, tomatoes, habanero chillies,
the hops vine you use as decoration.

○ **Signature**
Green strawberries and emerging flowers littered
over the garden and red smudges on their shirt.
No DNA testing necessary to find the perpetrator:
guilty as sin!

✕ **Prevention**
Lock them inside and put on a DVD

🗴 **Coping**
Feeding them properly so they don't have
to resort to eating fake plastic foliage.

⚡ **Eradicating**
There is no sure way of preventing a child from
destroying your veggie patch. Any parent knows
how erratic a child can be – one moment they're
sleeping on your shoulder like a saint, and the next
they're throwing your black Russian tomatoes to
the dog.

Identical to humans – albeit smaller, more erratic, and with
a hunger for strawberries and appetite for destruction –
the child is one of the veggie garden's greatest foes. This is,
however, a foe that will one day bring the garden benefits,
so some concessions need to be made. When dealing with
children it's important to strike a fine line between the damage
to the current crop versus a learning experience that will
benefit the future crops to come.

A child is known as a help hinderer, meaning that its offerings
of help are usually to the detriment of the garden. But you
need to accept that the best education is through experience,
so you should learn to accept certain outcomes. Your child will
one day repay your veggie patch by monopolising all the riper
strawberries.

EARWIG

	1	2	3	4	5
DAMAGE					
PROBABILITY					
PERSISTENCE					

☼ **Season**
Autumn through to later spring

⌂ **Optimal conditions**
Wet, cooler conditions

⚘ **Favoured plants**
Flowers and lettuce

○ **Signature**
They leave irregular holes and eat the edges
of the foliage that appears jagged.

✕ **Prevention**
Keep your garden hygienic as the main food for
earwigs is dead or decomposing plant matter.

⚱ **Coping**
Damage is usually minimal and semi-mature plants
will have enough foliage that they won't make much
of an impact.

⚡ **Eradicating**
You can make pit traps using olive or vegetable oil
and soy sauce. Use a plastic container and add
equal parts of the two ingredients, securing a lid
that has been punched with holes – roughly
5–10 mm (¼–½ in) in diameter. Bury the container in
the soil near where you've noticed damage, leaving
the lid at ground level. The soy sauce attracts the
earwigs, and the oil prevents them from escaping.

Despite its name, an earwig is not a toupee for people with unsightly ears. Rather, it gets the name from the belief they tunnel in through the ear canal and into the brain. It has what appears to be a double-sided body, with large pincers on one end that look as sinister as a bear trap. While not the best-looking pest to be found in the garden (or an ear), thankfully they remain largely hidden under bricks or pots and will only come out under the cover of darkness.

While there are a number of earwig varieties that roam the garden, few do any damage in the veggie patch. They prefer to snack on other insects or dead and decaying plant matter, and it is only the introduced European earwig that sometimes turns its attention on your young seedlings.

An earwig is usually more of a friend than a foe, helping control aphid numbers among others.

FRUIT FLY

	1	2	3	4	5
DAMAGE					
PROBABILITY					
PERSISTENCE					

☼ **Season**
Whenever it is warm

⌂ **Optimal conditions**
Warm, tropical conditions

⚘ **Favoured plants**
Stone fruit, gourds and tomatoes

◯ **Signature**
Rotting fruit on the ground

✕ **Prevention**
Don't let fruit over-ripen and consider planting
dwarf or espaliered trees so harvesting is easier.
Once fruit begins to set, use exclusion nets or bags.
However, these can be costly and time-consuming
to set up.

♟ **Coping**
As soon as you notice an outbreak, dispose of the
affected fruit. Use pheromone traps that will attract
and kill both females and males, and ensure you get
your neighbours on board with a larger scale effort.

⚡ **Eradicating**
Tough to eradicate, so unless using exclusion nets it
is best to stay diligent and adopt the use of lures or
traps to keep numbers in check.

If you live in the cooler southern states of Australia the fruit
fly is nothing more than a myth, a spooky story that farmers
read to their kids at night. But to those living in subtropical
and tropical parts of our country, as well as Western Australia
(WA), the fruit fly is real. In fact, there are three common types
of fruit fly that affect our crops. The Mediterranean species
is confined to WA, and then there are the Queensland and
cucumber varieties.

The cycle of a fruit fly becomes vicious if not broken. The female
lays its eggs within the skin of the fruit and then the larvae,
which resemble white maggots, eat the fruit from the inside
out. This causes the fruit to rot and then fall off the tree. Once
those larvae are fully cooked, they migrate and burrow into the
soil to pupate – becoming the next generation of infecting pest.

Once fruit fly infests, it can wreak huge damage on fruit crops,
and commercially costs farmers millions in lost revenue.
To control an outbreak in the home garden, it involves
a concerted effort from not only yourself, but your
neighbours, too.

SLATERS

	1	2	3	4	5
DAMAGE					
PROBABILITY					
PERSISTENCE					

☼ **Season**
Summer

⌂ **Optimal conditions**
Hot and dry

⚲ **Favoured plants**
Sweet, young seedlings

○ **Signature**
Seedlings disappearing overnight or their stems being ringed. Scratch under the mulch and you should see them scurrying about.

✕ **Prevention**
The slaters favour the dusty covering of traditional mulches for breeding, but you shouldn't stop mulching your patch, particularly in summer. An alternative worth trying is pellet mulches, which expand once watered, changing the dynamic of the cover.

⊗ **Coping**
Growing vertically, and off the ground, means there is far less chance of a slater problem. If growing at ground level, you may need to position decoys when you have young seedlings about. Potato peels covered by a cup is a tasty snack that should distract them. Chooks are pretty fond of slaters, so if you have chickens try rotating them through the garden to control numbers.

⚡ **Eradicating**
Place protective plant collars around your plants. The slaters will not be able to penetrate this defence and will turn their attentions elsewhere.

Slaters (also known as roly polys) are land-living crustaceans that commonly feed on decaying matter and help to build soils. So while they can be considered friendly under many circumstances, in hot, dry conditions when their food sources are scarce, they can turn their attention to your young seedlings.

Though not an issue in the eastern states of Australia, slaters have become problematic for growers in the west. It is believed that the warm, arid climate in conjunction with dusty, dry mulches, have provided the ideal breeding ground for slaters to become something of a nuisance.

LEAF MINER

	1	2	3	4	5
DAMAGE					
PROBABILITY					
PERSISTENCE					

☀ **Season**
Spring

⌂ **Optimal conditions**
Early spring

⚘ **Favoured plants**
Citrus

◯ **Signature**
Mine tracks through the affected leaves and small
bumps on their undersides, this being their eggs.

✕ **Prevention**
Maintaining healthy plants and having a diverse
range of herbs and flowers will mean that your
plants are better able to resist attack, and you will
have help from friendly predators to control the
perpetrators.

⚒ **Coping**
Yellow sticky traps will attract those flies that are
typically responsible for the leaf miners. Mulching
the soil will help to break the cycle as this will
create a barrier to the soil, which is where the larvae
pupate and hatch into mature, egg-laying insects.

⚡ **Eradicating**
Cut affected leaves and discard in a sealed bag
rather than throwing in the compost bin.

The leaf miner is the larvae of insects – typically of flies but
also of moths and sometimes beetles – that are burrowed into
the tissue of the leaf. Eggs will appear as small bumps on the
underside of the leaves. When hatched, they feed on the tissue,
leaving recognisable lines or mine tracks.

Because the larvae are nestled within the protection of the
leaf, they are largely resistant to sprays and predators. The
key is in controlling the numbers of the egg-laying pests and
maintaining healthy plants that are more resistant to attack.

Although the leaf miner won't wipe out your crop, it's unsightly
and particularly damaging to the plant's new growth so we're
always determined to keep them out of our veggie patch.

POSSUM/RACOON/ SQUIRREL

	1	2	3	4	5
DAMAGE					
PROBABILITY					
PERSISTENCE					

☀ **Season**
All year, but particularly winter and spring

⌂ **Optimal conditions**
A built-up garden in a built-up area with plenty of access points, such as trees and fence lines.

⚘ **Favoured plants**
Not fussy

◯ **Signature**
Significant damage to outer parts of leaves and fruits. Or when you go out at night and you catch a possum nonchalantly eating your citrus while looking right at you.

✕ **Prevention**
Netting is the best form of prevention and eradication. If you can find the access point, disrupting it may divert your possum friends elsewhere. Keep precious plants away from fence lines as the closest plants to the access points usually get picked on first. Don't get a pet dog – in particular, a cocker spaniel – that will bark at the possums from dusk to dawn, resulting in your tired and rather frightening-looking German neighbour knocking on your door at 3.30 am.

🖉 **Coping**
While young seedlings and ripe fruit are frustrating to lose, we are usually happy to share the more mature foliage with our possum friends. You can also try your hand at a number of sprays – chilli, garlic and eucalyptus – as well as sensor lights, high frequency transmitters and fake owls, but like us possums will quickly recognise a plastic owl when they see one.

⚡ **Eradicating**
Possums are territorial, but if you 'relocate' them, another will happily take its place. Not only that, but moving the animals is illegal. Remember that they were here first so we have to learn to live with them. Soundly constructed netting is the only sure way of keeping them out.

As long as there have been gardens there have been pests, and it feels like the possum is the most evolved, making them a formidable foe. Their opposable thumbs render them capable thieves, and their nighttime appetites are voracious. They are also the only pest that, when young, are cute enough to consider keeping as a pet. (Raccoons and squirrels are equally voracious but adorable pests in their respective regions of the world.)

Possums are also easily adaptable to deterrents set in their path, particularly when fully grown and well versed in the art of patch destruction. They have a particular love of ripe fruit, but are cheeky opportunists and don't mind sampling whatever is available. Like us, they have simple common sense. This means that the plastic fake owl hanging around the veggie patch may frighten them the first time. However, on the second, third and fourth encounter, the patch-wise possum won't bat an eyelid at a fake owl's frozen vigilance.

Take a look down the pest control aisle in the hardware store and you will find a suite of products ranging from chilli sprays to high-frequency audio devices – all claiming to be the definitive solution. Unfortunately, audio devices are much more likely to annoy your poodle than save your lettuce, and some possums seem to have a newfound fondness for sprays that traditionally repelled.

That's right, even for the pesky possum, a chilli can be an aphrodisiac. So, when they eat your habaneros they're not just depriving you of food – they're getting off on it, too.

RODENT

	1	2	3	4	5
DAMAGE					
PROBABILITY					
PERSISTENCE					

☼ **Season**
Summer and autumn

⌂ **Optimal conditions**
When it is warm and where there is food, water and shelter, also known as your veggie patch.

⚘ **Favoured plants**
Silverbeet (Swiss chard), parsley, beetroot (beets)

○ **Signature**
A seedling eaten down to its stem butt, a fruit that has done a Houdini, or mature plants that are littered over the patch as though a vandal has ripped them up and thrown them back down. Closer inspection will reveal the roots completely eaten out until the plant has been felled.

✕ **Prevention**
See Controlling Rats, opposite

☷ **Coping**
What will be will be! Pick fruit early, as rats – just like us – prefer ripening produce. Rats don't like noise, so perhaps plan a summer of all-night house parties. We've also had moderate success using menthol scent bombs, locating them in potential nesting spots.

⚡ **Eradicating**
Get a pet tomcat, python or owl

Everyone accepts the existence of and fights a battle with the neighbourhood possum; it's a war that's been raging for generations and it's one that we need. However, we could do without rats.

As homes and gardens become more and more congested, rats have become dexterous, well-trained veggie patch assassins. It's surprising how few people want to admit that the thing chomping on their parsley or uprooting and felling giant silverbeet (Swiss chard) is, in fact, a rat. Rats have always been associated with unhygienic conditions, but even the cleanest of homes and gardens are fighting this new battle.

Unlike the possum – that we can find a way to impede – our bag of tricks for this new competitor is in experimental mode. One method is to apply some simple garden procedures to create a neat, hygienic environment, making our veggie patches less appealing to rat attack.

Finally, enlist some help. See Controlling Rats (opposite) for more on your most powerful ally, the cat.

CONTROLLING RATS

Controlling rats is as ambitious as understanding the meaning of life, and if some higher power gave me a call on Monday morning and offered me either, I know which one I'd take. That's because we like a bit of mystery and until recently there was a fair bit of mystery in our veggie patch. Then we started finding rats.

To survive and indeed flourish (and then perhaps take over the world), rats need food, water and shelter. In a veggie patch, food and water are givens, but shelter – for a rat – can take a number of different forms. Buried in a sequence of tunnels throughout the soil, or nestled in the warm depths of your compost bin perhaps or, as was the case on our rooftop garden (Federation Square Pop Up Patch), within the polystyrene pods we used to reduce the loading on the car park.

The first sign was finding plants that had seemingly been pulled out and then thrown back on the soil, as if an act of vandals. Rats have an annoying habit of eating the stem base of mature plants – that of parsley, silverbeet (Swiss chard) and beetroot (beets) in particular – until they are felled to the ground, like a pine tree harvested for timber in a forest. The second sign was finding hundreds of dislodged polystyrene balls underneath that crate when we moved it, and the third and final giveaway was dropping it too swiftly with the pallet jack and dislodging three rats from underneath.

When you have a rat problem, it is a problem that requires action. So what are your options?

HYGIENE Keep your garden as hygienic as possible. Pick fruit regularly and don't let it overripen. Don't leave mess in the garden – need to make the place as neat as humanly possible. That includes cleaning the BBQ of all those delicious-smelling meaty oils (for a rat, that is). We know that keeping things clean is a real task for a lot of people, but the threat of a plague of rats (rather than the usual jibes by your partner) should be enough to send you into action.

FORTIFICATION Next, fortify the patch. Simple netting will be a deterrent for the lazy rat, but those with a bit more determination will chew right through or burrow underneath - like the ones that tunnelled under concrete to find an entrance to our compost bin. For the netting to be truly effective, it will need to be wire mesh and will have to extend underground, too. It's a lot of work, but it's worth it.

SCENT BOMBS You can try any number of scent bombs that will work with varying success, depending on the tastes of your rats (yes, yours). Try dipping cotton balls into a peppermint concentrate (like the one you use for desserts) and place them around their housing spots. Another more effective scent is ammonia. Mix 1 tablespoon of liquid detergent, ¼ glass of water and 1 glass of ammonia and place where they frequent.

PREDATORS Finally, enlist some hunters. We've always found that our rat problem has hinged on the amount of time our neighbourhood cat has spent around our property. When she's hanging out and happy, the rats seem to go on vacation. However, when she finds a better place to reside – as is the case now – they quickly return. If you're not a cat person, perhaps consider that they are the number one predator for rats. Cats can be a powerful ally.

ROOT-KNOT NEMATODES

	1	2	3	4	5
DAMAGE					
PROBABILITY					
PERSISTENCE					

☼ **Season**
All year round

⌂ **Optimal conditions**
A soil that has previously hosted the root-knot nematodes.

⚘ **Favoured plants**
Particularly tomatoes and potatoes, as well as silverbeet (Swiss chard) and lettuce.

○ **Signature**
Tumour-like swellings on the plant roots

✕ **Prevention**
Crop rotation is the best practice to prevent the eelworm from burrowing back in. The marigold is a great companion plant that will reduce their numbers.

♨ **Coping**
Make sure your soil is healthy with a good level of organic matter for strong plant growth. A healthy plant will cope much better with root-knot nematodes than a malnourished one.

⚡ **Eradicating**
Dig out all the root matter of the affected crops and dispose of them in a bin or burn them rather than composting.

Also known as the eelworm, the root-knot nematode is a tiny, translucent worm that operates in your soil, burrowing into the roots of preferred plant species. There it lays its larvae, which then feed on the plant's nutrients while restricting its ability to function properly.

It is almost impossible to identify the problem until season's end. The changeover of crops will reveal the tumour-like swellings or galls on the root matter, indicating where the worm has burrowed in and laid its eggs.

Anyone with a young child can tell you just how easy it is to pass a sickness around a family. The nightshade family is no exception and is particularly susceptible to root-knot nematodes. Practise crop rotation and don't follow your eggplant (aubergine), capsicum (bell pepper) and tomato plants with potatoes. Instead, rotate in something a little more potent like garlic and chives. Not only will this help to keep the garden parasites at bay, but your very own family will also benefit from their immune-boosting properties.

SCALE

	1	2	3	4	5
DAMAGE					
PROBABILITY					
PERSISTENCE					

☼ **Season**
Spring

⌂ **Optimal conditions**
Dry, warm environments

⚘ **Favoured plants**
Citrus

○ **Signature**
Shell- or oval-shaped dots attached to the underside of your plants, typically amongst the honeydew that ants have come in to feed on.

✕ **Prevention**
Growing healthy plants will make them more resilient and in better shape to deal with scale.

⚗ **Coping**
Small amounts of scale can be rubbed off with your fingernail or a hard-bristled toothbrush, while larger infestations should be trimmed from the plant. Cleaning the plant of the honeydew – with a soapy spray and sponge – will diminish the ants' interest in proceedings. Note that ants often protect and spread the scale to protect their food source.

⚡ **Eradicating**
Using a pyrethrin spray (a mix of the pyrethrin daisy extract and oil) will help smother and kill the soft scale; the hard scale, however, will resist such attempts. A homemade version of this can be made mixing 2 tablespoons of vegetable oil and 1 tablespoon of liquid soap with 1 litre (34 fl oz/ 4 cups) of water and spraying the affected foliage.

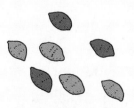

Scale is the name given to a range of sucking pests that feed on the sap of leaves and stems, mostly of citrus. Largely immobile, they do not often move over the plant, preferring rather to attach themselves and stay put, giving the appearance of a 'thing' – a tiny shell-like bump – rather than a pest. Left uncontrolled, they slowly reduce the health and productivity of plants.

They are broken into two groups, soft and hard (or armoured). Soft scale produces a honeydew as they feed and have a waxy protective coating over their body, whereas hard or armoured scale have a tough, shell-like cover and do not produce honeydew. As in the case of other sucking pests, it is the presence of ants (feeding on the honeydew) that is often the first alarm to an infestation of scale.

HOW TO MAKE MULTIPURPOSE ORGANIC SPRAYS

You can end up spending a fortune buying the remedies to safeguard your plants. While readily available, organic sprays don't come cheap – if you're not careful, those $2 heads of lettuce have cost you $5 extra in protection money. It feels that in an age where we demand a readily available solution to everything, we are losing one of the vegetable gardener's primary skills: that of resourcefulness.

Making homemade sprays to protect and clean your plants is a skill as ancient as gardening itself. Using simple combinations of basic household ingredients, you can concoct a spray to treat almost anything. Here are a few that you should definitely have in your repertoire.

SOAPY SPRAY

Shelf life 1 month

Aphids | Whitefly | Thrip | Caterpillars

HOW TO MAKE
Mix 1 tablespoon of biodegradable dishwashing liquid with 1 teaspoon of cooking oil in 1 litre (34 fl oz/4 cups) of water.

HOW TO APPLY
Spray over the foliage of plants, particularly on the underside of leaves where the pests often live.

MILKY SPRAY

Shelf life 24–48 hours

Powdery mildew | Honeydew

HOW TO MAKE
Mix 1 part full-cream (whole) milk to 10 parts water.

HOW TO APPLY
Spray on young and affected growth every week.

GARLIC + CHILLI SPRAY

Shelf life 2 weeks

Aphids | Whitefly | Thrip | Some possums | Snails and slugs

HOW TO MAKE
Combine 6 garlic cloves (crushed and roughly chopped), 10–12 chillies (thinly sliced) and 1 tablespoon of biodegradable dishwashing liquid into 1 litre (34 fl oz/4 cups) of boiling water (use a glass jar). Let it soak for 24 hours and then strain into a spray bottle for use.

HOW TO APPLY
Spray on the foliage of the affected plants, repeating the dosage after 3 days.

We are most certainly people of science, and for that reason we always encourage gardeners to use organic material. Growing food without the use of chemicals, particularly when dealing with pest and disease, will ensure we keep nature's balance in check. Don't forget that nature has a way of helping out in times of need, so waging chemical warfare that takes out everything will leave your veggie patch more susceptible to future attacks.

NETTLE SPRAY

Shelf life 4–6 weeks

Aphids | Leaf miners

HOW TO MAKE
Soak nettles in a large tub of water for approximately 1 week.

HOW TO APPLY
Use the liquid undiluted on the foliage of the plants. This also doubles up as a great plant tonic.

COFFEE SPRAY

Shelf life 2 weeks

Snails and slugs

HOW TO MAKE
Mix 1 part espresso coffee (the hard stuff) to 10 parts water.

HOW TO APPLY
Apply to leaves of affected plants as well as the surrounding soil.

BI-CARB SPRAY

Shelf life 1 month

Powdery mildew | Rust | Honeydew

HOW TO MAKE
Mix 1 teaspoon of bi-carbonate of soda (baking soda), 1 teaspoon of cooking oil, 1 tablespoon of biodegradable dishwashing liquid and 1 litre (34 fl oz/4 cups) of water.

HOW TO APPLY
Spray on young and affected growth every week.

SNAILS/SLUGS

	1	2	3	4	5
DAMAGE					
PROBABILITY					
PERSISTENCE					

☀ **Season**
All year, but mostly active in winter and spring

⌂ **Optimal conditions**
Damp, congested garden

⚘ **Favoured plants**
Strawberry, lettuce, young seedlings

◯ **Signature**
Slimy trail, or small clean holes on your fruits

✕ **Prevention**
Keeping a hygienic garden and depriving the mollusc of potential resting spots. They find it tougher to move over rougher ground, such as one that has recently been mulched. Nasturtium is a great decoy crop, providing a canopy that they will find a great shelter. You can then pick them out and throw them over your neighbour's fence. OK, not your neighbour's fence, but you know what we mean.

⚲ **Coping**
There are a number of coping techniques and strategies (see opposite).

⚡ **Eradicating**
There are a number of eradicating techniques and strategies (see opposite).

Snails and slugs are both from the mollusc family that once belonged in an aquatic environment. Although they have evolved into the annoying land-crawling creatures they are today, it gives us some clues as to which conditions they prefer.

For a snail or slug to move, it needs to produce a slime that it can then drag its disgusting slimy self over. This leaves behind a silky slime trail, which many moons ago we'd wake up to in our sharehouse living room. Other than sharehouse rugs, snails and slugs prefer the young, tender growth of your seedlings and are most active when conditions are damp. These night feeders tend to be gregarious and return to the same resting place. While snails have a protective shell, meaning they feel a little safer out in the open (as opposed to under my lowering boot), slugs don't enjoy the same protection and will burrow into the soil for shelter.

In our experience it's usually the slugs that do the most damage, in particular to our strawberry patch. They seem to have developed a sixth sense about when a strawberry is on the cusp of readiness.

ULTIMATE SNAIL/SLUG DEFENCE

SKILL UP!

Snails and slugs are not fast or particularly clever, but they make up for their shortcomings with a dogged persistence and by attacking your veggie patch while you sleep. This gives them 6–12 hours to slowly slime their way out, slime their way to your plants and then slime about all over them.

Rather than devouring a whole plant – although they can do so when food is lacking – they prefer to graze, taking little bites and leaving behind a glossy trail as their calling card. We like to call the damage they do to fruit 'spoilers', because in most cases they'll leave one or two solitary bites and then move on. How rude.

Yes, they are formidable and, yes, against the odds they always seem to win the race to the ripening strawberry – but we know we can defeat them.

MORNING REFRESHMENT Watering in the morning is a great starting point for avoiding all pests, as it means that there will be very little moisture left on the surface at nightfall. Snails are most active at night and are drawn to moisture, so when we water in the evening it creates an ideal environment for their nefarious activities.

WE'RE GOING ON A SNAIL HUNT Hunt and pick method is a garden treasure hunt. During the day, snails will hide in dark corners of the patch, but they can still be found. Under the foliage of low canopy plants – such as a nasturtium – is an ideal hiding place. Perhaps enlist some enthusiastic young kids by offering a prize for most collected.

THE PERFECT FOIL Copper tape and aluminium foil are like an electric fence for snails and slugs. When they come into contact with the metal, their mucus membranes have a bad chemical reaction that sends them in the opposite direction. It's a great technique for pots, to which the copper tape is easily attached and the mollusc will have to pass over to enter.

A VERY HAPPY ENDING Snails are drawn to the sweet, yeasty scent of beer as surely as gap year students to an open bar. Use traps or a glass that is partially filled with beer and some vegemite – for extra yeastiness! – and partially bury in the garden with the lip of the glass at ground level. When a slug or snail comes in for a taste, it will be their last drink.

THRIP

	1	2	3	4	5
DAMAGE					
PROBABILITY					
PERSISTENCE					

☼ **Season**
Spring and summer

⌂ **Optimal conditions**
Humid conditions that follow spring rains

⚘ **Favoured plants**
Beans, but really anything when conditions
are ideal.

◯ **Signature**
Brush up against a plant and a million tiny black
flies conduct a Mexican wave.

✕ **Prevention**
As thrips love to feast on damp and decaying matter,
try to keep your garden as hygienic as possible and
space out your plants so there is good airflow.

⚲ **Coping**
Naturally, once thrips appear (and whitefly and
aphids), you will notice ladybird numbers increasing.
This is the number one predator for thrips, so try
to encourage them into your patch with flowers
and herbs. You can use pheromone lures for the
ladybirds; otherwise, some kind words or a pat on
the back normally works.

⚡ **Eradicating**
Use a soapy spray to clean your plants of any food
and then apply two doses of a white or eco-oil a few
days apart.

Thrips are sucking insects – related to their cousins, the
whitefly and aphid – that cause damage by sucking the sap
from leaves and flowers. Most thrips are quite harmless,
whereas others will cause leaves and flowers to lose their
colour and they can also transfer viruses from plant to plant.

They feed off leaf litter, damp old wood, decaying matter and
fungi, bearing in mind that these things become tastier with
the warm and wet spring conditions. Much like the whitefly
and aphid, thrips are almost exclusively active in spring, when
their numbers fluctuate with the weather. Warm, humid
weather will see their numbers explode – there are days
when our plants at the nursery are stampeded on by them –
then days later, once conditions dry up, the thrips have
packed up and moved on.

The best treatment is, thankfully and reliably, from good
ol' Mother Nature herself. Thrip populations are heavily
influenced by the weather, and are driven away by hot,
dry/cool, windy conditions.

WHITEFLY

	1	2	3	4	5
DAMAGE					
PROBABILITY					
PERSISTENCE					

☼ **Season**
Spring

⌂ **Optimal conditions**
When conditions warm up and rains increase

⚘ **Favoured plants**
All gourds, tomatoes, eggplants (aubergine), mint

○ **Signature**
Brush against a plant and a million tiny white flies momentarily become airborne before returning to their sucking.

✕ **Prevention**
Ensure there is a high diversity of different border-plants and flowers, particularly nasturtiums, which attract predators that become your secret helpers. This is not just some pseudo-science stuff; professional growers constantly utilise this 'free labour' by strategically planting borders plants to attract certain bugs. The ladybird is a huge ally.

⏳ **Coping**
They are attracted to the colour yellow like girls to diamonds, moss to stones, snot to a toddler's nose. Hang yellow sticky traps around the concerned plants and they will fly onto them and get stuck. One sucker after another.

⚡ **Eradicating**
An organic white or eco-oil will help to eradicate the whitefly but always make sure to spray the underside of all leaves. Nicotine sprays have also been found to work. The old hippie method is to soak ciggies in water overnight and then use the water in a spray bottle.

First, some interesting facts about whiteflies:

- They are white.
- They are not flies.
- They suck. Literally.

They belong to the vampire order of the insect world, the sucking insects (*Hemiptera*) and, as such, are a close relative of aphids. The adults and their larvae simply love hanging out on the underside of leaves sucking sugary phloem juices all day. When disturbed they flutter about a bit but soon want to be back in sucking position. Not only do they suck the life out of plants, they are also vectors for viruses, which cause nasty plant diseases.

Adults live four to six weeks and lay more than 100 eggs each (onto the underside of the leaf), so an army of the white suckers can quickly populate each plant. All in all, you want to make sure they don't get too comfortable.

But remember that the whitefly is yet another seasonal pest that peaks when conditions are ideal and then quickly abates when the weather changes. This doesn't mean you should sit back and do nothing; it just means you shouldn't freak out and start panicking.

WHITE CABBAGE MOTH

THE LITTLE
VEGGIE PATCH CO
RATING
4.5

	1	2	3	4	5
DAMAGE					
PROBABILITY					
PERSISTENCE					

☼ **Season**
Autumn primarily, but also spring

⌂ **Optimal conditions**
The warm and relatively dry conditions of mid-autumn are their time to party.

⚘ **Favoured plants**
All brassicas

○ **Signature**
Quickly decimated brassica plants, with tiny black droppings in the base of the stems.

✕ **Prevention**
The moths are territorial, so dummy butterflies should deter them from laying their larvae. But if you're serious about preventing them, it's worth putting fine netting over the patch that will restrict landing space for the moths to lay their larvae. Make sure the netting is fine enough to prohibit them from entering the veggie patch and is not draped over the plants themselves, as this will render the netting useless.

☿ **Coping**
A search and destroy mission is useful. We like to reward our kids for caterpillar kills.

⚡ **Eradicating**
If you turn your back and things have gotten out of hand, dipel *bacillus thuringiensis*– a bio-insecticide spray – will drastically reduce their numbers. A couple of sprays, a few days apart when it is not raining, will kill all living caterpillars. But to ensure they don't come back, netting needs to be constructed.

It is important to discard any childhood misconceptions you may have about butterflies. No doubt they are pretty creatures, but they are not pretty when it comes to the vegetable garden. In particular, the white ones with the distinguishable black spot on one wing are nothing but trouble, hatching destructive green caterpillars that have a taste for sweet, cool-season crops.

The real strength of the white cabbage moth is its stealth. Its caterpillars are green – exactly like the foliage of your plants – and extremely difficult to spot. But when your eyes shift focus, there they are, all over your kale and broccoli and rocket (arugula) and their namesake, cabbage, getting fatter and fatter as each day passes.

As soon as you begin to spot the caterpillars, you realise what the black little dots are that collect in the stems of your plant. That's right, their shit! The eating habits of the caterpillars and breeding frequency of the moths are both so supreme that overnight – quite literally – a few tiny green caterpillars will transform into a green shitting army of brassica-eating machines.

DUMMY BUTTERFLY

If you are growing brassicas or greens in autumn and winter, then you may get to know the white cabbage moth pretty well. The first thing to do is remind yourself that leaves with holes in them are still edible. The next thing is to remember that every moth was once a caterpillar. Enlist some helping hands and offer a reward for the most caterpillars captured. If they are still harassing your patch, it's time to step up those defences.

Butterflies are territorial creatures – like the neighbourhood possum – and if a patch is occupied, they usually abide by the gentlemen's rule of 'do not enter, sir'. They also have very poor eyesight. This means they will be deterred by some simple bits of white plastic attached to rigid metal wire sitting in the patch.

When making your dummy butterflies, don't assume all white cabbage moths play fair. Rather than putting one in the patch, hoping the gentlemen's rule is followed, make it look extremely busy and intimidating.

BLOSSOM-END ROT

	1	2	3	4	5
DAMAGE					
PROBABILITY					
PERSISTENCE					

☼ **Season**
Early summer

⌂ **Optimal conditions**
When conditions are warm and watering has been erratic.

⚶ **Favoured plants**
Tomatoes and capsicum (bell pepper)

◯ **Signature**
The rotting of the tips of fruit

✕ **Prevention**
Keep watering consistent and mulch your garden beds. A calcium deficiency also increases the probability of infection; an application of rock minerals will help greatly. Don't overfertilise with nitrogen and potassium as this also swings probability in its favour.

⚱ **Coping**
Blossom-end rot is typically an early-season problem that abates.

⚡ **Eradicating**
Once you have it, it's a matter of following the prevention practices and in time the problem will abate.

Even once plants have flowered, there is still no certainty that they will bear fruit. Early-season plants can often suffer from blossom-end rot, whereby the fruit will develop a dry sunken decay at the end opposite its stem. This is not a pest, parasite or disease process, but a physiological problem.

We find that patience is generally the best remedy and blossom-end rot seems to abate naturally as plants mature and the season progresses. Nevertheless, a consistent daily watering practice, mulching and supplemental calcium help to avoid this problem.

LEAF BLIGHT

THE LITTLE VEGGIE PATCH CO RATING

3.5

DISEASE!

	1	2	3	4	5
DAMAGE					
PROBABILITY					
PERSISTENCE					

Season
Spring and summer

Optimal conditions
Damp, humid conditions

Favoured plants
Tomatoes, potatoes, strawberries

Signature
Discoloured, yellow leaves that also typically curl up

Prevention
As damp, humid conditions greatly increase the potential for this disease, correct watering and spacing of your plants is paramount. Try to use a drip irrigation instead of fan spray so that the soil and its roots are watered rather than the foliage. The disease may be carried in the seed, so source from a reputable supplier and don't save seed from affected plants the year before. Crop rotation is also advisable.

Coping
Pick off the affected leaves and if the plant looks terminal dispose of it. Bicarbonate of soda (baking soda) and milk sprays will have some effect on containing it, as will a compost tea made with worm wee or compost juice.

Eradicating
Disposing of the affected leaves and plants is the only way to eradicate the disease.

A fungal infection that causes the discolouration of leaves and can often be terminal to a plant, leaf blight is one of those diseases that sinks your heart. Often affecting your tomato crop, it is commonly referred to as tomato blight or potato blight, another crop it gravitates towards.

Blight will usually appear early in the season and is given away by yellowing or dying leaves. However, it will also strike around fruiting time and limit the plant's ability to photosynthesise. Usually the result of damp, humid conditions, it is exacerbated by overcrowding crops and keeping the leaf foliage too wet.

If you notice blight on your cherished summer crop, don't be defeatist and pack it in. Some simple but tough measures – such as culling overcrowded plants and watering in the morning rather than at night – will greatly reduce the chances of further infestation.

LEAF ROLL/CURL

THE LITTLE
VEGGIE PATCH CO
RATING
3.8

DISEASE!

	1	2	3	4	5
DAMAGE					
PROBABILITY					
PERSISTENCE					

☼ **Season**
Early spring

⌂ **Optimal conditions**
When there is a lack of airflow, the spores are more likely to infect.

⚘ **Favoured plants**
Peaches and other stone fruit

◯ **Signature**
Leaves turn a paler green colour and then begin to curl and 'bubble' and turn darker.

✕ **Prevention**
The infection jumps from tree to tree, so keep an eye on neighbouring plants for signs and keep your plant healthy and strong.

⌛ **Coping**
Remove any infected leaves, from both the tree and the ground and dispose in the bin (not compost bin). You will also need to give the tree some extra love to limit stress. Apply a seaweed solution to the soil and to the leaves every month and keep it well watered.

⚡ **Eradicating**
Just before bud burst, spray your trees with copper hydroxide or copper oxychloride, ensuring thorough coverage over all branches and leaves. If your tree was severely infected the previous season, it doesn't hurt to spray in mid-winter and then again just before bud-swell.

Leaf curl is a fungal disease that is quite common in peach trees, but will also affect other stone fruit such as nectarines, apricots and almonds.

The fungal spores of the disease lie dormant on the tree's bark and then infection begins at bud burst. The first signs are seen on the new leaf growth; leaves start out a paler green colour and quickly begin to curl. As it develops, the leaves turn a pinky-purple, followed by a white bloom on their surface, and finally they fall off the tree.

Unfortunately, peach leaf curl can also affect the fruit, restricting their growth and causing them to drop before ripening. The tree will keep growing, but will seriously weaken if the disease is not controlled.

Unfortunately (again), by the time the symptoms are noticed it's too late for significant control measures to be applied that year. Treatment needs to be applied just prior to bud burst in spring, so get out your veggie patch calendar and make an important note for next year. But, what to do now?

Peach leaf curl does not mean a year of stone fruit abstinence, because a little more care and nurturing now can salvage some results. However, it's a prolonged effort to put the tree back into its full swing and that means being more organised and diligent than you otherwise would.

MAGNESIUM DEFICIENCY

	1	2	3	4	5
DAMAGE					
PROBABILITY					
PERSISTENCE					

☼ **Season**
Spring

⌂ **Optimal conditions**
It will mostly affect warm-season plants during the cooler, wetter times of the year.

⚘ **Favoured plants**
Citrus, tomatoes, potatoes

◎ **Signature**
Yellowing leaves on the lower, more mature stems of the plant.

✕ **Prevention**
Consistent watering practices and routine testing of pH. Worm castings and juice are both great soil conditioners that allow easier passage of nutrition in the soil to the plant. Incorporate sparingly in the patch.

⌀ **Coping**
Keeping plants properly watered and mulched allows greater access to the nutrients within the soil. Warmer-season plants tend to slow their uptake of water and nutrients when temperatures drop, so it is most common for leaves to turn yellow in cool conditions. Once soil temperatures increase, they begin to repair.

⚡ **Eradicating**
An application of Epsom salts to the foliage and the roots will quickly begin to repair the plants as they absorb the salts.

The telltale sign of magnesium deficiency is chlorosis – that is, the leaves of the plant becoming paler and paler, turning yellow and sometimes brown. It will show up in lower, more mature plant growth and then begin to spread. While being unsightly to the veggie patch and lowering the overall colour tone of the garden, magnesium deficiency will also stunt plant and fruit growth.

Typically a result of wetter- and cooler-than-usual conditions, it will also be more prevalent in acidic soils, so testing of your pH is advisable if you start to notice your leaves turning. It will also target those plants that require high levels of potassium to produce fruit – such as tomatoes and citrus – that will make magnesium unavailable.

POWDERY MILDEW

THE LITTLE VEGGIE PATCH CO RATING
3.0

DISEASE!

	1	2	3	4	5
DAMAGE					
PROBABILITY					
PERSISTENCE					

☼ **Season**
Late spring to early autumn

⌂ **Optimal conditions**
Late spring, with its warm weather and humid conditions.

⚘ **Favoured plants**
Cucurbita family, which includes squash, zucchini (courgettes), pumpkin (winter squash) and cucumber.

○ **Signature**
Circular, powdery-looking blotches on the tops of the leaves.

✕ **Prevention**
Adequate spacing of plants and using drip irrigation, as surface water connecting with the leaf increases the probability of infection.

⌷ **Coping**
Cutting off affected leaves and culling overcrowded plants.

⚡ **Eradicating**
Apply a milk spray of 1 part full-cream (whole) milk to 10 parts water.

Sometimes a disease is more of a visual inconvenience than a functional inconvenience, and such is the case of powdery mildew. Easily identified as the powdery-looking blotches on your plants' leaves, it tends to affect the Cucurbita family – squash, zucchini (courgettes), pumpkin (winter squash) and cucumber – and is caused by poor airflow and humid conditions.

While it can affect plants in the early stages, it is more common (almost inevitable) in the latter stages of a cucurbita plant's life. When removing these plants from the patch in late summer and early autumn, it would be unusual not to have some powdery mildew affecting the leaves.

Although not commonly terminal to the plant in question, it can affect its ability to photosynthesise and therefore produce fruit, and is embarrassing for the plant when at public functions and dinner parties.

ROOT ROT/STEM ROT

THE LITTLE
VEGGIE PATCH CO
RATING
3.2

DISEASE!

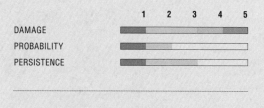

	1	2	3	4	5
DAMAGE					
PROBABILITY					
PERSISTENCE					

☼ **Season**
All year round

⌂ **Optimal conditions**
When a patch has been overwatered and mulched too deeply.

⚘ **Favoured plants**
Eggplants (aubergines), capsicums (bell peppers)

◯ **Signature**
Stems turning to a dark colour and then beginning to rot.

✕ **Prevention**
Get your watering practices right, particularly when you have boggy, water-holding soil, which will make plants more prone to the condition. When mulching, leave a clear area around the stem.

♟ **Coping**
It's almost impossible to reverse the damage of stem rot and you will lose those plants affected.

⚡ **Eradicating**
Mulch to no deeper than 5 cm (2 in) and allow the stems to breathe.

There's probably not a more frustrating condition than stem rot, as it's usually terminal for your plants and you're 99% to blame. Stem rot is exactly as it sounds – the rotting of a plant's stem. It is the result of overwatering, and in most cases over-mulching, which creates humidity around the stem of the plant that will eventually cause it to rot.

Thankfully, it is easily avoided in warm climates like Australia, as long as you take some care with your watering practices. If you're working in boggy or clay-based soils, monitor the soil and its water retention carefully and then set your watering schedule accordingly. Then, when mulching your plants, keep its depth to no more than 3–5 cm (1¼–2 in) and keep a wide berth of the stems of susceptible plants.

There's enough to get frustrated about in life without having to heighten it through unnecessary stem rot.

RUST

	1	2	3	4	5
DAMAGE					
PROBABILITY					
PERSISTENCE					

☀ **Season**
Mid- to late summer and early autumn

⌂ **Optimal conditions**
Following a wet summer

⚶ **Favoured plants**
Mint, broad bean, pear

◯ **Signature**
Coloured spots on the leaves, typically
a rust-like colour.

✕ **Prevention**
Regularly fertilise with seaweed extract that
contains plenty of potassium, sulphur, and other
trace elements (including copper) that boost the
plants' immune systems. However, don't overfeed
with nitrogen, as the young, soft plant growth is
more likely to host the spores.

⅁ **Coping**
For mild cases of rust, remove damaged parts of
the affected plant and burn these, or dispose of
them in a sealed plastic bag. Don't ever compost
them, as the spores may not be killed.

⚡ **Eradicating**
You can make an organic fungicide using 100 parts
water, 10 parts bicarbonate of soda (baking soda),
1 part oil and 1 part liquid detergent. The bicarbonate
is the active ingredient that helps to kill the fungal
spores, while the oil and detergent help to fix and
spread the mix over the leaf foliage respectively.

Rust is a fungal infection that causes pale leaf spots called
pustules to develop on the leaves. These are spore-producing
structures that can be yellow, orange, black, brown or white,
but are most commonly a rust-like colour, from which it
gets its name.

Like humans and animals, plants are more prone to diseases
when they have a poor diet, and rust disease is essentially
a sign of malnutrition. It can be avoided by keeping plants
growing vigorously and by the use of drip irrigation as
opposed to overhead watering. Letting water sit on the plant's
leaves allows the fungal spores to germinate with greater ease.

INDEX

pulverised mulch 28
pumpkins 112, 164, 165, 219, 280

Making a book is truly a team sport and it would not have been possible without a lot of very talented people who patiently turned our crude cave paintings into this Sistine Chapel of gardening (so the critics are saying). The following people were absolutely essential in creating this book (in order of appearance in this project):

Thank you to our publisher, Hardie Grant, for your dedication to making great books and your excellent team of passionate and talented staff. Specifically, Jane Willson for your new vision and complete lack of bullshit (and your ability to cut through ours). Thank you to Andrea O'Connor for being our editor, project manager and reluctant talent. You have always conveyed confidence and ease, and even though we repeatedly threw you a tangled line with no hook, you still caught us a fish. Thank you to Mark Campbell for Pete (and your design vision).

The shoot(s): Thank you to John Laurie, our favourite photographer and storyteller. Your talents are too great for shooting vegetables and high-fives, but we are thrilled that you keep saying yes. Thanks to Marlowe and Emi for your continual appearances in our books, which will one day be used to embarrass you in front of your dates. Thank you to Sam and Charlie for your enthusiasm and cat wrangling. Thanks to Eli and Shane for sharing your sons and letting us take over your garden. Also, thank you to Annette for volunteering your home and aquaponics expertise. So nice to stumble on your garden playground and learn about the local fried possum windsock.

The nitty gritty: The reading experience of this book was largely determined by Susie Ashworth. Susie is an extraordinary editor who is as talented as she is patient. Thank you for channeling our torrent of information into a functional irrigation system. A very special thanks to Evi O for giving us a fresh look and your wholehearted embrace of our ideas. Your playfulness and humour are what make this book so much fun and it would be nothing without your work. Thanks to Tyler Cameron for sharing your mycelial passion and consulting on the finer points of gourmet mushroom cultivation.

Marketing/Publicity: Thank you to Roxy Ryan for being our spiritual leader and always giving us the best opportunities to succeed. We refuse to make another book (despite many lucrative offers) until you return from maternity leave. Thank you to Kasi Collins and Jessica Speight for having faith in this book and putting us in front of the right people.

Thank you to Mile End Bagel for providing the perfect venue and snack for book writing.

Finally, thank you to anyone who bought this book. Your choice shows extraordinary character and excellent taste.

Love,
Dillon and Mat

MAT PEMBER is Australia's best-selling gardening author, so it's strange that he doesn't consider himself a gardener. After hanging a commerce degree on his parents' wall many springs ago, he flirted with the idea of getting a real job before making his Nonna and Nonno proud by creating The Little Veggie Patch Co in 2008. Now a father of two girls, Emiliana and Marlowe, he is striving to achieve what the naysayers call unachievable – running a thriving Melbourne business from a farm south of Hobart. When he's not writing books he's blunting his pencil contributing to publications such as *Gourmet Traveller* and Melbourne's *Herald Sun*, or otherwise trying to catch Tasmanian flathead.

DILLON SEITCHIK-REARDON identifies as multi-passionate and is a firm believer in doing as many different things as possible, regardless of ability. Although he was educated as an environmental scientist, Dillon quickly became disillusioned with research when he realised that most of it is conducted in air-conditioned, artificially lit laboratories. In 2012 he began working for The Little Veggie Patch Co as an environmental consultant, where he finally found the place to channel his scientific prowess while still working outside. Dillon was raised in New Mexico and has lived back and forth between the US and Australia since 2007.

Mat and Dillon met in a past life as landscapers and professional hole diggers. While crawling on their hands and knees through rose gardens they formed a strong friendship based not only on their mutual love of growing food, but also a shared passion for music, relationship philosophising and a collaborative approach to work.

Published in 2017 by Hardie Grant Books,
an imprint of Hardie Grant Publishing

Hardie Grant Books (Melbourne)
Building 1, 658 Church Street
Richmond, Victoria 3121
hardiegrantbooks.com.au

Hardie Grant Books (London)
5th & 6th Floors
52–54 Southwark Street
London SE1 1UN
hardiegrantbooks.co.uk

A Cataloguing-in-Publication entry is available from the catalogue of the
National Library of Australia at www.nla.gov.au

Grow. Food. Anywhere.
US ISBN 978 1 74379 377 0
UK ISBN 978 1 74379 378 7

Publishing Director: Jane Willson
Managing Editor: Marg Bowman
Project Editor: Andrea O'Connor
Editor: Susie Ashworth
Design Manager: Mark Campbell
Designer: Evi O. / OetomoNew
Illustrator: Evi Oetomo
Photographer: John Laurie
Production Manager: Todd Rechner
Production Coordinator: Rebecca Bryson

Colour reproduction by Splitting Image Colour Studio
Printed in China by 1010 Printing International Limited

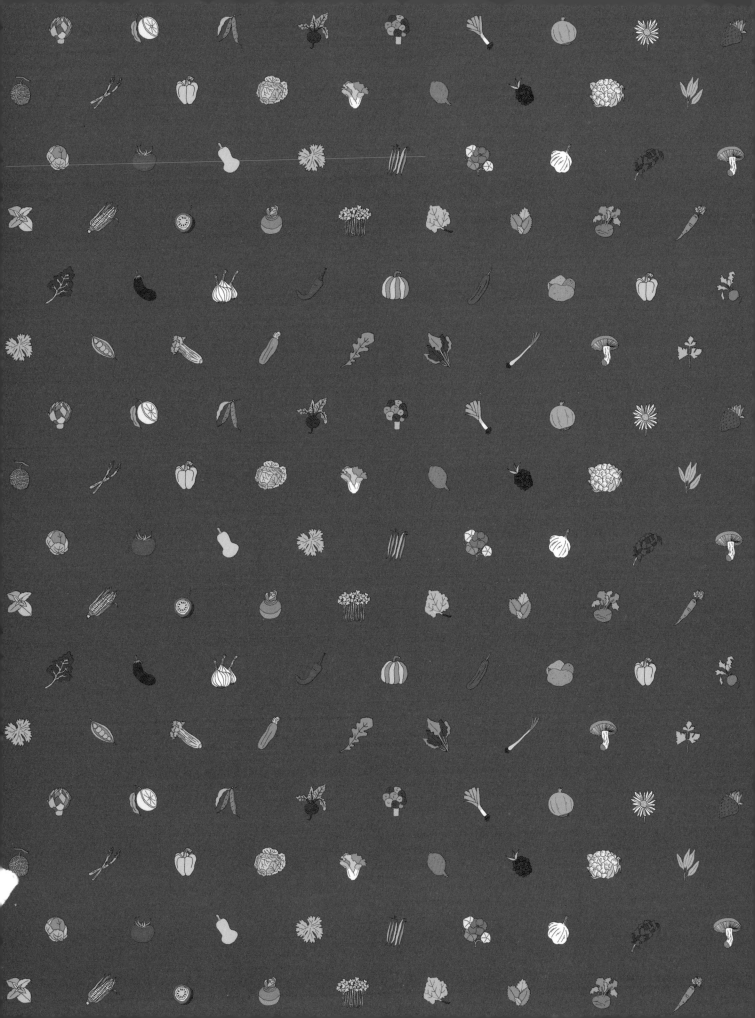

PLANTING CALENDAR

	JAN	FEB	MAR	APR	MAY	JUN	JUL	AUG	SEP	OCT	NOV	DEC
Apple	•	•	••	••••	••••	•••			••	••••	•••••	•
Artichoke	•	•		•••	•••	•••	••					
Asparagus	•	•		•••	•••	•••	••					
Basil	•		••	••	••	••					•	•
Beans		•	•••	•••	••	••	•••	•••	••			
Beetroot	•	•••	••••	••••	••	••	••	•	••••	•••	••	•
Blackberry	•		••	•••	•••	••						•
Blueberry	•		••	•••	•••	••						•
Borage	•	••	•••	••	••	•••	•					
Broad beans			••	•••	•••	•		•	••••	••••	••	
Broccoli	••		•••	•••	•••	••			•••	•••	••	•
Brussels sprouts	•		••	•••	•••	•	•		•••	•••	••	•
Cabbage	•	••	••	•••	•••	•	•		•••	•••	••	•
Capsicum	•	•	•••	•••	••••	•••			•	•	•	
Carrot	••	•••	••••	••••	••	••	••	•	•••	•••	••	•
Cauliflower	•		••	•••	•••	••	•		••	•••	•	•
Celeriac	•		••	•••	•••	•••	••				•	•
Celery	•		••	•••	•••	•••	••				•	•
Chamomile	•	••	•••	•••	•••	•••	•					
Cherry				••••	•••	•••			••	•••••	•••••	
Chilli	•	•	•••	•••	••••	•••			•	•	•	
Citrus	•	•	••	•••	••	•••			•	•	•	•
Coriander	•	••	••	•••	•••	••			••	•••	••	•
Cornflower	•	•	••	•••	•••	•••	•					
Cranberry	•		••	•••	•••	••						
Cucumber	•	••	•••	••••	•••	•••						
Eggplant	•	•	•••	••	•••••	•••			•	•	•	
Fennel	•	•	••	••••	•••				••	••	•	•
Fig	•	•	••	•••	•••	••			•	••	•	•
Garlic	•	•	•••	•••	•				••	•••	••	•
Ginger	•	•	••	•	••	•						
Herbs	•	•••	••••	••••	•••••	••••	••	••	••••	•••	•••	•
Hyssop	•	••	•••	•••	•••	•••	•					
Horseradish				••••	••••	•			•	••	•	
Kale	••	••	••	•••	•••	••	••	•	•••	•••	••	•
Kohlrabi	•	••	••	••••	•••	•••			••	•••	••	•
Lavender	•	••	•••	•••	•••							